Customs Valuation and Transfer Pricing

Series on International Taxation

VOLUME 28

Series Editors

Prof. Ruth Mason, University of Virginia School of Law
Prof. Dr Ekkehart Reimer, University of Heidelberg

Introduction & Contents

The Series on International Taxation deals with a wide variety of topics in the global tax arena. The authors include many of the field's leading experts as well as talented newcomers. Their expert views and incisive commentary has proven highly useful to practitioners and academics alike.

Objective

The volumes published in this series are aimed at offering high-quality analytical information and practical solutions for international tax practitioners.

Readership

Practitioners, academics and policy makers in international tax law.

Frequency of Publication

2-3 new volumes published each year.

The titles published in this series are listed at the end of this volume.

Customs Valuation and Transfer Pricing

Is It Possible to Harmonize Customs and Tax Rules?

Second Edition

Juan Martin Jovanovich

Wolters Kluwer

Published by:
Kluwer Law International B.V.
PO Box 316
2400 AH Alphen aan den Rijn
The Netherlands
Website: www.wolterskluwerlr.com

Sold and distributed in North, Central and South America by:
Wolters Kluwer Legal & Regulatory U.S.
7201 McKinney Circle
Frederick, MD 21704
United States of America
Email: customer.service@wolterskluwer.com

Sold and distributed in all other countries by:
Quadrant
Rockwood House
Haywards Heath
West Sussex
RH16 3DH
United Kingdom
Email: international-customerservice@wolterskluwer.com

ISBN 978-90-411-6134-5

e-Book: ISBN 978-90-411-6142-0
web-PDF: ISBN 978-90-411-8068-1

For my father ...

Table of Contents

Preface

There is an overlap between the transfer pricing concepts that apply under tax and under customs regimes. This book aims to demonstrate (i) that customs and tax laws often share common principles in respect of related-party transactions; (ii) that transfer pricing as agreed to under one discipline should be recognized under the other; (iii) that the OECD Transfer Pricing Guidelines constitute a body of rules that is appropriate to supplement the related-party provisions of the GATT/WTO Valuation Code ("GVC"); and (iv) that such guidelines are generally in accordance with the provisions of the GVC and its general principles and objectives. This book also analyzes the tax and customs value of imported goods, and identifies which additions to or deductions from customs value might have to be taken into account in comparing tax and customs results. The book concludes with an analysis of the circumstances and conditions under which the introduction of transfer pricing year-end adjustments to transaction value would be consistent with Article 1 of the GVC.

Preface

Acknowledgments

First and foremost, I would like to thank my thesis supervisor, Professor Armand L.C. De Mestral, for his assistance, ideas and guidance.

I greatly appreciate the support and patience of Lorena Minoretti, who was by my side during countless hours of work on this book.

I also wish to express my gratitude to my esteemed advisor and mentor, Dr. Graciela L.T. de Wurcel and to the University of Buenos Aires.

I am also indebted to Mr. Adam Kramer for assisting me with the editing of this thesis; to Mr. Peter Jarosz and Mr. François Vincent for providing me with material and input; and to Mr. Pablo Dukarevich for believing in and supporting my project.

Next, my grateful thanks to the Faculty of Graduate Studies and Research, McGill University and, especially, to Professor Stephen Smith, for granting me a DFW which allowed me to take my time and do my best in completing this thesis.

Finally, I would like to thank my parents, María Angélica and Juan Carlos, who instilled in me a desire to learn.

Introduction

There is an overlap between the transfer pricing concepts that apply under the customs and tax regimes. As a consequence of this, a lawyer who practices in both tax and customs fields frequently faces a dilemma: how to apply two systems of valuation to the same transaction.

Rates of duty are usually established on an *ad valorem* basis. Consequently, it becomes necessary to establish the value of the goods for determining what duty to assess. Valuation constitutes, therefore, one of the main fields of Customs law.

In determining income taxes, it is also necessary to establish the value of imported goods. In effect, the tax rate is applied to taxable income (i.e., the tax base of income taxes) to determine the amount of tax payable. Many of the elements which are necessary to determine taxable income (e.g. sales price, cost of goods sold, adjusted cost base, inventory cost, etc. [hereinafter "tax value" or "value for tax purposes"]) are calculated on the basis of the value of goods (which are involved in income-producing activities). Hence, valuation also constitutes one of the main fields of Income Tax law.

Under both tax and customs laws, the transaction value usually governs in determining the value of goods sold or acquired (although sometimes, pursuant to statutory or treaty provisions, certain elements are to be included in or excluded from transaction value in calculating the tax bases of duties or income taxes). In other words, transaction value is the point of departure to calculate tax and customs values of such goods.

However, transactions agreed upon by and between related parties (hereinafter "related-party transactions") present a particular problem: the relationship between the parties may permit them to establish special conditions in their "intra-group" relations that differ from those that would have been established had the parties been acting as independent enterprises. In other words, when associated enterprises deal with each other, their commercial and financial relations may not be directly affected by external market forces. Thus, associated enterprises could manipulate their profits and prices to ensure the most favorable tax and customs treatment for their transactions.[1] Consequently, when transfer pricing does not reflect market forces, the tax and customs liabilities of the associated enterprises and the tax and customs revenues of the host countries could be distorted.

Tax and Customs administrations are each pulling the importer/ taxpayer in opposite directions. The larger the gain, as measures in the context of resales after importation, the greater the tax revenue. Thus, tax administrations will generally insist on a low transfer price to ensure the greatest income in their countries. Customs administrations are charged with a similar collection mission. The higher the dutiable value of the imported goods, the greater the duty revenue for Customs.[2]

This means the importer/taxpayer could be squeezed in the middle if neither customs nor tax law recognized transfer pricing as agreed to under the other discipline.[3]

Chapters 1, 2 and 3 of the present work will be aimed at demonstrating that

(i) customs and tax laws often share common principles in respect of related-party transactions;
(ii) transfer pricing as agreed to under one discipline should be recognized under the other;
(iii) the OECD Transfer Pricing Guidelines[4] constitute a body of rules that is appropriate to supplement the related-party provisions of the GATT Valuation Code;[5]
(iv) the provisions of the OECD Guidelines are generally in accordance with the provisions of the GVC, their notes and their general principles and objectives.

They will also be aimed at determining the particular conditions that must be observed in applying the OECD Guidelines and their methodologies in the customs context.

1. Associated enterprises seeking to achieve the most favorable tax and customs treatment, would often set their transfer prices considering, among others, the following factors: income tax rates in the country of exportation and in the country of importation, customs-duty rate in the country of importation; existence of statutory or treaty relief for underlying foreign taxes in the country of importation or exportation (e.g., tax credits, exempt dividends, exempt surplus, etc.), existence of withholding tax on dividends paid to foreign beneficiaries, etc.
2. This, however, may not be true in particular economic circumstances. For instance, in countries applying exchange control regulations with double or multiple foreign exchange rate systems, Customs administrations may be charged with the mission of controlling that the transaction values declared by importers are not higher than those fixed between independent parties. This is because, in this type of economies, benefits from special foreign exchange rates applicable to payments of imports of goods outweigh the incremental cost represented by the import duties. As an example of this, we can mention the case of the exchange control system and economic policy implemented in Argentina from 2012 to 2015.
3. *See* Levey, M., *Taxation of Foreign Controlled Business*, (WL, 2000) at 8.05[1]. Online: WL (Levey, Taxation of Foreign Controlled Business, Tax Treatises).
4. Organization for Economic Cooperation and Development (2017), *OECD Transfer Pricing Guidelines for Multinational Enterprises and Tax Administrations 2017*, OECD Publishing, Paris. http://dx.doi.org/10.1787/tpg-2017-en [hereinafter "OECD Guidelines"].
5. *Agreement on Implementation of Article VII of the General Agreement on Tariffs and Trade 1994* included in *The Final Act Embodying the Results of the Uruguay Round of Multilateral Trade Negotiations*", 15 April 1994, at 171, online: <http://www.wto.org:80/wto/english/ docs_e/ legal_e/final_e.htm> (date accessed: 3 August 2000) [hereinafter "GVC"].

The objective of Chapter 4 will be significantly different. As indicated above, statutory additions to or deductions from the transaction value are sometimes required to calculate the tax base of customs duties (i.e., the customs value) or the relevant element of the tax base of income taxes (i.e., the value of the goods for tax purposes).

For instance, certain assists provided by the buyer to the seller free of charge might not be regarded as part of the tax value of the imported goods. In contrast, the same assists might be considered to be part of the customs value of such goods. In these cases, a comparison between tax and customs values would not provide consistent results unless appropriate adjustments were made to account for differences in the calculation of such values. This comparison may be useful for many purposes. For example, it could avoid double scrutiny of the same transactions by tax and customs authorities. (It should be taken into account that importers/ taxpayers usually provide tax and customs administrations with information concerning tax bases.) It could also prevent customs and tax administrations from adopting inconsistent approaches regarding the appropriate determination of arm's length prices.

Therefore, Chapter 4 will be aimed at analyzing the tax base of customs duties and at identifying which additions to or deductions from customs value might have to be taken into account (and eventually adjusted) in comparing tax and customs figures.

Finally, in Chapter 5 we will address a practical problem that multinational enterprises may face in determining and declaring appropriate arm's length prices to customs, through the application of certain methodologies. One consequence of the application of a transfer pricing methodology could be a year-end adjustment. For example, when there is a cost-plus pricing and the entry is made when the costs have not been finalized, the transaction value declared to customs would only be estimated or provisional, since some of the elements that are necessary to calculate an appropriate arm's length transaction value will not be known until later.

Whether such provisional or estimated price is arm's length will usually depend on whether or not a year-end adjustment is finally necessary. Therefore, in such circumstances, an importer would only be able to declare to Customs an appropriate arm's length transaction value, if the customs legislation permitted the introduction of year-end adjustments to a transaction value that has already been declared.

Consequently, in Chapter 5, it will be analyzed in which circumstances and under which conditions the introduction of year-end adjustments to transaction value would be consistent with GVC Article 1.

The first edition of this book was written between 1999 and 2001, and published in 2002. At that time, just a few countries had transfer pricing legislation in force. A few others had recently started to draft or implement OECD-type transfer pricing rules. Also, a large number of countries had recently become WTO members and, consequently, were just starting to apply the GVC in their territories. The overlap between customs and tax transfer pricing rules was, at that time, not really evident. That first edition was mentioned by one delegate at the 18th Session of the Technical Committee on Customs Valuation ("TCCV") as she suggested the inclusion of this topic in the Program for the Theme Meeting to be held during the 20th Session. This is when the transfer pricing aspects of customs valuation, and the examination of the possible use of the OECD Guidelines in such a context, became an important part of the Agenda of the TCCV. Since then, the World Customs Organization ("WCO") and the TCCV produced important works and instruments and, in many countries, the issue was addressed in information papers, rulings and decisions. This second edition reaffirms, and expands on, the ideas expressed in that first edition, in the light of more than a decade of international developments.

CHAPTER 1
General

1 RULES TO BE HARMONIZED

In the customs valuation field, we will examine the provisions of the GVC (especially, those applicable to related-party transactions). The GVC's definition of "customs value" constitutes the basis on which the WTO members have drafted the definitions of such terms in their own customs statutes. In the European Community, the basic customs valuation rules and definitions may be found in Chapter 3 of Title II of the Union Customs Code[6] and in Chapter 3 of Title II of the Commission Implementing Regulation 2015/2447.[7] In the United States, the valuation provisions have been introduced in 19 U.S.C. 1401a.[8] The Canadian valuation rules may be found in Sections 44–56 of the *Customs Act*.[9] In some countries, like Argentina, the GVC's provisions – being part of an international convention approved by Congress – are directly applicable and binding on the government pursuant to Constitutional principles.

In the tax field, no multilateral tax convention establishes principles of valuation or methodologies. However, a great number of countries (including, but not limited to, those which are members of the OECD) have drafted their tax conventions based on the OECD Model Tax Convention[10] ("MTC") ") and United Nations Model Tax Convention ("UNMTC"), where one can identify certain basic rules regarding related-party

6. EU, *Regulation No 952/2013 of the European Parliament and of the Council of 9 October 2013 laying down the Union Customs Code*, O.J.L 269/1 10 October 2013 [hereinafter "UCC"].
7. EU, Commission Implementing Regulation 2015/2447 of 24 November 2015 laying down detailed rules implementing certain provisions of Regulation (EU) No 952/2013 of the European Parliament and the Council laying down the UCC, O.J.EUL 343/558 29 December 2015 [hereinafter "IRUCC"].
8. 17 June 1930, ch. 497, title IV, Sec. 402, as added 2 August 1956, ch. 887, Sec. 2(a), 70 Stat. 943, amended Pub.L. 96-39, title II, Sec. 201(a), 26 July 1979, 93 Stat. 194 Pub.L. 96–490, Sec. 2, 2 December 1980, 94 Stat. 2556.
9. R.S.C. 1985, C.1 (2nd Supp) [hereinafter "*Customs Act*"].
10. OECD, Committee on Fiscal Affairs, *Model Tax Convention on Income and on Capital*, June 1998 condensed version (Paris: OECD, 1998) [hereinafter "MTC"].

transactions and, thus, transfer pricing. The arm's length principle has been included in Article 9 of the MTC – which is replicated in Article 9 of the UNMTC – and gained acceptance as the fundamental principle governing international transfer pricing in all OECD member countries, both in bilateral treaty networks as well as in those countries' tax statutes and implementing regulations.[11] Interestingly, the arm's length principle was included not only in the tax conventions between OECD countries but also in those between OECD countries and non-OECD countries. This created a large treaty network among a great number of countries where related-party transactions are governed by a common principle: the arm's length standard.

One can suggest, therefore, that our object of study in this field seems to be a number of concordant international instruments. However, neither the tax conventions nor the MTC elaborate on the arm's length standard. They merely embrace the arm's length principle for the tax treatment of transactions among associated enterprises. (Where a treaty country has made a transfer pricing adjustment to a multinational enterprise, these conventions also provide for corresponding adjustments by the other treaty-country.)

The OECD Committee on Fiscal Affairs has issued a number of reports on transfer pricing. The first major report, published in 1979, was "Transfer Pricing and Multinational Enterprises".[12] Subsequent OECD reports analyzed specific transfer pricing issues. In 1993 the OECD started revising the 1979 OECD Report. The first five chapters of the revised version were approved by the OECD Council in July 1995 and, consequently, released to the public. This new version was entitled "*Transfer Pricing Guidelines for Multinational Enterprises and Tax Administrations*" (OECD Guidelines).[13] It included the definition of the arm's length principle, the various methodologies for determining prices that would be in accordance with this principle, as well as the guidelines regarding documentation and penalties. Competent authority and mutual agreement, simultaneous examinations, burden of proof, advance pricing agreements and arbitration were also covered. The OECD Council adopted three more chapters of the Guidelines in 1996 and 1998. Two revised versions were adopted first in 2010 and afterwards in 2017.

The OECD is a consultative body, and its decisions and pronouncements are advisory and instructive, not mandatory. It is not a legislative body that can dictate to its members. Nonetheless, the OECD enjoys a high level of prestige among its members and most non-member states. Each of its positions evolves out of multinational

11. *See* Hammer *et al.*, *International Transfer Pricing – OECD Guidelines*, (WL, 2000), at 3.01, online: WL (Hammer, Lowell, Burge & Levey, Transfer Pricing Treatises). Note that, in the European Community, the profit allocation principle laid down in the Arbitration Convention (E.C., *Convention 90/463/EEC of 23 July 1990*, [1990] O.J. L 225, 20.8.1990, at 10) is the principle of arm's length dealing and separate accounting. Profits of associated enterprises, and of branches and their head offices, should be determined as if they were dealing wholly independently from each other. The Arbitration Convention, however, does not specify which arm's length method it adheres to (*See* Terra, B. and Wattel, P., *European Tax Law*, 2nd ed. (London, Kluwer Law International, 1997) at 289).
12. OECD, Committee on Fiscal Affairs, *Transfer Pricing and Multinational Enterprises* (Paris: OECD, 1979) [hereinafter "1979 OECD Report"].
13. *See* OECD Guidelines *supra* note 4.

dialogues and deliberations and represents a consensus on any particular topic under study.[14] In addition, a vast number of member and non-member countries have introduced in their tax legislation most of the principles and methodologies recommended in the OECD Guidelines.[15] This broad recognition makes the OECD Guidelines at least comparable to the GVC for the purposes of this analysis. Therefore, in the tax field, we will examine the MTC (which is a representative of the treaty network that supports the arm's length principle) and, especially, the OECD Guidelines.

Since the OECD Guidelines are far more detailed than the provisions of the GVC regarding related-party transactions, our analysis will basically consist in the study of the OECD Guidelines in order to determine whether the latter may complement the GVC's provisions on related-party transactions. For such purposes, we will also examine advisory opinions, commentaries, explanatory notes, case studies, memorandums and rulings that have been issued by national agencies, courts and international organizations in interpreting the GVC.

2 IS IT NECESSARY OR, AT LEAST, ADVISABLE TO HARMONIZE BOTH TAX AND CUSTOMS TRANSFER PRICING REGIMES?

When facing the question whether harmonization of tax and customs transfer pricing regimes is necessary or advisable, we find a number of problems which arise from (i) the existence of heterogeneous norms and international instruments, and (ii) the fact that tax and customs laws often have different objectives and principles.

The origin and development of the tax transfer pricing regimes compared to those of the customs valuation system have been radically different, what resulted in the different kinds of international and national norms and instruments governing each field. A comparison and subsequent harmonization of these norms and instruments may not be easy, since each of them has different legal authority (or no legal authority at all) and scope of application.

However, although all these particularities may cause some problems in the context of a process of harmonization, they are not a reason to reject the whole idea of harmonization of tax and customs transfer pricing laws. There are many reasons to think that harmonization is not only advisable but also necessary.

A first argument seems to be based on the idea of consistency. If two systems adopt common principles, the results derived from their implementation should be, to the greatest extent possible, substantially consistent. (Implementing should not, in principle, change the substance of the rule being implemented.)

As we will see, both customs and tax valuation systems have chosen the arm's length standard as the principle that must govern the relations between related parties. Therefore, a harmonized implementation of such principle seems to be necessary to obtain consistent results. Implementing standards and principles in different and often

14. *See* Hammer *supra* note 11 at 1.02[1].
15. *See*, e.g., *Ley de Impuesto a las Ganancias, t.o. 1997 y sus modificaciones* (Argentina), Article 15, as amended by *Ley 23.239* (B.O. 31 December 1999) [hereinafter "Argentine Income Tax Law"].

inconsistent manner is a problem described by the Corporate Customs Counsel of General Motors USA, Mr. Peter Zubrin, as follows:

> A couple of other issues that we encounter in several countries point out the limitations of a global code such as the Valuation Agreement. When this *uniform agreement is implemented in any one country it becomes only a small portion of the whole set of laws and regulations affecting import transactions* within that country.
>
> For example, the Valuation Agreement specifies that retroactive payments may be dutiable under certain circumstances. It is silent, however, on the procedures for reporting such payments to the customs authorities. In the United States, thanks to the Customs Modernization Act, for which GM was a strong proponent, importers will soon have the flexibility to file entry declarations based on estimated values and reconcile those entries within 15 months thereafter by means of a post-importation review process. If additional duty is due for retroactive payments or any other adjustment, we will be required to pay it with interest. In other countries paying additional duty to amend an entry after its original due date automatically exposes the importer to substantial monetary penalties. A mod-act styled provision in the WTO Agreement would facilitate an efficient valuation reporting process by allowing all transactions covering a specific trade flow during a one-year period to be reviewed as a single project.[16]

A second argument appears to be more practical in character. This argument is often presented by members of the international business community and, especially, by multinational enterprises ("MNEs"). Zubrin explains such practical argument as follows:

> Continuing with related party transactions, GM and other global traders are required to devote more attention to the special requirements for sustaining related party prices for both customs and tax purposes. The complexities and shortage of expertise has made this difficult and very costly since independent analyses must be done. Like us in the customs and trade profession, the tax professions and organizations such as the OECD are leading an effort towards transparent taxation rules. What amazes me, however, is how little interest the tax and customs authorities in most countries have for developing a harmonized approach for establishing the bona fides of a related party transaction. I might also add, there seems to be relatively little interest in the private sector for this.
>
> There should be no reason why a **transfer price** established under OECD guidelines that passes the arms-length test under the income tax laws of the exporting and importing country should not be acceptable as a price actually paid or payable for customs purposes. Amending the Valuation Agreement to allow importers the alternative of applying tax rules for this purpose would be a major breakthrough for traders, saving them the additional cost and work of doing two parallel valuation analyses of the same transaction.[17]

16. WTO, Council for Trade in Goods, *WTO Trade Facilitation Symposium (9/10 March 1998), Report by the Secretariat, Panel 2 – Import and export procedures and requirements, including customs and border crossing problems – D – Compendium of all presentations – "Practical Problems for traders in the area of customs valuation"*, WTO Doc. G/C/W/115 (19 May 1998), online: <http://www.wto.org/wto/ddf/ep/public.html> (date accessed: 3 August 2000) [hereinafter "Practical Problems"].
17. *Ibid.*

In effect, transfer pricing and customs valuation analyses are often complex, expensive and time-consuming. It does not appear to be reasonable (or at least, economically efficient) for an MNE to undertake two parallel valuation analyses of the same transaction.

On the other hand, sometimes an adjustment to transfer prices by the tax authorities may be rejected by the customs authorities and vice versa. Since the arm's length principle is the common standard governing related-party transactions for both tax and customs purposes, it should be necessary to identify whether such rejection arises from actual differences between the tax and customs regimes (which, as we will demonstrate, cannot be found in the rules regarding examination and acceptability of related-party transactions, but in specific rules which define the tax bases of customs duties and income tax) or simply from different opinions of the tax and customs officials.[18]

In 2005, the Technical Committee on Customs Valuation invited me as speaker to make a presentation on customs valuation and transfer pricing at the 20th Session's Theme Meeting. As the Theme Meeting created great interest in most delegates, the WCO's Secretariat decided to organize, jointly with the OECD, a conference on transfer pricing and customs valuation in May 2006. Interestingly, the agenda of such conference included an open discussion on the following questions:

- To what extent is it acceptable to have different rules because the policy objectives are different?
- Do different answers to the same question "what is the arm's length price" alter the credibility of the assessing authorities?
- If converging standards are found desirable, would the 1995 Transfer Pricing Guidelines form a suitable basis?[19]

We expressed the view that having converging standards for tax and customs purposes was not only a desirable and feasible objective, but also an obligation of those countries which have adopted the arm's length standard for tax purposes and which were members to the WTO Valuation Agreement. We said that the Valuation Agreement has clearly adopted the arm's length standard under GVC Article 1.2(a), although without the detailed set of guidelines proposed by the OECD in order to implement such standard. Therefore, even if the policy objectives of tax and customs laws were different, both systems sought to determine at which price independent parties would have sold the goods in comparable circumstances. From such perspective, it appeared to be unacceptable that customs and tax administrations – which are agencies of the

18. Where customs and tax administrations are parts of the same agency (e.g., Federal Administration of Public Revenue of Argentina), adjustments based on different opinions of tax and customs officials could be blatantly arbitrary.
19. *See* the Program of the WCO/OECD Joint Conference on Transfer Pricing and Customs Valuation online: http://www.wcoomd.org/en/media/newsroom/2006/may/international-conference-on-transfer-pricing-and-customs-valuation.aspx.

same government (and sometimes departments of the same agency) – arrive at different conclusions. This was clearly contrary to the elemental principles of justice, good faith and legality.

We mentioned that it could very well happen that the analysis conducted by one agency did not provide useful elements for the investigation conducted by the other. But what certainly should not happen is that such agencies arrive at opposite conclusions. That is the reason why we needed converging standards primarily in the domestic legislation of each country and, hopefully, also at an international level, because this would help achieve uniformity in the implementation of the Valuation Agreement, which was one of its objectives.

In his closing remarks, Mr. Kunio Mikuriya – WCO Deputy Secretary General – proposed the following as a way forward:

> At national level, we need to encourage more dialogue between customs and tax authorities, in close consultation with business, possibly establishing a mechanism for liaison. At international level, customs and tax administrations through the WCO and the OECD should create an appropriate joint forum for dialogue, study and possible liaison, with invitations being extended to the WTO, business and academics. The issues for dialogue and study might include a more thorough comparison between the two sets of rules, the identification of areas for possible convergence of rules and coordinated approaches, including possible development of guidelines or explanatory notes, the degree of acceptability by one agency of a value determination of the other, Advance Pricing Agreements, joint audits, the consequences of a re-adjustment of the value made by one agency on another, the exchange of information, and cooperation between customs and tax agencies. As noted during the deliberations, we have to take into account regional variation for needs and strategies in developing possible guidelines and coordinated approaches. We also have to accept that this joint initiative would mean a long road ahead, because this course of action will involve the review of own processes and systems by customs, tax and business.[20]

3 IS HARMONIZATION FEASIBLE?

3.1 Circumstances That Make the Comparison and, Thus, the Harmonization Difficult

As indicated above, the instruments involved in the present analysis are different in nature and legal status. As well, the fields of the law in question present different objectives. Thus, certain conclusions could work perfectly well in the tax field and be, however, not applicable in the customs field.

Briefly, we can mention the following general objectives of customs law:

20. WCO/OECD Joint Conference on Transfer Pricing and Customs Valuation, Brussels (Belgium), 3–4 may 2006. Closing remarks by Kunio Mikuriya, WCO Deputy Secretary General. Online: http://www.oecd.org/ctp/transfer-pricing/36740073.pdf.

(1) Regulate a country's foreign trade;[21]
(2) Revenue objective. (Nowadays, revenue objectives are secondary in most developed countries.)[22]

We can also mention the following general principles of customs valuation law:

(1) not to be an obstacle to international trade;
(2) simplicity;
(3) ease of trade;
(4) uniformity;
(5) avoid arbitrariness and protectionism through valuation.[23]

Bear in mind that customs duties are taxes. Therefore, the general principles of tax law are also applicable to them.

There are two fundamental objectives of tax law:

(1) Revenue objective;
(2) Non-fiscal (economic or budgetary) objectives (e.g. tax expenditures, etc.)

One can mention the following general principles of tax law:

(1) equity;
(2) fairness;
(3) neutrality;
(4) ability to pay;
(5) economic efficiency.[24]

Simplicity and ease of trade can also be regarded as principles of tax law. Therefore, when pursuing harmonization through implementing measures, one should take into account the existence of non-symmetric objectives. Otherwise, the application of the measure might undermine the main objective of customs law, i.e., the regulation of foreign trade. This would be clearly unacceptable since countries would lose an important economic instrument, which is often granted to them by the countries' constitutions.[25]

---

21. Alsina, *et al.*, *Codigo Aduanero. Comentarios – Antecedentes – Concordancias*, Vol. 4 (Buenos Aires, Abeledo Perrot) at 154.
22. *Ibid.* at 634–635 (*see*, especially, footnote 10).
23. Most of these principles can be found in the Preamble of the GVC. *See* Sherman, S. and Glashoff, H., *Customs Valuation. Commentary on the GATT Customs Valuation Code* (New York, Kluwer Law and Taxation Publishers, 1988) at 60.
24. *See* generally Krishna V., *Fundamentals of Canadian Income Tax* (Toronto, Carswell, 1993) at 12–29 (Krishna mentions "equity" as an objective of the tax system). *See* Jarach, D., *Finanzas Publicas y Derecho Tributario* (Buenos Aires, Ed. Cangallo, 1985) at 299–307 [hereinafter "Finanzas"]. In relation to the principle of "ability to pay" (capacidad contributiva), *see* Jarach, D., *El Hecho Imponible*, 3rd ed. (Buenos Aires, Abeledo-Perrot, 1982) at 91.
25. *See*, e.g., *Constitución de la Nación Argentina*, Article 75(1), as amended in 1994.

These differences in objectives were pointed out by many delegates during the two Transfer Pricing and Customs Valuation Conferences organized jointly by the WCO and the OECD in 2006 and 2007 and in subsequent TCCV's Sessions. For example, in Annex II to Document VT0914E1a, China expressed the following view:

> 3. Firstly, we should bear in mind the different focuses between the tax authority and the customs administration. As we know, the Tax authority focuses on the annual profits, i.e., net margin of the importers, and we focus on the import price of each cargo. A lower declared price may lead to a lower import cost and then a higher profit, which might be on the benefit of the tax authority but not on ours. So a transfer pricing report accepted by the tax authorities may not be accepted by the customs in the decision that the relationship doesn't influenced the price. That's why we suggest that APA is not necessary in this case.
>
> 4. Secondly, TNMM is an easy approach for the tax authority but not an appropriate one for customs. Due to the different focuses of the tax authority and customs administration, different preferences may exist in choosing appropriate methods concerning transfer pricing study. For the tax authority, TNMM is proved to be an appropriate way because it focuses on the net margin, which would be very easy for the tax authority to draw a conclusion whether it's in the arm's length range. But for the customs administration, TNMM may not be a suitable one..."

As it will be explained in 3.2 below, the differences in objectives and focuses should not be an obstacle, with respect to the specific treatment of related-party transactions, because both the GVC and the OECD Guidelines have a common objective in this aspect. The Administration must apply the rule of law. This means that it should not attempt to charge the taxpayer a tax that is either less or more than the one prescribed by the law. That is why the argument of China in Document VT0914E1a is not acceptable. First, a price is not declared on the benefit of the tax or customs authorities. A price is at arm's length irrespective of whether it generates more revenue for the tax administration or for the Customs Service. The government is a single entity which must apply the law, which means that its different agencies may not choose what method is appropriate on the basis of their revenue preferences. A method is appropriate not because it raises more revenue for one agency or another, but because it is the most reliable one.

Another argument that was repeatedly raised against harmonization is the fact that tax administrations focus on annual profits and customs administrations focus on individual transactions. This argument may also be found in a publication issued by the U.S. Customs and Border Protection in April 2007 on related-party transaction[26]:

> Importers sometimes claim that a related party transaction value is acceptable because it satisfies the Section 482 arm's length principle as determined using the best transfer pricing method. Sometimes, a copy of an APA or transfer pricing study is submitted along with the claim. In various rulings addressing this issue, CBP has determined that an APA or transfer pricing study by itself is not sufficient to show that a related party transaction value is an acceptable transaction value. CBP has noted that although the broad goal of both the relevant provisions of the

26. U.S. Customs and Border Protection. Determining the acceptability of transaction value for related-party transactions. April 2007.

> customs and the tax law is the same, i.e., to ensure that related party transactions are at arm's length, there are substantial differences in the legal requirements.
>
> For example, the customs laws require that a customs value must be determined for every imported article. Different rates of duty apply to specific imported goods on the basis of their classification and value. Therefore, U.S. importers are required to declare the customs value on an entry-by-entry and product-by-product basis. Moreover, in order to determine whether a related party transaction value is acceptable, each import transaction must be considered. If an importer purchases different products from a related company, it is necessary to determine the correct customs value for each product, not for all the products as a whole. Therefore, the determination of whether transaction value is acceptable must also be made on a product-by-product basis.
>
> In contrast, Section 482 seeks to properly allocate income between related parties to prevent the evasion of taxes and achieve the clear reflection of income. The IRS's goal of clear reflection of income does not necessarily require a valuation of each transaction for each product, and the IRC Section 482 regulations allow for aggregation of transactions and offsetting adjustments in appropriate circumstances. This is consistent with the fact that U.S. taxpayers are required to file annual income tax returns based on aggregate tax results for the year.
>
> In view of these significant differences between the two determinations of value, it is difficult to make any direct comparisons between those made under the tax laws and those laws made under the customs laws.

It is true that importers are required to declare the customs value on an entry-by-entry basis, and that each transaction must be examined in order to determine if the price was influenced. However, it does not necessarily mean that, in order to examine a particular transaction, we cannot consider the effects of the relationship on a group of transactions, for example, all the transactions of the same product in the fiscal year. One thing is the obligation to declare the customs value transaction-by-transaction and product-by-product and a completely different thing is how we examine the effect of relationship on prices.[27]

In fact, the third example of the note to Article 1.2(a) requires the examination of a group of transactions, not just the transaction being valued. And surprisingly, this is recognized by the U.S. CBP a couple of paragraphs down in the publication. There, it indicates that the so-called "all cost plus method" of the Circumstances-of-Sale Test requires that the transfer price be adequate to ensure recovery of all costs plus a profit equivalent to the firm's overall profit realized over a representative period of time in sales of goods of the same class or kind. As one can observe, this cannot be done just by examining the particular transaction being valued. In order to determine the profit obtained in the particular transaction, one needs to calculate the costs of the company and such costs, of course, will have to be calculated for a period of time, which is, probably, the fiscal year. One cannot just calculate the cost for a particular transaction because we have to consider initial inventories, purchases and final inventories. Once have we calculated the cost for the relevant period of time, we can then allocate the cost to the particular transaction. Then, we have to compare the profit margin with the

27. Jovanovich, J. M., "Comparison between Customs Valuation and OECD Transfer Pricing Guidelines", Chapter 6 in "Transfer Pricing and Customs Valuation. Two worlds to tax as one" edited by Anuschka Bakker and Belema Obuoforibo, IBFD, 2009.

firm's overall profit realized over the relevant period of time in sales of goods of the same class or kind. Obviously, if the price of the goods being valued has not changed during the relevant period, the aggregated analysis will be valid for any transaction made during such period.[28]

In fact, a transfer pricing study is generally the way in which the price in question is arrived at and, consequently, what the customs administrations should examine.

The main obstacle found by the U.S. CBP to accept transfer pricing studies appears to be the Comparable Profits Method, which compares the overall profit margin of the importer with the overall profit margin of comparable companies. The OECD Guidelines should not be a problem in this respect because they have adopted the Transactional Net Margin Method ("TNMM"), which is transactional in character. It requires segmentation of the financial statements so as to compare the profit margin obtained in a particular transaction or in a particular line of products. If the profits in that particular line of products have been stable, and if there is no economic support to argue that profits should vary from product to product in each line, then there would be no reason to reject the TNMM for customs purposes. If we segment the financial statements so as to show the profits obtained in a single transaction, the result will probably be the same as if we compare the overall profit of the line of products. In our view, a Customs Service should not say that it will not accept transfer pricing studies in the context of the Circumstances-of-Sale Test. Rather, it should say that the transfer pricing study should follow a few important guidelines to be useful for customs purposes.[29]

3.2 Circumstances That Facilitate the Comparison and, Thus, the Harmonization

With respect to the treatment of related-party transactions, both the GVC and the OECD Guidelines, have a common objective: determining whether the relationship between buyer and seller in a particular transaction has influenced the price or, in other words, whether the price is arm's length.

The existence of common objectives and principles may be regarded as a basic premise of harmonization processes. We believe that the GVC and the OECD Guidelines share such objectives and principles (e.g. the arm's length standard), at least in relation to related-party transactions. This constitutes the grounds on which the present work is based.

A second step in the harmonization process would be the definition of the methodologies for applying the arm's length principle. Where the methodologies defined in one system are different from those defined in the other, harmonization is still possible. However, the prices resulting from the application of one method could sometimes be significantly different from those resulting from the application of another method. Where the systems do not provide flexibility for applying such

28. *Ibid.*
29. *Ibid.*

methods (e.g., existence of a mandatory sequential order of application), the only way to reconcile the results is to identify the elements of the methodologies, which produce the differences.

The GVC is flexible in respect of the methodologies that can be used by the importer to demonstrate that the relationship did not influence the price. However, such flexibility disappears when such circumstance cannot be shown by the importer. Where the price is not acceptable, the GVC defines methodologies to substitute the price agreed upon by the related parties. Such methodologies are not always flexible and, in addition, must be applied in a sequential order. (In other words, the "best method rule" is not applicable once the customs administration has determined that the relationship influenced the price.)

3.3 Other Important Considerations Regarding Harmonization

It is important to recognize that determining arm's length prices - i.e., prices which are not influenced by the relationship between buyer and seller - is a difficult task for a multinational enterprise (MNE). The OECD Guidelines indicate that, in applying the principles of taxation of MNEs, one of the most difficult issues that has arisen is the establishment for tax purposes of appropriate transfer prices.

There is no easy way to determine an arm's length price. Many elements make this task difficult. For example, difficulties appear when:

- the seller does not sell or the buyer does not buy comparable products to or from any unrelated party;
- comparable products are only traded among related parties;
- there are trademarks;
- comparable products are traded on different commercial levels; or
- the functions, assets and risks of the related buyer are not comparable to those of other buyers of comparable goods (levels of advertising and promotion expenses, etc.).

The GVC provides three simple examples to illustrate how to examine the circumstances of the sale and how to determine whether the relationship influenced the price. It may be argued that, from an economic perspective, it does not make sense to attempt to solve a complex pricing problem in the light of three simple examples. In fact, uniformity in the solution of this type of cases cannot be expected using just those three simple examples. And more importantly, importers cannot have certainty on the methodology that the customs services will apply. Uncertainty is generally a major obstacle to trade.

We need to bear in mind the Preamble to the GVC which indicates that the GVC's objective is the creation of a fair, uniform and neutral system for the valuation of goods that precludes the use of arbitrary values. The GVC requires certainty and uniformity.

If the Customs Service examines the arm's length character of a price without sufficient economic analysis, the result would likely be unfair. There are many approaches on how to determine an arm's length price. Without clear rules, the importer cannot predict what the customs administration will expect from him in determining transfer prices. And if there are many different approaches on how to determine arm's length prices, MNEs would need guidance to achieve a uniform application of the Circumstances-of-Sale Test.

In the context of Article 1.2(a) we have to consider all these elements: comparability standards, functional analysis, statistical ranges and arm's length methodologies. All of them are required to be examined if one wants to perform a sound economic analysis or, in other words, if one wants to achieve fairness, certainty and uniformity. But to consider all these elements, which are part of the circumstances of the sale, we need guidelines to examine them methodologically. The question is whether we should start developing a set of guidelines for customs valuation purposes from scratch, or whether there is any other alternative available.

The answer is, in our view, that the OECD Guidelines have been developed for this exact purpose and, consequently, that we can take advantage of the OECD's work. They have nine chapters and annexes and include rules on economic and comparability analyses, transfer pricing methodologies and special chapters for intangibles and services.

It is interesting to consider the summary remarks of the Deputy Secretary General of the WCO, Mr. Kunio Mikuriya, in the first WCO/OECD Joint Conference on Transfer Pricing and Customs Valuation:[30]

> Those who are in favor of convergence point out that a credibility question could arise if two sets of rules on value determination exist within one government. They hold that this situation results in greater compliance costs for business and greater enforcement costs for government. The proponents suggest that since the provisions on related party transactions in the WTO Agreement on Customs Valuation [the GVC] are relatively concise, compared to the more precise and comprehensive OECD Guidelines on Transfer Pricing, there might be a room for developing guidelines or explanatory/interpretative notes for their better application. They maintain that this approach does not imply the revision of the WTO Agreement, but is rather intended to facilitate and complement the proper implementation of the existing WTO rules. The approach should provide Customs administrations with a choice, instead of imposing an obligation. They encourage customs, in particular, to follow the functional analysis epitomized in the OECD Guidelines in determining whether the relationship influenced the price. They also suggest that inputs from the customs area would be beneficial for the future review of OECD guidelines.[31]

Considering the different types of instruments (domestic tax laws, tax treaties, the OECD Guidelines and the GVC, which is a multilateral trade agreement), the possibility of having a single valuation system for tax and customs purposes is not realistic (or even desirable). This has been recognized in the Guide to Customs Valuation and Transfer Pricing published by the WCO:

30. First Joint WCO/OECD Conference on Transfer Pricing and Customs Valuation, Brussels, 3–4 May 2006.
31. OECD, online: http://www.oecd.org/ctp/transfer-pricing/36740073.pdf.

> The relationship between Customs valuation and transfer pricing has been discussed in various national and international fora over the past few years... The business community has raised the issue as a matter of concern, in particular advocating that Customs take into account available transfer pricing information prepared for direct tax purposes when examining related party transactions and also give consideration to the impact of transfer pricing adjustments on the Customs value. It has been recognized that at this stage any alignment or merger of tax and Customs methodologies is not a realistic proposition given the particulars of the existing legal frameworks upon which they are based.[32]

What is actually desirable is to have a set of guidelines in order to apply Article 1.2(a) of the GVC in a uniform manner and to provide certainty to MNEs. The OECD Guidelines are, in most aspects, compatible with the GVC. In the First WCO/OECD Joint Conference, the delegate of the Canada Border Services Agency, Mr. Paul Allan, indicated that, in Memorandum D13-4-5, his agency had already accepted, for valuation purposes, a price paid or payable which is derived from one of the methods set out in the OECD Guidelines, unless there is information on prices available which is more directly related to the specific importations. Mr. Allan made a very interesting comment: he said that it was not the intention of the Canada Border Services Agency to reinvent the wheel on this matter.

If one reads the OECD Guidelines in the light of the GVC's Preamble, the principles underlying the General Introductory Commentary and the General Interpretative Note, the limitations of Article 7 and the principles underlying the test values and the secondary methods, one can observe that they are consistent with the GVC's primary sources of interpretation.

Like Article 1.2(a), the OECD Guidelines are based on the comparison between related and unrelated transactions. Ideally, they should be applied on transaction-by-transaction basis. They have adequate comparability standards (even higher than the comparability standards that we can find in most provisions of the GVC). The methodologies do not seem alien to the GVC's language and, as in the case of Article 1.2(a), they are not subject to a strict hierarchical order of application.

If we can find a set of guidelines detailed and thorough enough to tackle the complex transfer pricing problems in a fair and economically sound manner, consistent with the GVC's principles and objectives, such guidelines may help to achieve a worldwide uniform implementation of the GVC's related party provisions. In our view, we can find such guidelines in the OECD's work and one can see that, to some extent, the TCCV shared this view in Commentary 23.1 and Case Study 14.1. The WCO, in the abovementioned Guide to Customs Valuation and Transfer Pricing expressed the following view:

> The essence of the issue is therefore contained in the following question: to what extent can information contained in transfer pricing documentation, primarily developed for taxation purposes, provide useful information for Customs to

32. WCO, *Guide to Customs Valuation and Transfer Pricing* (2015 – WCO). Available at: http://www.wcoomd.org/en/topics/key-issues/revenue-package/~/media/36DE1A4DC54B47109514FFCD0AAE6B0A.ashx.

> determine whether or not the price declared for imported goods has been influenced by the parties' relationship, in order to make a final determination of the Customs Value?
>
> The Technical Committee on Customs Valuation has confirmed the basic principle that transfer pricing documentation may provide useful information for Customs in respect of related party transactions, on a case by case basis... The focus is now on providing further guidance to Customs on how to examine and interpret transfer pricing documentation which may be helpful in this regard. The other key question is the impact of adjustments made (after importation) for transfer pricing purposes; in which cases, if any, should such adjustments be taken into account by Customs in determining the Customs value of the imported goods?[33]

3.4 Conclusions Regarding Feasibility of Harmonization

The GVC and the OECD Guidelines present many important differences which, in most cases, derive from the inhomogeneous characteristics and nature of the instruments and taxes in question. However, such differences appear not to be so important where the interpreter focuses on the related-party rules of the GVC. The fact that tax and customs rules share a common standard in relation to related-party transactions, facilitates the process of harmonization. Where broad and flexible constructions of tax and customs rules are adopted, an interpreter can achieve an acceptable degree of harmonization. A harmonized approach to the analysis of related-party transactions under the OECD Guidelines and the GVC would consist of:

(1) Use of common standards for determining arm's length values and for examining whether the relationship influenced the transaction value. This part of the analysis will be undertaken in Chapters 2 and 3.
(2) Identification of the differences between the customs duties' tax base and the relevant elements (e.g. inventory cost of imported property) of the tax base of income taxes. This part of the analysis could involve the examination of possible adjustments and reconciliation of results. This will be explored in Chapter 4.

The single determination of arm's length transaction values for customs and tax purposes constitutes one of the objectives of the present work. Once such transaction values have been so determined, appropriate upward or downward adjustments should be made separately for tax and customs purposes, in order to account for the differences in the regimes. Another possibility would be the determination of the arm's length transaction value of the imported goods for either tax or customs purposes and, once such transaction value has been determined under one of the systems (e.g.

33. *See supra* note 32 at 5. The issue about the impact of transfer pricing adjustments made after importation was first raised in Chapter V of the first edition of this book and, subsequently, in a paper submitted to the TCCV at its 20th Session (published in *Periódico Económico Tributario* (Nbr. 333, 334, 335 y 336), La Ley, Buenos Aires, 2005).

customs), subsequent upward or downward adjustments should be made, as required by the other system (e.g. tax), to arrive at the statutory value.

It is important to indicate, however, that once the customs administration has determined that the importer has not been able to demonstrate that the relationship had not influenced the price, the possibilities to obtain consistent results through customs and tax methodologies decrease. In this respect, the role of the customs administrations in the determination of the appropriate arm's length value will determine the extent and degree of harmonization that could be actually achieved.

CHAPTER 2

The Arm's Length Principle

4 DEFINITION: OECD GUIDELINES

The arm's length principle is defined in the Glossary of the OECD Guidelines as follows:

> The international standard that OECD Member countries have agreed should be used for determining transfer prices for tax purposes. It is set forth in Article 9 of the OECD Model Tax Convention as follows: where "conditions are made or imposed between the two enterprises in their commercial or financial relations which differ from those which would be made between independent enterprises, then any profits which would, but for those conditions, have not so accrued, may be included in the profits of that enterprise and taxed accordingly.

An arm's length price is the price which would have been agreed upon between unrelated parties engaged in the same or similar transactions under the same or similar conditions.[34] Levey explains that this has been the Guidelines' guiding principle since the issuance of the 1979 OECD Report.[35]

The Guidelines indicate that, when independent enterprises deal with each other, the conditions of their commercial and financial relations ordinarily are determined by market forces.[36] When transfer prices agreed upon between associated enterprises do not reflect market forces and the arm's length principle, the tax liabilities of such enterprises and tax revenues of the host countries can be distorted. OECD Member countries have adopted the arm's length principle as the standard on which any adjustment to correct such distortions should be based.[37]

34. *See* OECD Guidelines *supra* note 4, at 1.3.
35. Hammer *supra* note 11 at 3.02[1][a].
36. *See* OECD Guidelines *supra* note 4, at 1.2.
37. *Ibid.* at 1.3.

5 RECOGNITION OF THE ARM'S LENGTH PRINCIPLE IN THE GVC

5.1 Structure of the GVC: Application of the Provisions of the GVC to Related-Party Transactions

As a general principle, in determining customs values in cases of related-party transactions, Customs administrations must apply, in first term, the provisions of GVC Article 1.2. Where Customs administrations determine that the importer has not demonstrated that the relationship had not influenced the price, then the provisions of GVC Articles 2, 3, 5, 6 and 7 are applicable (in sequential order) to determine a substitute value.[38]

5.2 GVC Article 1.2: Recognition of the Arm's Length Principle

GVC Article 1.2 contains general rules regarding related-party transactions. Such rules should not be used to establish substitute values. Rather, their purpose is to determine whether the transaction value agreed upon between related parties is acceptable for customs valuation purposes.[39]

GVC Article 1.2 sets out a general principle: "the transaction value shall be accepted provided that the relationship did not influence the price". The principle adopted under the GVC is clearly similar to the one adopted by the OECD Guidelines.[40] In effect, the only possible way to determine whether the relationship has influenced the price in any given controlled transaction is to compare such transaction with similar uncontrolled transactions (in comparable circumstances). We can illustrate this idea with the following example (which has been simplified for purposes of illustration. It does not involve economic or valuation analyses):

The transaction value of the imported goods in a given controlled transaction has been determined through the following formula:

$$A + X = D$$
$$X = B + C$$

38. World Customs Organization (WCO), Technical Committee on Customs Valuation, *Customs Valuation Compendium* (Brussels, WCO, 1997) [hereinafter "CVC"] at Com14.1/1–CS10.1/1 (Commentary 14.1 and Case Study 10.1 of the Technical Committee on Customs Valuation).
39. *See* GVC Article 1.2 and its Interpretative Note. *See* also Sherman *supra* note 23 at 191.
40. Joseph S. Kaplan indicates that "this statutory language is an invitation to transaction-by-transaction analysis as to whether the circumstances of sale rule out the possibility that the relationship between buyer and seller has influenced the price. This is as close as customs valuation law comes to providing an arm's-length test. The lack of clear guidelines as to whether the circumstances of sale justify the conclusion that the related-party price is not influenced by the relationship can be overcome by obtaining a binding ruling to this effect from the Headquarters Office of Customs." (Paper delivered at the Transfer Pricing Seminar organized by Insight Information Co., 26–27 April 1999). We believe that the problem of the absence of guidelines in the GVC may be solved if the OECD Guidelines are used to interpret and supplement the related-party provisions of the GVC.

where
A = Cost of goods sold (COGs).
X = Amount for profits and general expenses.
D = Transaction value.
B = Amount for profits and general expenses (not influenced by relationship).
C = Other elements present in controlled transactions (which therefore, are not present in open market conditions) (this number may be positive or negative).

In order to accept the transaction value, C must be equal to (or closely approximate) zero.

In this equation, there will always be two variables that we do not know (or if we do know, whose accuracy cannot be proven, in principle): (1) X and (2) D. To solve the equation we need to know at least one of them.

A system of valuation can adopt different methodologies or standards to determine or discover the value of either X or D.

One possibility can be the, so-called, global formulary apportionment, which would allocate the global profits of an MNE group on a consolidated basis among the associated enterprises in different countries on the basis of a predetermined and mechanistic formula.[41] This method has obviously not been adopted by the authors of the GVC. First, the GVC does not provide any formula to determine the value of any element of the price. Second, the GVC does not authorize the use of such a formula. Rather, it appears to prevent such formulae from being used, since it expressly prohibits the use of arbitrary or fictitious values.[42]

By putting the emphasis on the "influence of the relationship", it seems that the GVC has adopted the arm's length standard on the basis of which the unknown elements are discovered through comparison of comparable controlled and uncontrolled transactions. In effect, to determine whether the relationship has influenced the price (element C in our equation), we must determine such facts by examining similar uncontrolled transactions (i.e., transactions in which there is no relationship between the parties).

This approach has also been taken by the Canada Border Services Agency for Customs valuation purposes. In effect, paragraphs 6 to 9 of Memorandum D13-4-5,[43] which explains and illustrates the treatment of sales between related persons in determining the value for duty under Section 48 of the Customs Act, states:

> 6. Neither the Act nor the international customs valuation agreement adopted by the World Trade Organization (WTO), upon which the valuation provisions of the Act are based, detail the information to be used in establishing that a relationship has not influenced the price in a sale of goods for export. Regardless of how an importer chooses to establish the acceptability of the price, the importer's conclusion that the price is acceptable should be supported by factual evidence. For example, showing that the price is adequate to ensure recovery of all costs plus a

41. *See* Hammer *supra* note 11, at 4.06.
42. *See* Preamble and Article 7.2(g) of the GVC.
43. Canada Border Services Agency, Memorandum D13-4-5 "Transaction value method for related persons" (17 September 2015) [hereinafter "Memorandum"] online: <http://www.cbsa-asfc.gc.ca/publications/dm-md/d13/d13-4-5-eng.html> (date accessed: 8 July 2017).

profit which is representative of the firm's overall profit realized over a representative period of time in sales of goods of the same class or kind, would demonstrate that the price had not been influenced.

7. The CBSA accepts the transaction value method in most importations involving sales between related persons. It is also expected that importers will be able to assure themselves more easily and more often of the acceptability of prices between related persons than they would be able to demonstrate that the transaction value closely approximates a test value.

8. A transfer price agreement submitted by the importer may be a good source of information if it contains relevant information about the circumstances surrounding the sale. A transfer price (i.e., a price charged for the goods by the related entity) is an acceptable starting point for determining the value for duty of imported goods.

9. The Organisation for Economic Co-operation and Development (OECD) sets out several methods of pricing goods in order to achieve a price which could reasonably have been expected in similar circumstances had the vendor and the purchaser not been related. The CBSA will accept a price paid or payable which is derived from one of the methods set out by the OECD, unless there is information on prices available which is more directly related to the specific importations.

As one can clearly see, Revenue Canada has interpreted GVC Article 1.2 and its Note as laying down the arm's length standard (as defined by the OECD Guidelines) for determining whether related-party transactions are acceptable under the provisions of GVC Article 1.1.

6 THE OECD GUIDELINES CAN BE USED TO DETERMINE WHETHER TRANSACTION PRICE IS ARM'S LENGTH UNDER GVC ARTICLE 1.2

6.1 General Considerations

It is under GVC Article 1.2(a) and its Note, where the OECD Guidelines may be primarily and broadly applied. As we will see, they can provide rules and principles for determining whether the transaction value has been influenced by the relationship and guide the examination of the circumstances surrounding the sale. In other words, the detailed provisions of the Guidelines could complement the more general provisions of GVC Article 1.2(a) and its Note.

The transaction value of sales between related parties forms the basis for determining the customs value of the imported goods (i.e., no substitute value must be determined under the provisions of GVC Articles 2, 3, 5, 6 or 7) only if it is established that the price has not been influenced by the relationship. Under GVC Article 1.2, the responsibility for demonstrating that the relationship has not influenced the prices lies with the importer.[44] GVC Article 1.2(a) provides that, in determining whether the

44. *See* CVC *supra* note 39 at Com14.1/1–CS10.1/1 (Commentary 14.1 and Case Study 10.1 of the Technical Committee on Custom Valuation). *See also* United States Customs Service (USCS), *Customs Valuation Encyclopedia* (USCS, 1998) at chapter XXXIV [hereinafter "CVE"] (*see* especially Rulings 544686 (31 August 1994), 545813 (11 September 1996), 545638 (13 February

related-party transaction value has not been influenced by the relationship (i.e., whether such value is acceptable for the purposes of GVC Article 1.1), the circumstances surrounding the sale should be examined. Customs administrations should give the importers an opportunity to supply further detailed information as may be necessary to enable them to examine such circumstances.[45]

The Note to GVC Article 1.2 gives some guidance in relation to the circumstances that Customs administrations should examine and to the information that importers should submit. However, such guidance is very general. Customs administrations and importers cannot be expected to solve complex transfer pricing problems solely on the basis of such general provisions. This might produce an inconsistent application of the related-party provisions of the GVC from one country to another, which is clearly contrary to the principle of "uniformity and certainty" in the implementation of GATT Article VII.[46]

Furthermore, the Note to GVC Article 1.2 only provides examples of circumstances or aspects of the transactions which could be examined by Customs administrations. Such examples do not constitute the only circumstances or aspects that Customs administrations might explore.[47] Sherman and Glashoff indicate that "[i]t is extremely important that the Notes be taken only as a starting point and as illustrative."[48] They add that "[t]he Code does not confine itself to the facts regarding the sale - it deals with the broader concept of an inquiry into 'the circumstances surrounding' the sale. This language plainly speaks of the entire context of the transaction and not just of the transaction itself."[49] Interestingly, these authors explain that "if the pricing is done pursuant to a formula which has been accepted by the taxing authorities of either the country of export or the country of importation, evidence to that effect should help to establish that the TV [transaction value] is acceptable."[50] We need to make some comments on such assertion. In some cases, the acceptance by the Customs of a transaction value calculated pursuant to a formula which has been accepted by the tax authorities may also lead to non-uniform implementation of the GVC. In effect, where

1995) and 546449 (6 January 1998)). But *see ESSO S.A.P.A.* v. *A.N.A. s/ recurso de apelacion*, (7 October 1993) Tribunal Fiscal de la Nacion, Sala G, File No. 6872-A (Argentina).

45. Note to paragraph 2 of GVC Article 1.
46. *See* Preamble of the GVC.
47. This has been recognized, for example, by the U.S. CBP in Ruling HQ H037375 (11 December 2009). The U.S. CBP said: "The Customs Regulations specified in 19 CFR Part 152 set forth *illustrative examples* of how to determine if the relationship between the buyer and the seller influences the price. In this respect, Customs will examine the manner in which the buyer and seller organize their commercial relations and the way in which the price in question was derived in order to determine whether the relationship influenced the price. If it can be shown that the price was settled in a manner consistent with the normal pricing practices of the industry in question, or with the way in which the seller settles prices with unrelated buyers, this will demonstrate that the price has not been influenced by the relationship... In addition, Customs will consider the price not to have been influenced if the price was adequate to ensure recovery of all costs plus a profit equivalent to the firm's overall profit realized over a representative period of time ... *These are examples to illustrate that the relationship has not influenced the price, but other factors may be relevant as well.*" [emphasis added]
48. Sherman *supra* note 23, at 193.
49. *Ibid.*
50. *Ibid.*

the tax authorities do not use common or consistent standards to evaluate the arm's length character of the transaction, the acceptance of such values for customs purposes might produce an inconsistent implementation of the related-party provisions of the GVC. Therefore, such transaction values should only be accepted for customs purposes if the tax authorities have used common and consistent standards to determine whether the transaction was arm's length or whether the formula (for determining the price) produced arm's length results. We believe that the OECD Guidelines may provide these common and consistent standards.

The Note to GVC Article 1.2 provides that "the customs administrations should be prepared to examine relevant aspects of the transaction, *including* the way in which the buyer and seller organize their commercial relations and the way in which the price in question was arrived at, in order to determine whether the relationship influenced the price" [emphasis added]. This involves a complete analysis of the transaction in question and uncontrolled transactions in order to determine whether the relationship influenced the price (the examination of those aspects should always have a comparability purpose, since it appears to be the only mechanism authorized by the GVC to determine whether the relationship influenced the price). We can conclude that the language of the Note to GVC Article 1.2 is broad enough to permit a transfer pricing analysis under the more detailed rules of the OECD Guidelines for determining whether the relationship influenced the transaction value. Being a detailed set of rules which has been (totally or partially) adopted by a great number of countries, the OECD Guidelines appear to be an adequate complement to GVC Article 1.2 and its Note for determining the arm's length character of related-party transactions. They could also facilitate an appropriate and uniform implementation of the related-party rules of the GVC, which is one of the clear purposes of its Preamble.

The Canada Border Services Agency ("CBSA") has adopted this approach for customs purposes. In effect, paragraph 9 of Memorandum D13-4-5 states:

> 9. The Organisation for Economic Co-operation and Development (OECD) sets out several methods of pricing goods in order to achieve a price which could reasonably have been expected in similar circumstances had the vendor and the purchaser not been related. The CBSA will accept a price paid or payable which is derived from one of the methods set out by the OECD, unless there is information on prices available which is more directly related to the specific importations.[51]

This approach of the CBSA constituted a major step towards harmonization of customs and tax transfer pricing laws.

Another interesting effort towards harmonization may be found in the United States. The Internal Revenue Service ("IRS") and the US Customs Service ("USCS") – which come, both within the jurisdiction of the Treasury Department – have collaborated when the USCS participated in Advance Pricing Arrangement ("APA") negotiations and, as a result of such involvement, ruled that the importer may declare values for products imported from a related party on the basis of the results of the APA. Meyer

51. Memorandum *supra* note 44.

and Outman[52] indicate that the importer had filed a ruling request with the USCS to validate its declared values on the basis of the transfer pricing method included in its request for a bilateral APA. Since the USCS ruling request and the request for APA had identical subject matters, a USCS representative participated in the APA process which facilitated the issuance of a favorable USCS ruling. Accordingly, the USCS indicated its willingness to accept the transaction value proposed by the importer and reflected in the APA request provided the importer could demonstrate that the circumstances of sale - i.e., the test laid down in GVC Article 1.2(a) - would produce an arm's length transaction value. The USCS found that such test was satisfied stating:

> Our review of the information, including attending the APA prefiling conference and review of information submitted to the IRS ... allows us to conclude that we have examined the relevant aspects of the transaction, including the way in which the importer and its related suppliers organize their commercial relations, as well as the way in which the price in question was arrived at between the parties. Based on this review, we hold that the importer has demonstrated that the price has not been influenced by the relationship for purposes of the COS [*circumstances of sale*] test.[53]

This type of collaboration between Customs and tax agencies constitutes another way to approach the problem of harmonization of customs and tax transfer pricing rules. It implies prior recognition of the overlapping between such areas of law and of the fact that uniformity between tax and customs valuation is desirable and feasible.

In Ruling HRL 548482 (23 July 2014) the United States Customs Border Protection ("U.S. CBP") accepted that the information supplied to Customs in a transfer pricing study could be relevant in examining the circumstances of sale, but the weight to be given to this information would vary depending on the details set forth in the study. The U.S. CBP also indicated that whether the products covered by the study are comparable to the imported products and the type of methodology used in the transfer pricing study were important considerations. The U.S. CBP found the information of the transfer pricing studies to be relevant in the examination of the circumstances of the sale in, among others, Rulings HQ H037375 (11 December 2009) and HQ H219515 (11 October 2012).

6.2 The Transfer Pricing Issue at the TCCV: From the First Debates at the 20th Session to Commentary 23.1 and Case Study 14.1[54]

Transfer pricing was first discussed at the TCCV at the Theme Meeting of its 20th Session, where we submitted a paper entitled "Transfer Pricing for Customs and Tax

52. Dennis I. Meyer and William D. Outman, "U.S. Tax and Customs Consequences of Dealing with a Related Foreign Supplier", (November 2001) 12 J.Int'l Tax'n 30, online: <http://www.bakernet.com> (date accessed: 25 April 2002).
53. Wrappe, Pike and Chung, "Joint APA Effort Signals New Level of IRS-Customs Coordination", (29 November 2000) 9 Transfer Pricing 551.
54. *See* Jovanovich *supra* note 28.

Purposes".[55] At that time, many of the participants struggled in comparing the GVC's methods and the methods of the OECD Guidelines. We insisted in pointing out that Articles 2, 3, 5, 6 and 7 of the GVC are not transfer pricing provisions. We emphasized that, if one was facing the application of these Articles, it was because the discussion about transfer pricing had already finished and the transaction value method had been rejected. Therefore, we tried to make it clear that there was no point in comparing the methods laid down in Articles 2 through 7 of the GVC with the methods described in the OECD Guidelines.

In 2006 and 2007, the WCO and the OECD organized two joint conferences on transfer pricing and customs valuation. In both conferences, some delegates expressed the view that convergence of tax and customs transfer pricing rules was not possible because tax and customs laws had different objectives. In the panel discussions, we indicated that we did not agree with such a statement. On the one hand, the general objective of customs law is the regulation of the international trade of goods. To be more specific, the GVC's objective is for a fair, uniform and neutral system for the valuation of goods for customs purposes that precludes the use of arbitrary or fictitious values. To be even more specific, we can say that the objective of the GVC's related-party provisions (Article 1.2) is to determine whether the relationship between buyer and seller influenced the price. On the other hand, the general objective of tax law is, of course, to raise revenue. In turn, the objective of income tax legislation is to impose a tax upon a specific exteriorization of ability to pay (or wealth), which is the income of a person. But then, if we focus on the transfer pricing provisions of income tax legislation, we can observe that their objective is to determine whether an element of the tax base of income taxes (i.e., the sales price or the acquisition cost) is subject to conditions which differ from those which would be made between independent enterprises. As we become more specific, the objectives converge to one single objective: determining whether the relationship influenced the prices. One can conclude, therefore, that it is not relevant if the general objectives are different. The specific objectives are the same both in the customs and in the tax context.

As a sequel to the second joint WCO/OECD conference, it was proposed that a Focus Group on Transfer Pricing be set up to take the issue forward. Besides the representatives of the WCO and the OECD, the said Focus Group contained representatives of the WTO, customs administrations, tax authorities and the private sector. The first meeting of the Focus Group was held on 26 October 2007 on the sidelines of the meeting of the 25th Session of the TCCV. One of the purposes of this initiative was that the TCCV had the benefit of interacting with the members of the Focus Group as some of the members of the TCCV, including the chairperson and the vice-chairperson, were also in the Focus Group and this would enable effective coordination between the two bodies.

The materials developed by the Focus Group were put on the WCO website for consideration by WCO members.[56] Among these materials there were eleven draft case

55. *See* Jovanovich, J. M. Paper submitted to the TCCV at its 20th Session (published in *Periódico Económico Tributario* (No. 333, 334, 335 y 336), La Ley, Buenos Aires, 2005).

56. *See* TCCV, Doc. VT0647E1a.

studies submitted to the Focus Group by the author of this book, the purpose of which was to set a basis for the discussion on how to use the OECD Guidelines in the context of the Circumstances-of-Sale Test of Article 1.2(a) of the GVC. Furthermore, the issue was raised of how year-end adjustments introduced by the tax authorities could be treated for the initial customs declarations under price review clauses under Commentary 4.1. We had previously raised this issue in Chapter 5 of the first edition of this book in 2002 and in a paper submitted at the 20th Session of the TCCV[57] and also in one of the abovementioned draft case studies. This issue is reflected in Subchapter 5.3.1 of the WCO Guide to Customs Valuation and Transfer Pricing.

The Focus Group made the following recommendations:

(i) The summary of these recommendations to be presented to the TCCV at the 26th Session for the information of members;
Presentations and case studies presented to the Focus Group to be made available to the members of the TCCV for their information;
(ii) A proposal be made to the TCCV at their next session that the following technical points be taken up for examination and consideration of the need for further instruments:
- the phrase "circumstances of sale" in Article 1.2(a) of the GVC in respect of its application to transfer pricing situations.
- consideration of the customs valuation treatment of situations where a transfer pricing agreement indicates that the declared customs value will be adjusted as necessary at a later date to achieve a predetermined profit margin (known as price review clauses). This could be a development of earlier work of the TCCV on price review clauses.
(iii) Members of the Focus Group from the private sector could contribute to TCCV discussions on these issues, via the International Chamber of Commerce (ICC) or by invitation (by the chairperson of the TCCV).
(iv) Greater dialogue between customs and tax administrations to be encouraged.
(v) Continued support by the OECD.

Following the recommendations of the Focus Group, during the intersession, the WCO Secretariat prepared working document VT0604E1a, containing a summary of the Focus Group meeting, which was presented to the 26th Session of the TCCV in April 2008.

The WCO Secretariat suggested that the TCCV needed to identify the objectives, the core issues, the ultimate goal and the way forward on the subject of customs valuation and transfer pricing. As possible core issues, it suggested the following:

- How to accept and utilize transfer pricing methods for customs purposes in order to examine the circumstances of sale under Art. 1.2(a) of the GVC, as a tool which would demonstrate that the transaction value is not influenced by the relationship between buyer and seller.

57. *See supra* note 56.

- How to treat compensating or the year-end adjustments of the tax authorities for adjusting the customs value by modifying the customs declarations at the point of importation, with reference to Commentary 4.1 dealing with price review clauses.

The Secretariat suggested that 3 of the 11 draft case studies be presented to the TCCV during the 27th Session.[58] These case studies concerned how Customs could accept the transaction value between related parties as the customs value, by utilizing the transfer pricing methods under the OECD Guidelines. Case study 1 dealt with the cost-plus method, case study 2 related to the resale price method and case study 3 included both the issue of the transactional net margin method (TNMM) and price review clauses. The WCO Secretariat invited members to comment on the case study approach. Prior to the 27th Session, the Secretariat received comments from Colombia, Japan and the United States. The three presented draft case studies were at the very origin of the discussion and drafting process of Case Study 14.1. The rationale underlying the example in item (i) of Subchapter 5.2.2 of the WCO Guide also corresponds to one of the said draft case studies.

The WCO Secretariat, on behalf of the TCCV, invited the OECD and the ICC to make presentations at the 27th Session. It also invited members' comments as to the establishment of a working group on the issue of transfer pricing. The initiative received immediate support from Japan, which was of the view that the establishment of a working group would facilitate discussions on the issues of transfer pricing and customs valuation. Japan agreed to focus the TCCV's discussions on the two core issues suggested by the Secretariat. The working group, however, was finally not established as some members considered that, due to the importance of the issue and in order to be inclusive, the issue should be dealt within the TCCV.

As indicated above, the objective of the case studies that we submitted to the Focus Group and presented during the 27th Session was to illustrate how to utilize the OECD transfer pricing methods in order to examine the circumstances of sale under Article 1.2(a) of the GVC (i.e., as a tool which would demonstrate that the transaction value is not influenced by the relationship between buyer and seller). Case study 3 introduced the discussion about the use of price review clauses, in order to allow the application of year-end transfer pricing adjustments to transaction value within the context of Article 1 of the GVC.

Of course, the methodologies of the OECD Guidelines are not expressly contemplated in Article 1.2(a) of the GVC. The fact that they are not expressly contemplated does not mean that the GVC prevents the use of them. It is necessary to "interpret" the GVC and determine whether such methodologies are in accordance with it. The proposal to the TCCV was that one way to do so was by means of case studies. The TCCV could analyze, on a case-by-case basis, the application of the OECD Guidelines and methods to specific situations, keeping in mind the objectives underlying the GVC. In this way, the importers and customs administrations would be provided with additional guidance on how to solve the transfer pricing problems in a uniform and

58. These three case studies were included as Annex III to document VT0647E1 of the TCCV.

predictable way, and in a progressive manner. This would give the chance to all the customs administrations to gradually understand the OECD methods and how to approach transfer pricing in an economically sound way. The idea of moving forward by means of case studies was generally accepted by the members during the TCCV's 27th Session.

In previous sessions, the idea of a "convergence" between tax and customs rules was always present in the discussions. As from the 27th Session, the TCCV's approach to this topic gradually changed. The discussions started to be focused on whether the OECD Guidelines could be utilized to interpret or supplement Article 1.2(a) of the GVC or, from a different perspective, whether the information of a transfer pricing study prepared in accordance with the OECD Guidelines may be used by customs administrations and importers in determining whether the relationship between buyer and seller influenced the price.

The 27th Session had a very important outcome: upon a proposal made by the delegate of Japan, this issue was shifted to the Agenda Item V "Specific technical questions" for the next sessions. In other words, this subject was no longer a "question raised during the Intersession", and become a permanent subject in the TCCV's agenda. Consequently, item V of the Agenda for the 28th Session presented the issue under the following title: "Related party transactions under the Agreement and Transfer Pricing".

At the 27th Session, the TCCV adopted the following approach as a way forward: (i) key issues on how to examine the transaction value between related parties should be highlighted and discussed; and (ii) the TCCV would start to work on a new, single case study which could include all considerations on the issue of related-party transaction in relation to transfer pricing. The delegate of the United States offered to prepare a draft case study, which could be circulated to members for comments.[59]

The United States submitted a draft case study during the intersession, which was circulated to members by the Secretariat. In the draft case study, the Customs Service evaluated the acceptability of transaction value on the basis of the third example of paragraph 3 of the Interpretative Note to Article 1.2(a) (i.e., "where it is shown that the price is adequate to ensure recovery of all costs plus a profit which is representative of the firm's overall profit realized over a representative period of time (e.g., on an annual basis) in sales of goods of the same class or kind, this would demonstrate that the price had not been influenced"). As it harbored doubts about the acceptability of the price, the Customs Service examined the transfer pricing study provided by the importer, which was prepared on the basis of the TNMM of the OECD Guidelines. Interestingly, the draft case study prepared by the United States indicated that the language of Interpretative Note to Article 1.2 was broad enough to permit the use of the OECD Guidelines in determining whether the relationship influenced the price. This idea had already been introduced in Subchapter 6 of the first edition of this book in 2002 and in the case studies that we submitted to the Focus Group and that we presented to the

59. *See* TCCV, Doc. VT0675E1a.

TCCV during the 27th Session.[60] In fact, the draft case study submitted by the United States follows, in essence, a fact pattern and a rationale similar to that introduced in the said case studies.

Among the key issues proposed by the Secretariat for discussion for the 28th Session, it is interesting to highlight the treatment of price adjustments after importation when the transaction value is adjusted by the tax authorities after importation and, in this respect, the relevance of the price review clauses under Commentary 4.1. This will be examined in detail below in Chapter 5.

The draft case study prepared by the United States was first discussed at the 28th Session of the TCCV. Several members had questions and asked for clarifications as a result of a paragraph-by-paragraph examination. Finally, the TCCV decided to cease examination in order to prepare a revised case study for the next session.

During the intersession, the Secretariat prepared a new working document along with the revised case study taking into account the discussions at the 28th Session. At the 29th, the TCCV continued to discuss the issue and asked the Secretariat to prepare a new working document incorporating, among other things, the revised case study and basic background and fundamental principles of related-party transactions relating to transfer pricing. The TCCV also proposed that a case study be submitted based on the traditional OECD transfer pricing methods (the comparable uncontrolled price (CUP), cost-plus and resale price methods). The Secretariat incorporated Case Study 1 which was presented by the author of this book to the Focus Group in 2007 and which was presented to the TCCV in Annex III to TCCV Doc. VT0647E1a.

At the 30th Session, the TCCV agreed to continue discussions for drafting a new instrument on the issue at its 31st Session. In addition, Members decided to temporarily suspend the examination of the case study presented by the United States. The Secretariat prepared a draft Commentary, the purpose of which would be to provide guidance to members on the issue of related-party transactions and transfer pricing.

At the 31st Session, the discussions were mainly focused on the draft Commentary prepared by the Secretariat. After a thorough examination, the TCCV adopted it as Commentary 23.1 entitled "Examination of the expression 'circumstances surrounding the sales' under Article 1.2(a) in relation to the use of transfer pricing studies". We will examine this Commentary in Section 6.3 below.

At the 32nd Session of the TCCV, the Ministry of Strategy and Finance of the Republic of Korea was invited to make a presentation on this subject. That presentation was mainly focused on transfer pricing adjustments and its effects for customs valuation purposes and, in particular, on whether customs administrations should accept upward or downward transfer pricing adjustments. The ICC was also invited to make presentations at this session, which was mainly focused on the ICC's work in formulating a policy statement by the business sector and the desire for formal recognition of the arm's length principle.[61]

60. *See* TCCV, Annex III to Doc. 0647E1 of the TCCV and Annex I to Doc. VT0675E1a.

61. *See* https://iccwbo.org/publication/icc-policy-statement-transfer-pricing-and-customs-value-2012/.

As a way forward, some delegates suggested to examine the information available in transfer pricing studies and how they should be presented to customs administrations in order to provide useful information in determining whether the relationship influenced the prices. At this session, it was agreed to create an informal working group to continue the analysis of this subject.

At the 33rd Session of the TCCV, some delegates expressed the view that, as a way forward, the case study submitted by the United States could be re-examined. Therefore, the TCCV agreed to reexamine a simplified version of the case study (to be prepared by the informal working group) submitted by the United States, which followed the structure and rationale of the three draft case studies presented at the 27th Session of the TCCV.[62]

During the 34th Session of the TCCV, the United States presented their proposed new national policy regarding post-importation adjustments and the ICC presented their policy statement on customs valuation and transfer pricing. Also, the TCCV discussed the simplified version of the case study prepared by the informal working group (which was based on the earlier case study submitted by the United States).

The issue analyzed in this simplified version of the case study was whether the examination of external comparables - discussed in an MNE's transfer pricing study and supported by a bilateral advance pricing agreement (APA) - could be regarded in certain cases as being consistent with the process of examining the normal industry pricing practices under the Interpretative Note to Article 1.2(a) of the GVC, which would allow Customs to conduct an analysis of profitability of similar companies in the industry. As in the earlier version, the transfer pricing study submitted by the importer used the TNMM, which compared the importer's operating margin with the operating margins of comparable uncontrolled transactions. This simplified version also kept the idea that the language of Interpretative Note to Article 1.2(a) of the GVC was broad enough to permit the use of the OECD Guidelines in determining whether the relationship influenced the price.

This simplified version of the case study represented a considerable improvement over the earlier version. However, the reference to the existence of an APA - approving the transfer pricing study submitted by the importer - did not appear to provide any relevant information to solve the case. Rather, it created some confusion as to whether a transfer pricing study needs to be approved by way of an APA in order to be considered by the customs administration in examining the circumstances of the sale. The relevant development in the simplified case study was whether the information and methodologies of the transfer pricing study (including other technical aspects, like the use of external comparables) were useful and sufficient to demonstrate that the relationship did not influence the price. If one wanted to go one step further, it would have also been relevant to address how the information should be presented by the importer to Customs and the level of segmentation of the financial data that may be required to permit the examination of a transaction or series of transactions (e.g. on an annual basis) of one particular product. In contrast, the existence of an APA indicated

62. *See* TCCV, Annex III to Doc. VT0647E1a.

that other governmental authorities have audited and approved the information and methodologies included in the transfer pricing study, but in no way did that mean that Customs would rely on such audit and approval processes. In fact, the case study did not explain why the APA was important, or even relevant, in the analysis performed by the customs administration. Again, as the case study made reference to the APA, this could be interpreted by the customs administrations as a requirement to accept transfer pricing documentation when examining the circumstances of the sale which was not the original purpose of the draft case studies that we submitted to the Focus Group and to the TCCV at its 27th Session.

At the 38th Session of the TCCV, the case study continued to be discussed, with some delegates expressing ongoing concerns regarding the use of the transactional net margin methodology in the customs valuation context and in particular (i) the impact that variations in operating expenditure may have, (ii) the use of the importer as the "tested party", (iii) the non-transactional use of the TNMM as observed in practice by many officials and (iv) the comparables observed in practice. During this session a representative of the World Bank Group gave presentations on the implementation of transfer pricing rules in practice and outlined the importance of providing clearer guidance on the interface of transfer pricing and customs valuation to trade and tax and customs officials. Furthermore, preliminary discussions concerning another draft case study, based on an application of the resale price method, took place during this session, after the draft case study was submitted for consideration by a delegate country.

At its 42nd Session, the TCCV finally adopted the case study as Case Study 14.1, which will be discussed below in Subchapter 12.3.3.

6.3 Commentary 23.1 of the TCCV: The Bridge Between the Tax and Customs Transfer Pricing Worlds[63]

Commentary 23.1 is the first official instrument which builds a real bridge between the tax and customs transfer pricing worlds. In Commentary 23.1, the issue is whether a transfer pricing study prepared for tax purposes (in accordance with the OECD Guidelines), and provided by the importer, can be utilized by the customs administration as a basis for examining the circumstances surrounding the sale.

The underlying issue is whether the OECD Guidelines may be used in order to interpret or supplement the provisions of Article 1.2(a) of the GVC (i.e., the Circumstances-of-Sale Test) and, if so, under which conditions.

The TCCV recognizes that a transfer pricing study may be a good source of information if it contains relevant information about the circumstances surrounding the sale.

However, it also recognizes that it might not be relevant or adequate in examining the circumstances surrounding the sale because of the substantial and significant differences which exist between the methods in the GVC to determine the

63. *See supra* note 28.

value of the imported goods and those of the OECD Guidelines. This second statement is the result of a recurrent mistake of many TCCV's members. They struggle in comparing the GVC's methods and the methods of the OECD Guidelines. As indicated above, Articles 2, 3, 5, 6 and 7 of the GVC are not transfer pricing provisions. If one is facing the application of these Articles, it is because the discussion about transfer pricing has already finished and the transaction value method has been rejected. Therefore, there is no point in comparing the methods laid down in these Articles with the methods described in the OECD Guidelines.

It is true that the information contained in a transfer pricing study may not be relevant or adequate in examining the circumstances surrounding the sale, but this is not due to differences in the methodologies. The information in a transfer pricing study may not be relevant or adequate for customs purposes if it is presented, for example, without sufficient segmentation in the financial statements in order to show the results or profits in sales of a particular product realized over a representative period of time (e.g., on an annual basis). Lack of segmentation is one of the main obstacles when attempting to use a transfer pricing study in demonstrating that relationship did not influence the price. However, this obstacle may be easily removed if a transfer pricing study, or additional financial information, is prepared with a view at supporting the arm's length character of a transaction for customs purposes (or, in other words, with a view at demonstrating that relationship did not influence the price).

What is remarkable is the conclusion of Commentary 23.1. This is, as we pointed out, the first bridge between the two worlds. It says that "the use of a transfer pricing study as a possible basis for examining the circumstances of the sale should be considered on a case by case basis." What is important to highlight is the use of the word "should". It means that, if the importer provides Customs with a transfer pricing study prepared for tax purposes, Customs should consider the transfer pricing study and, if the information is relevant, it should use it as possible basis for examining the circumstances of the sale.

The TCCV meant that it could not give general guidance as to the acceptability of transfer pricing studies in the customs valuation arena but that such acceptability should be evaluated on a case-by-case basis. But the underlying principle is that Customs must consider a transfer pricing study prepared in accordance with the OECD Guidelines or, in other words, that it cannot reject transfer pricing documentation (prepared in accordance with the OECD Guidelines) provided by the importer just because it was prepared for tax (as opposed to customs) purposes.

Commentary 23.1 concludes that any relevant information and documents provided by an importer may be utilized for examining the circumstances of the sale, and a transfer pricing study could be one source of such information.

Transfer pricing documentation prepared in accordance with the OECD Guidelines may, in effect, be the source of information referred to in Commentary 23.1 provided that the documentation is prepared considering the specific facts to be proven in the customs valuation arena (the proof of which may not be necessary in a tax transfer pricing controversy). This was also the view of the National Director of Customs of Chile in recent cases involving the importation of certain printing cartridges, where a transfer pricing study (with a supplementary analysis prepared for customs purposes) - which used the TNMM - was accepted as evidence that the relationship did not influence the price.[64]

COMMENTARY 23.1

Examination of the Expression "Circumstances surrounding the sale" Under Article 1.2(a) in relation to the use of Transfer Pricing Studies

1. This Commentary seeks to provide guidance on the use of a transfer pricing study, prepared in accordance with the OECD Transfer Pricing Guidelines, and provided by importers as a basis for examining "the circumstances surrounding the sale" under Article 1.2 (a) of the Agreement.
2. Under Article 1 of the Agreement, a transaction value is acceptable as the Customs value when the buyer and the seller are not related, or if related, provided that the relationship did not influence the price.
3. Where the buyer and seller are related, Article 1.2 of the Agreement provides different means of establishing the acceptability of the transaction value:

1. the circumstances surrounding the sale shall be examined to determine whether the relationship influenced the price (Article 1.2 (a));
2. the importer has an opportunity to demonstrate that the price closely approximates to one of the three test values (Article 1.2 (b)).

4. The Interpretative Note to Article 1.2 of the Agreement provides that: "It is not intended that there should be an examination of the circumstances in all cases where the buyer and the seller are related. Such examination will only be required where there are doubts about the acceptability of the price. Where the Customs administration has no doubts about the acceptability of the price, it should be accepted without requesting further information from the importer."
5. In light of this, where the Customs administration has doubts about the acceptability of the price, the administration will examine the circumstances surrounding the sale, based on information provided by the importer.
6. The Interpretative Note to Article 1.2 states that where the Customs administration is unable to accept the transaction value without further enquiry, it should give the importer an opportunity to supply such further detailed information as may be necessary. The Note also sets forth illustrative examples of how to determine if the relationship between the buyer and the seller does not influence the price.
7. The question which then arises is whether a transfer pricing study prepared for tax purposes, and provided by the importer, can be utilized by the Customs administration as a basis for examining the circumstances surrounding the sale.

---

64. *See* Resolutions 59 (10 March 2011 - Claim 721/18.12.2007) and 212 (20 April 2012 - Claim 088/09.01.08) of the National Director of Customs of Chile- Online: https://www.aduana.cl/aduana/site/artic/20110324/pags/20110324155551.html https://www.aduana.cl/aduana/site/artic/20120503/pags/20120503105051.html.

8. On one hand, a transfer pricing study submitted by an importer may be a good source of information, if it contains relevant information about the circumstances surrounding the sale. On the other hand, a transfer pricing study might not be relevant or adequate in examining the circumstances surrounding the sale because of the substantial and significant differences which exist between the methods in the Agreement to determine the value of the imported goods and those of the OECD Transfer Pricing Guidelines.
9. Accordingly, the use of a transfer pricing study as a possible basis for examining the circumstances of the sale should be considered on a case-by-case basis. As a conclusion, any relevant information and documents provided by an importer may be utilized for examining the circumstances of the sale. A transfer pricing study could be one source of such information.

7 GUIDANCE FOR APPLYING THE ARM'S LENGTH PRINCIPLE: USE OF SUCH GUIDANCE UNDER GVC ARTICLE 1.2

7.1 Comparability Analysis

The OECD Guidelines indicate that the application of the arm's length principle is based on a comparison of the conditions in a controlled transaction with the conditions that would have been made had the parties been independent and undertaking a comparable transaction under comparable circumstances. They explain that there are two key aspects in such an analysis: the first aspect is to identify the commercial or financial relations between the associated enterprises and the conditions and economically relevant circumstances attaching to those relations in order that the controlled transaction is accurately delineated; the second aspect is to compare the conditions and the economically relevant circumstances of the controlled transaction as accurately delineated with the conditions and the economically relevant circumstances of comparable transactions between independent enterprises.[65] To be comparable means that none of the differences between the situations being compared could materially affect the condition being examined in the methodology or that reasonably accurate adjustments can be made to eliminate the effect of any such differences.[66]

GVC Article 1.2(a) does not make any reference to comparability analyses. However, the idea of "comparability" is inherent in the provisions of such article. If determining whether the relationship influenced the price implies a comparison of a controlled transaction and an uncontrolled transaction which have been undertaken under the same or similar conditions, then logically the results would not be reliable unless the economically relevant characteristics of the situations being compared were sufficiently comparable.

65. *See* OECD Guidelines *supra* note 4, at 1.33.
66. *Ibid* at 3.47.

An analysis of the Note to GVC Article 1.2 indicates that the idea of comparability is clearly present in its provisions. The examples provided by the Note show a clear preference for internal comparables.[67] This same preference is reflected in paragraph 2.33 of the OECD Guidelines:

> When the resale price margin used is that of an independent enterprise in a comparable transaction, the reliability of the resale price method may be affected if there are material differences in the ways the associated enterprises and independent enterprises carry out their business ... These types of characteristics should be analyzed in determining whether an uncontrolled transaction is comparable for purposes of applying the resale price method.

This principle is also applicable in determining whether a transaction is a comparable uncontrolled transaction for the purposes of the cost-plus method. If the Note to GVC Article 1.2 and its examples are interpreted in the light of this principle, it appears that the examples that have been selected by the authors of the GVC involved a choice for situations which reflected a high degree of comparability. In other words, the examples chosen by the authors involved a standard of comparability. In applying the arm's length methods, this standard should be regarded as a requisite to be met. Therefore, it could be suggested that the application of any method (either those from which the examples are derived or any other method consistent with the provisions of the Note[68]) should always be supplemented by an appropriate comparability analysis (to ensure an adequate degree of comparability between the transactions being examined).

In Ruling 546285[69] (7 June 1996), the US Customs Service undertook an analysis to determine whether the uncontrolled transactions used for the purposes of GVC Article 1.2 were sufficiently comparable. A related buyer received from the seller a higher trade discount than the related US distributors and unrelated US retailers. The US Customs Service examined the following facts: (i) the trade discounts to both the related buyer and unrelated US distributors were based on the volume of their purchases from the foreign seller; (ii) the larger trade discount given to the related buyer was due to the increased warehousing costs incurred by stocking a larger and more extensive line of the foreign seller's products than the unrelated US distributors; and (iii) the related buyer also marketed and advertised the foreign seller's merchandise in the United States. On the basis of these facts, the US Customs Service concluded that it did not appear that the relationship affected the price of the merchandise and that the parties bought and sold from each other as if they were unrelated. It is clear that the US Customs Service evaluated the differences between the transactions (which required some adjustments for comparability purposes – e.g., volume) in determining whether the relationship had influenced the price.

67. The preference for internal comparables is reflected by the second example provided by the Note: "where it is shown that the price is adequate to ensure recovery of all costs plus a profit which is representative of the firm's overall profit realized over a representative period of time ... in sales of goods of the same class or kind, this would demonstrate that the price had not been influenced."
68. Bear in mind that the examples provided by the Note are only illustrative.
69. *See* CVE *supra* note 45 at chapter XXXIV.

This ruling shows how material differences must be taken into account when making comparisons for customs purposes. This is also suggested in paragraph 1.33 of the OECD Guidelines. This is necessary to establish the degree of actual comparability and to make appropriate adjustments to establish arm's length conditions.[70]

The requirement of "comparability" is also introduced in GVC Article 1.2(b) in applying the test values. The relevant part of GVC Article 1.2(b) reads:

In applying the foregoing tests, due account shall be taken of demonstrated differences in commercial levels, quantity levels, the elements enumerated in Article 8 and costs incurred by the seller in sales in which the seller and the buyer are not related that are not incurred by the seller in sales in which the seller and the buyer are related.[71]

Although not directly applicable for the purposes of GVC Article 1.2(a), the provision quoted above (in addition to the provisions of GVC Articles 2.1(b) and 3.1(b)) reflects the general structure and principles underlying the GVC.[72] It is important to bear in mind that the factors to be examined under a comparability analysis in the context of GVC Article 1.2(a) are not limited to those mentioned in GVC Article 1.2(b). The application of the arm's length standard – as introduced in the Note to GVC Article 1.2 – requires Customs administrations to undertake a thorough and complete analysis of comparability.

Determining the degree of comparability requires an understanding of how unrelated parties evaluate potential transactions.[73] This may be regarded as part of the circumstances surrounding the sale that shall be examined to determine whether the relationship influenced the price under GVC Article 1.2. Levey explains that one enterprise is unlikely to accept a price that an independent enterprise offers for a product if it knows that other potential customers will pay more under similar conditions. He indicates that this point is relevant to the question of comparability, because independent enterprises would generally take into account any economically relevant differences between the options realistically available to them (e.g., differences in the levels of risk).[74]

We can therefore conclude that under GVC Article 1.2(a) as well as under the OECD Guidelines all material differences should be taken into account, since this is

70. *See* OECD Guidelines *supra* note 4, at 3.47.
71. The fact that the degree of comparability required under GVC Articles 2 and 3 is lower than that required under Article 1.2 does not mean that a minimum degree of comparability is not required at all. In effect, in applying GVC Articles 2 and 3, the transaction value of identical or similar goods in a sale at the same commercial level and in substantially the same quantity as the goods being valued shall be used to determine the customs value. Where no such sale is found, the transaction value of identical goods sold at a different commercial level and/or in different quantities, adjusted to take account of differences attributable to commercial level and/or to quantity shall be used, provided that such adjustments can be made on the basis of demonstrated evidence which clearly establishes the reasonableness and accuracy of the adjustment.
72. Commentary 10.1 of the Technical Committee on Customs Valuation reads: "Although the wording in Article 1.2(b) is somewhat different from that found in Articles 2.1(b) and 3.1(b), it is clear that the principles involved are the same: account has to be taken of differences attributable to commercial level or quantity and it must be possible to make the necessary adjustment on the basis of demonstrated evidence which clearly establishes its reasonableness and accuracy." (CVC *supra* note 39, at Com10.1/1.)
73. *See* Hammer *supra* note 11, at 3.03[1][a].
74. *Ibid.* at 3.03[1][b].

necessary to first, establish the degree of actual comparability, and thus to make appropriate adjustments to establish arm's length conditions. In order to do so, it is necessary to identify the economically relevant characteristics of the commercial or financial relations that would affect conditions in arm's length transactions.[75] The OECD Guidelines refer to the following economically relevant characteristics or comparability factors:

(i) characteristics of the property;
(ii) functions performed by the parties (taking into account assets used and risks assumed including how those functions relate to widen the generation of value by the MNE group to which the parties belong, the circumstances of the transaction and industry practices);
(iii) contractual terms;
(iv) economic circumstances of the parties and of the market in which the parties operate;
(v) business strategies pursued by the parties.[76]

The circumstances of the transaction (e.g., sale) and the industry practices are evidently the same aspects that must be examined under GVC Article 1.2(a) and its interpretative note.

7.1.1 Characteristics of the Property

Differences in the specific characteristics of the property often account for differences in their value in the open market. Consequently, these features should usually be examined in determining comparability of controlled and uncontrolled transactions.[77] This principle also underlies most of the provisions of the GVC. For instance, the second example provided by the Note to GVC Article 1.2(a) requires a comparison between the profit realized in the related-party transaction and the firm's overall profit realized in sales of goods of the same class or kind. GVC Article 15.3 defines the term "goods of the same class or kind" as "goods which fall within a group or range of goods produced by a particular industry or industry sector, and includes identical or similar goods." One can suggest that the term "goods of the same class or kind" has been introduced in the second example to require an adequate level of comparability between the transactions or profit margins being examined in relation to characteristics of the goods involved.

The example mentioned in the foregoing paragraph is not the only case in which the GVC introduced comparability requisites concerning characteristics of the property. GVC Articles 1.2(b), 2 and 3 require even higher degrees of product comparability than that required by the example cited above. Under such articles, transactions must involve identical or similar goods. In relation to the concept of identical and similar goods, GVC Article 15 provides:

75. *See* OECD Guidelines *supra* note 4, at 1.35.
76. *Ibid.* at 1.36.
77. *Ibid.* at 1.39.

(a) "identical goods" means goods which are the same in all respects, including physical characteristics, quality and reputation. Minor differences in appearance would not preclude goods otherwise conforming to the definition from being regarded as identical;
(b) "similar goods" means goods which, although not alike in all respects, have like characteristics and like component materials which enable them to perform the same functions and to be commercially interchangeable. The quality of the goods, their reputation and the existence of a trademark are among the factors to be considered in determining whether goods are similar;
(c) the terms "identical goods" and "similar goods" do not include, as the case may be, goods which incorporate or reflect engineering, development, artwork, design work, and plans and sketches for which no adjustment has been made under paragraph 1(b)(iv) of Article 8 because such elements were undertaken in the country of importation;
(d) goods shall not be regarded as "identical goods" or "similar goods" unless they were produced in the same country as the goods being valued;
(e) goods produced by a different person shall be taken into account only when there are no identical or similar goods, as the case may be, produced by the same person as the goods being valued.

We can conclude that product comparability is a general requisite in applying the methods laid down in GVC Articles 2, 3, 5 and 6 (certain methods require a higher degree of product comparability than others) and in applying the test values under GVC Article 1.2(b). Product comparability is also evident in the examples of the Note to GVC Article 1.2(a). Consequently, it could be regarded as a general condition in applying the arm's length standard under GVC Article 1.2(a). This is consistent with paragraph 1.107 of the OECD Guidelines.

The OECD Guidelines suggest that, among the transfer pricing methods, the requirement for comparability of property or services is the strictest for the comparable uncontrolled price method, because any material differences in the characteristics of property or services can have an effect on the price and would require an appropriate adjustment to be considered. The OECD Guidelines suggest that the effects of differences in the characteristics of the property when determining comparability under resale price method and the cost-plus method are not as significant as under the comparable uncontrolled price method. In turn, the effects of such differences under the transactional profits methods is less significant than under the cost-plus and resale price methods. The OECD Guidelines indicate that "... [u]nder the resale price method and cost plus method, some differences in the characteristics of property or services are less likely to have a material effect on the gross profit margin or mark-up on costs ... Differences in the characteristics of property or services are also less sensitive in the case of the transactional profit methods than in the case of traditional transaction methods ... This however does not mean that the question of comparability in characteristics of property or services can be ignored when applying transactional profit methods, because it may be that product differences entail or reflect different functions performed, assets used and/or risks assumed by the tested party."[78] This is

78. *Ibid.*

also consistent with the structure of GVC Articles 2, 3, 5 and 6 and the degree of product comparability required under each of these provisions. In effect, the methods of GVC Articles 2 and 3, which are similar (but not identical) to the CUP method require the use of transaction values of identical or similar goods respectively (i.e., a high degree of product comparability). The methods of GVC Articles 5 and 6, which are based on profit margins, require a lower degree of product comparability. In effect, they use the "profit and general expenses in connection with sales of imported goods of the same class or kind." The GVC recognizes that the impact of product similarity is less significant under Articles 5 and 6, under which profit margins are used.

Among the characteristics to be considered, the OECD Guidelines include the following: the physical features of the property, its quality and reliability, and the availability and volume of supply. The characteristics of the property mentioned in the GVC should also be examined. The fact that the goods being compared are identical, similar, or of the same class or kind, should be properly taken into account vis-à-vis the arm's length method used by importers and tax and customs administrations.[79]

In paragraph 22 of Case Study 14.1 (*see* Subsection 11.3.4 below) it can be observed that the TCCV took specifically into account the characteristics of property as a relevant comparability factor to accept the use of the transfer pricing information supplied by the importer. Paragraph 22 reads: "... Accordingly, since all the comparable companies sell goods of the same class or kind, the transfer pricing study supports a finding that the price between ICO and XCO was settled in a manner consistent with the normal pricing practices of the industry." This can also be observed in the case studies No. 2 (*see* 11.3.3. below, paragraph 8), No. 3 (*see* 11.3.3 below, paragraph 20), No. 4 (*see* 11.3.3. below, paragraph 8) and No. 5 (*see* below 11.2.6. below, paragraph 21), among others.[80]

The OECD Guidelines also refer to the characteristics to be considered in case of provisions of services and transfers of intangible property.

These recommendations may be useful for customs purposes when provisions of services and transfers of intangibles are closely connected to the sale of the imported

79. Commentary 1.1 of the Technical Committee on Customs Valuation provides useful guidance and examples to illustrate the application of the principles for determining whether goods are identical or similar in accordance with GVC Article 15 (*See* CVC *supra* note 39, at Com1.1/1). We understand that such examples could supplement the rules set forth in the OECD Guidelines.

80. Likewise, the U.S. CBP took into account the characteristics of property as a relevant comparability factor to accept the use of the transfer pricing information supplied by the importer in Ruling HQ H037375 (11 December 2009). The U.S. CBP said: "...In this respect, we reviewed the information contained in CH 303's transfer pricing study and conclude that the products sold by the comparable companies are of the same class or kind as the imported merchandise. All comparable companies distribute medical products and supplies, and most importantly, these companies are direct competitors of Cardinal Health, Inc. Under these circumstances, the comparison between CH 303 and the other comparable companies, as stated in the transfer pricing study, may be considered to be consistent with the market as a whole, thereby demonstrating that the price between CH 317 and CH 303 was settled in a manner consistent with the normal pricing practices of the industry. An adequate level of product comparability was observed. Thus, the gross margins on the resale of the imported merchandise were shown to be generally the same to those in the medical product and supplies industry. On the basis of the transfer pricing study, we are satisfied that the circumstances of the sale establish that the price was settled in a manner consistent with the normal pricing practices of the industry."

goods. The Customs administrations should be prepared to examine these other characteristics as a part of the circumstances surrounding the sale.

7.1.2 Functional Analysis

The OECD Guidelines indicate that, in transactions between two independent enterprises, compensation usually will reflect the functions that each enterprise performs, taking into account assets used and risks assumed.[81] These functions are clearly among those circumstances surrounding the sale that should be examined by the Customs administrations under GVC Article 1.2. If, in the customs valuation context, the issue is whether the relationship influenced the price – and pricing in uncontrolled transactions usually reflects the functions that each enterprise performs – then the analysis of the distribution of such functions in both controlled and uncontrolled transactions is necessary to determine whether the controlled and uncontrolled transactions are sufficiently comparable and, therefore, whether the relationship influenced the price. In Case Study 14.1, one can see how the TCCV took into account the results of the functional analysis in the Circumstances-of-Sale Test:

> The functional analysis showed that there were no significant differences in functions, risks, and assets between ICO and the eight unrelated distributors. In addition, an adequate level of product comparability was observed. The comparable companies were chosen from the electrical apparatus, and electronic parts industries (companies that sell goods of the same class or kind as the imported goods). Thus, the operating profit margin on the resale of the imported goods was shown to be generally the same as in the electrical apparatus and electronic parts industries. Specifically, the transfer pricing study found that the arm's length range of the comparable companies' operating profit margins was 0.64 % to 2.79 %. As previously noted, ICO's operating profit margin was 2.50 %. Accordingly, since all the comparable companies sell goods of the same class or kind, the transfer pricing study supports a finding that the price between ICO and XCO was settled in a manner consistent with the normal pricing practices of the industry.

Differences in functions may produce different prices in the open market. If the uncontrolled transaction – selected for comparison purposes – reflected a different distribution of functions than that of the controlled transaction in question, a price derived from a comparison between these transactions would not be likely to be at arm's length. Therefore, it will provide no useful data for demonstrating that the relationship did not influence the price.

We can illustrate this with the following example:

> A, B and C are distributors of product M in country X. Product M is supplied by seller D, who is a resident of country Z. A and D are related parties. A and B do not undertake marketing and advertising activities and keep low levels of inventory of product M. In contrast, C undertakes marketing and advertising activities and keeps in inventory a large number of units of product M. A and C purchase product M from seller D at a price of 10 c.u. per unit, while B purchases the same product from seller D at a price of 13 c.u. per unit. If the Customs administration does not

81. *See* OECD Guidelines *supra* note 4, at 1.51.

> undertake a functional analysis and compares the controlled transaction (A–D) with the transaction between C and D, it will arrive at the erroneous conclusion that the price of the controlled transaction has not been influenced by the relationship. Had the Customs administration undertaken an appropriate functional analysis, it would have determined that the transaction between C and D was not sufficiently comparable to the transaction between A and D. The transaction that was actually comparable to the transaction between A and D was the transaction between B and D, which provided sufficient grounds to determine that the relationship did influence the price.[82]

Functional analysis seeks to identify the significant activities and responsibilities undertaken, assets used or contributed and risks assumed by the parties to the transactions. The economic significance of the functions in terms of their frequency, nature, and value to the respective parties to the transactions is what must be taken into account.[83]

The OECD Guidelines provide that:

> The analysis focuses on what the parties actually do and the capabilities they provide. Such activities and capabilities will include decision-making, including decisions about business strategy and risks. For this purpose, it may be helpful to understand the structure and organisation of the MNE group and how they influence the context in which the MNE operates. In particular, it is important to understand how value is generated by the group as a whole, the interdependencies of the functions performed by the associated enterprises with the rest of the group, and the contribution that the associated enterprises make to that value creation. It will also be relevant to determine the legal rights and obligations of each of the parties in performing their functions.[84]

82. Note that, where the commercial level and quantities involved are similar, the test values of GVC Article 1.2(b) could be used at the initiative of the importer A. In such a case, the transaction value would have to be accepted since C and D were unrelated parties and there were no differences in commercial level, quantity level, elements enumerated in GVC Article 8 or "costs incurred by the seller in sales in which the seller and the buyer are not related that are not incurred by the seller in sales in which the seller and the buyer are related." In this case, the tax and customs transfer pricing rules would not be consistent, being one of the situations where harmonization appears not to be feasible. However, there are two important considerations: (i) the test values can only be used at the initiative of the importer, constituting a sort of safe harbor; and (ii) an adequate interpretation of the provision that requires that "due account shall be taken of demonstrated differences in … costs incurred by the seller in sales in which the seller and the buyer are not related that are not incurred by the seller in sales in which the seller and the buyer are related" could provide a good instrument – in most of the cases – to prevent importers from using test values which do not comply with minimum standards of comparability (other than commercial level and quantity). Unfortunately, Commentary 10.1 of the Technical Committee on Customs Valuation did not address the adjustments in relation to this element of Article 1.2(b). Paragraph 4 of the Commentary states that the examples provided therein do not include other adjustments such as for differences in distances and modes of transport. Functional analysis is, however, addressed in Case Study 14.1. We would be glad to see the Technical Committee addressing this issue in more detail in further Commentaries or Advisory Opinions.
83. *See* OECD Guidelines *supra* note 4, at 1.51.
84. *Ibid.* at 1.51.

The following assets used should be considered: plant and equipment, valuable intangibles, etc. The nature of such assets, such as age, market value and property right protections available, among others, should be properly taken into account.[85]

Even though many of these elements (under certain circumstances) may be excluded from transaction value (e.g., advertising and marketing expenses incurred by the importer in the country of importation) or are not to be added to the price paid or payable for customs purposes,[86] there is nothing in GVC Article 1.2(a) preventing such elements from being analyzed in the context of a comparability analysis. Since comparability is one of the most significant features for determining whether a controlled transaction is arm's length (and a specific standard provided for in the Note to GVC Article 1.2), the examination of such elements should be specifically required in the context of a comparability (functional) analysis under GVC Article 1.2.

Note that the examination of the circumstances surrounding the sale, under the Note to GVC Article 1.2, involves the use of the most appropriate methodology - i.e., there is no sequential order of application - and, thus, the examination of a broader scope of uncontrolled transactions. Therefore, a complete functional analysis - whereby all relevant functions, assets and risks are examined - is necessary to choose the adequate arm's length methodology or the appropriate uncontrolled transaction for determining whether the relationship influenced the price. In our view, this is recognized in paragraph 22 of Case Study 14.1. The functional analysis was specifically introduced in the 11 draft case studies that we submitted to the Focus Group on Customs Valuation and Transfer Pricing in 2007, and it was present in all the drafts that were discussed at the TCCV prior to the adoption of Case Study 14.1.[87]

An analysis of the structure and principles underlying the GVC indicates that any adjustment (e.g., adjustments to account for any material differences in the functions performed by the enterprises being compared) have to be made on the basis of demonstrated evidence which clearly establishes their reasonableness and accuracy. (As indicated above, this has been identified by the Technical Committee on Customs Valuation as a general principle underlying the provisions of GVC Articles 1.2(b), 2.1(b) and 3.1(b).[88] This principle can also be found in GVC Article 8.3, the Note to GVC Article 8.1(b)(iv), the Note to GVC Article 8.3 and GVC Article 15.1(c).)

As indicated above, what is important is the economic significance of the functions performed by the enterprises being compared. Therefore, an adjustment should only be made where the differences in functions are economically significant.[89]

---

85. *Ibid.* at 1.54.
86. Further discussion of this issue will be found in Chapter IV.
87. It was also present in many rulings issued by the U.S. CBP where transfer pricing information was examined for purposes of the Circumstances-of-Sale Test. *See*, for instance, Rulings HQ H037375 (11 December 2009) and HQ H219515 (11 October 2012).
88. *See* CVC *supra* note 39, at Com10.1/1.
89. In a different context, the Technical Committee on Customs Valuation indicated that the mere existence of differences in commercial level or quantity would not by itself require that an adjustment be made; an adjustment will be necessary only if a difference in the price or value results from a difference in commercial level or quantity. *See* CVC *supra* note 39, at Com10.1/1 (Commentary 10.1). One can infer, therefore, that the Technical Committee follows the same principle: "adjustments should be made where the differences are economically significant."

In relation to risks assumed, the OECD Guidelines explain that, in the open market, the assumption of increased risk will also be compensated by an increase in the expected rate of return.[90] They also provide that in making comparisons between controlled and uncontrolled transactions and between controlled and uncontrolled parties it is necessary to analyze what risks have been assumed, what functions are performed that relate to or affect the assumption or impact of these risks and which party or parties to the transaction assume these risks.[91] Likewise, Customs administrations should always undertake risk analyses where the comparability between controlled and uncontrolled transactions is at stake, since its omission may lead to erroneous conclusions as to whether or not the relationship influenced the price. Levey illustrates the issue with the following example:

> DistCo is an unrelated distributor of the optical and camera products that MafCo manufactures. DistCo takes on responsibility for marketing and advertising this line of products by use of its own resources.
>
> Here, it would be assumed that in the open market, DistCo would be entitled to a commensurately higher anticipated return from the activity than if it were simply acting as an agent without financial responsibility for the marketing and advertising expenses. Similarly, a contract manufacturer ... or a contract research provider that takes on no meaningful risk would be entitled to only a limited return.[92]

The Note to GVC Article 1.2 provides that "if the price had been settled in a manner consistent with the normal pricing practices of the industry in question ... this would demonstrate that the price had not been influenced by the relationship." This provision has usually been interpreted as allowing the use of posted prices as a basis for comparison in demonstrating that the relationship did not influence the price.[93] However, this is clearly not the only meaning of this provision, which is reflected in paragraphs 20 and 22 of Case Study 14.1. It also means that the price should be settled taking into account *all the elements* that independent enterprises of the industry in question take into account when establishing or negotiating their prices. Since the risk element is usually one of these elements, customs administrations and importers can find authority in the Note to GVC Article 1.2 to undertake risk analysis for customs valuation purposes.[94] The OECD Guidelines provide some guidance as to which types of risks may be pertinent to examine. Paragraph 1.72 includes the following: (a) Strategic risks or marketplace risks; (b) Infrastructure or operational risks; (c) Financial risks; (d) Transactional risks; and (e) Hazard risks.[95] Bear in mind that these elements are examined for comparability purposes and not for the purposes of establishing

90. *See* OECD Guidelines *supra* note 4, at 1.56.
91. *Ibid* at 1.58.
92. Hammer *supra* note 11 at 3.03[2][b].
93. *See* Sherman *supra* note 23, at 192. "The transaction value of imported merchandise sold between related parties may be based upon 'posted prices' which reflect the normal pricing practices of the industry in question" (CVE *supra* note 45, at chapter XXXI (Ruling 542261 – TAA No. 19 (11 March 1981)).
94. Note, e.g., that the Note to GVC Article 6 refers to the usual pricing policies in the branch of industry concerned, when comparing the exporter's profit figures with those of other producers.
95. *See* OECD Guidelines *supra* note 4, at 1.72.

additions to or deductions from the customs value of the imported goods. (These additions and deductions can be made only - under GVC Articles 1 and 8 - once the price has been found to be arm's length under GVC Article 1.2, which requires a previous examination of the elements indicated above for comparability purposes only.)

Finally, the OECD Guidelines suggest that it is necessary to consider whether a purported allocation of risk is at arm's length.[96]

7.1.3 Contractual Terms

When analyzing a related-party sale and its circumstances under GVC Article 1.2(a) or under transfer pricing provisions, the examination of the contractual terms of such transaction will generally be of utmost importance. The OECD Guidelines read:

> A transaction is the consequence or expression of the commercial or financial relations between the parties. The controlled transactions may have been formalised in written contracts which may reflect the intention of the parties at the time the contract was concluded in relation to aspects of the transaction covered by the contract, including in typical cases the division of responsibilities, obligations and rights, assumption of identified risks, and pricing arrangements. Where a transaction has been formalised by the associated enterprises through written contractual agreements, those agreements provide the starting point for delineating the transaction between them and how the responsibilities, risks, and anticipated outcomes arising from their interaction were intended to be divided at the time of entering into the contract. The terms of a transaction may also be found in communications between the parties other than a written contract.[97]

According to the OECD Guidelines, where the written contractual terms between the related enterprises are not consistent with the actual characteristics of the transaction, the latter should generally be delineated for purposes of the transfer pricing analysis in accordance with the characteristics of the transaction reflected in the conduct of the parties. This may be particularly relevant from a customs standpoint. For example, certain royalty payments must be added to the transaction value where they are a condition of sale of the goods being imported.[98] The European Community Customs Code Committee indicated that "[w]hen goods are purchased from one person and a royalty or license fee is paid to another person, the payment may nevertheless be regarded as a condition of sale of the goods under certain conditions... The seller, or a person related to him, may be regarded as requiring the seller to make the payment when, for example, in a multinational group goods are bought from one member of the group and the royalty is required to be paid to another member of the same group ..."[99] The OECD Guidelines conclude that it is particularly important in considering the

96. *See* OECD Guidelines *supra* note 4, at 2.76.
97. *Ibid.* at 1.42.
98. *See* below Section 16.2.4.
99. E.C., European Commission, Directorate General XXI - Customs and Indirect Taxation, Customs Code Committee, Commentary No. 3, *Compendium of Customs Valuation Texts*, Brussels, E.C. Customs Code Committee, 1997, at 13 [hereinafter "CCVT"].

commercial or financial relations between associated enterprises to examine whether the arrangements reflected in the actual conduct of the parties are substantially consistent with the terms of any written contract, or whether the related enterprises' actual conduct indicates that the contractual terms have not been followed or are a sham. Where conduct is not fully consistent with economically significant contractual terms, further analysis is required to identify the actual transaction.[100]

The importance that must be given to the examination of the contractual terms when analyzing a related party and its circumstances of sale under GVC Article 1.2(a) may be observed in Case Study 1 of the draft case studies that we submitted to the Focus Group on Customs Valuation and Transfer Pricing in 2007.[101]

7.1.4 Economic Circumstances

The OECD Guidelines indicate that arm's length prices may vary from market to market even for transactions involving the same property or services. Therefore, to achieve comparability, the markets in which the independent and related enterprises operate must be comparable. To ensure comparability, any differences in the markets should not have a material effect on price unless appropriate adjustments can be made to account for such differences.[102]

Since the analysis of these circumstances constitutes a part of the comparability analysis, it should also be part of the analysis undertaken under GVC Article 1.2. Only comparable uncontrolled transactions in comparable economic circumstances can provide valuable information to determine whether the relationship influenced the price.

Note that some of the restrictions contained in GVC Article 7.2 are based on economic circumstances derived from differences between markets.[103] GVC Article 7.2 provides:

> No customs value shall be determined under the provisions of this Article on the basis of: (a) the selling price in the country of importation of goods produced in such country; ... (c) the price of goods on the domestic market of the country of exportation; ... (e) the price of the goods for export to a country other than the country of importation ... .

100. *See* OECD Guidelines *supra* note 4, at 1.46.
101. *See* 11.1.3. below.
102. *See* OECD Guidelines *supra* note 4, at 1.110. *See also* Hammer *supra* note 11, at 3.03[4].
103. GVC Article 7 is not directly applicable under GVC Article 1.2(a). However, it provides general principles that may be applicable to interpret most of the provisions of the GVC. Article 7 applies where Articles 1, 2, 3, 5 and 6 cannot be applied. It provides for a flexible application of the methods established in those Articles. However, such flexible application is subject to the conditions imposed by Article 7.2. We understand that the conditions imposed by Article 7.2 must necessarily be met in all the methods established by the GVC (including Article 1), since Article 7.1 only provides for a flexible application of them. Consequently, if the "flexible" application of the methods cannot exceed certain limits, the "original" application thereof (i.e., under Articles 1, 2, 3, 5 and 6) cannot exceed such limits either.

These restrictions clearly reflect the purpose of preventing customs administrations and importers from comparing transactions of independent and related enterprises which operate in different (and non-comparable) markets.

For example, the price of a product in transactions between unrelated buyers and sellers on the domestic market of the country of exportation would be probably different from the price of such product when sold for export to the country of importation (or from the price of such product on the domestic market of the country of importation).

The OECD Guidelines mention the following economic circumstances that may be relevant to determine market comparability: (i) geographic location; (ii) the size of the markets; (iii) the extent of competition in the markets and the relative competitive positions of the buyers and sellers; (iv) the availability (risk thereof) of substitute goods and services; (v) the levels of supply and demand in the market as a whole and in particular regions, if relevant; (vi) cost of production, including the costs of land, labor and capital; (vii) transport costs; (viii) the level of the market (e.g. retail or wholesale); (ix) consumer purchasing power; and (x) the date and time of transactions.[104] One can also add to the list the nature and extent of government regulation of the market.[105] Among the government policies that have a significant impact in comparability, we can mention exchange controls, subsidies and import restriction measures.[106]

The determination of the geographic market is extremely important, especially in large countries or customs unions like the European Community and Mercosur. The economic circumstances in one country or region within a country may vary from those of another country or region within such country. For example, there may be a significant difference in consumer purchasing power, cost of production and governmental intervention in the markets of the North-east region of Brazil, the state of São Paulo (Brazil), the Province of Buenos Aires (Argentina) and the Province of Tierra del Fuego (Argentina). (Note, e.g., the special tax and customs provisions laid down in national and Mercosur legislation for Tierra del Fuego and Manaus (Brazil).) The extent of competition, the availability of substitute goods and the levels of supply and demand may be radically different.

When comparing either prices or profit margins, the economic circumstances have to be examined. Where it is necessary and possible, adjustments should be made to account for such differences.

When drafting the GVC, the negotiators took into account the effect that economic circumstances had on pricing. This is reflected not only in the provisions of GVC Article 7, but also in the Note to GVC Article 6. It provides, in the context of the

104. *See* OECD Guidelines *supra* note 4, at 1.110.

105. *See* Hammer *supra* note 11, at 3.03[4]. The OECD Guidelines consider this factor in Subchapter D.4.

106. *See* OECD Guidelines *supra* note 4, at 1.132. For instance, performing a comparability analysis in Argentina between 2012 and 2015 was a difficult challenge due to the exchange control rules and the import restrictions applied by the Government. The government imposed measures affecting importation which, in general terms, required importers to export domestic goods for an amount equivalent to the annual value of the their imports. *See* WTO, "Argentina – Measures affecting the import of goods" – AB-2014-9 (WT/DS438/AB/R, WT/DS444/AB/R, WT/DS445/AB/R).

computed value method, for the examination of economic circumstances when determining whether the producer's figures "for profit and general expenses" are consistent with those usually reflected in sales of goods of the same class or kind – as the goods being valued – which are made by producers in the country of exportation for export to the country of importation.[107] Where the producer can demonstrate that a low profit on sales of the imported goods is due to particular commercial circumstances, the producer's actual profit figures should be used to determine customs value under the computed value method. The Note to GVC Article 6 adds that the "*producer's pricing policy must reflect usual pricing policies in the branch of industry concerned.*" The Note indicates that such a situation might occur, e.g., where producers have been forced to lower prices temporarily because of an unforeseeable drop in demand. Bear in mind that the Note to GVC Article 1.2(a) indicates that the controlled price would have not been influenced by the relationship if "*the price had been settled in a manner consistent with the normal pricing policies of the industry in question.*" As one can observe, the wording of the Notes to GVC Articles 1.2 and 6 is similar. We can conclude, therefore, that the example given by the Note to GVC Article 6 provides valid guidance to interpret the Note to GVC Article 1.2. In other words, the provisions of such example, in the context of the Note to GVC Article 1.2, authorizes the examination of the economic circumstances surrounding the sale in determining comparability under GVC Article 1.2.

7.1.5 Business Strategies

Under the OECD Guidelines, the analysis of business strategies of an MNE group constitutes an important element in determining comparability for transfer pricing purposes.[108] The concept of business strategies in this context would be far-reaching, including:

- innovation and new product development;
- degree of diversification;
- risk aversion;
- assessment of political changes;
- input of existing and planned labor laws;
- duration of arrangements;
- other factors bearing upon the daily conduct of business;[109]
- market penetration schemes.[110]

An important element in evaluating the legitimacy of a taxpayer/ importer's claim that is following a specific business strategy is the strategy's timing and likely returns. Some business strategies, such as those involving market penetration or

107. *See* paragraphs 4 and 5 of the Note to GVC Article 6.
108. *See* OECD Guidelines *supra* note 4, at 1.114.
109. *Ibid* at 1.115. *See also* Hammer *supra* note 11, at 3.03[5].
110. OECD Guidelines *ibid.*, at 1.115.

expansion of market share, involve reductions in the taxpayer's current profits in anticipation of increased future profits.[111] Consideration should also be given as to whether the taxpayer can plausibly explain that following such a business strategy will, in fact, produce a return sufficient to justify its costs within a period of time that would be acceptable in an arm's length situation.[112]

The analysis of the business strategies of the parties is another element that must be necessarily included in comparability analyses undertaken under GVC Article 1.2. The authors of the GVC paid special attention to this issue, when – in the context of the GVC Article 6 – they established in which cases the producer's profit figures were to be acceptable.[113] In effect, the Note to GVC Article 6 provides:

> 5. It should be noted in this context that the "amount for profit and general expenses" has to be taken as a whole. It follows that if, in any particular case, the producer's profit figure is low and the producer's general expenses are high, the producer's profit and general expenses taken together may nevertheless be consistent with that usually reflected in sales of goods of the same class or kind. Such a situation might occur, for example, if a product were being launched in the country of importation and the producer accepted a nil or low profit to offset high general expenses associated with the launch. Where the producer can demonstrate a low profit on sales of imported goods because of particular commercial circumstances, the producer's actual profit figures should be taken into account provided that the producer has valid commercial reasons to justify them ... Such a situation might occur, for example, ... where [producers] sell goods to complement a range of goods being produced in the country of importation and accept a low profit to maintain competitivity ...

The principles laid down in the Note to GVC Article 6 in respect of business strategies are clearly consistent with those of the OECD Guidelines. Paragraph 1.115 of the OECD Guidelines states that "a taxpayer seeking to penetrate a market or to increase its market share might temporarily charge a price for its product that is lower than the price charged for otherwise comparable products in the same market. Furthermore, a taxpayer seeking to enter a new market or expand (or defend) its market share might temporarily incur higher costs (e.g. due to start-up costs or increased marketing efforts) and hence achieve lower profit levels than other taxpayers operating in the same market."

Levey explains that some business strategies raise a threshold issue of which party bears the strategy's economic risk. It is important to determine whether a manufacturer incurs lower margins or loss by charging a lower price to its distributor, or the distributor does this by its selling at a lower price than comparable products or incurring extraordinary marketing and promotion expenses. In the former situation the economic risk is on the manufacturer; in the latter, on the distributor.[114]

In the context of a comparability analysis, Customs and tax administrations and importers should be prepared to examine all these circumstances as circumstances

111. *See* OECD Guidelines *supra* note 4, at 1.115. Hammer *supra* note 11, at 3.03[5].
112. *Ibid* at 1.118.
113. Bear in mind that the examples given by the Note to Article 6 are generally applicable in the context of the Note to Article 1.2, as indicated in the last paragraph of Section 7.1.4.
114. *See* Hammer *supra* note 11 at 3.03[5][a].

surrounding the sale. If the success of a strategy was unreasonable at the time of the adoption, or if such a business strategy is unsuccessful but nonetheless is continued beyond a period of time that an independent enterprise would accept, the taxpayer/importer's strategy may be disregarded.[115] In this kind of cases, final determination of the Customs value might have to be delayed. We will explore these issues in Chapter 5.

Another issue that arises in a market penetration context (and that – consequently – should be taken into account for customs valuation purposes) concerns which associated enterprise is the appropriate party to take the economic risk of the market penetration strategy. This should be the party that will also earn the economic return if the strategy is successful.[116] In essence, what occurs in a market penetration situation is the development of marketing intangibles relating to the product and the market in question.[117] When related-party transactions are being scrutinized for customs valuation purposes, this fact cannot be disregarded. The fact that marketing activities undertaken by the importer in the country of importation that benefit the exporter are not included in transaction value,[118] does not mean that such activities must also be disregarded when examining whether the relationship influenced the price or when establishing comparability between controlled and uncontrolled transactions. Any adjustment to the price (including or excluding elements) is to be made after it has been determined that the related-party transaction value is acceptable under GVC Article 1.2. For the purposes of determining such facts, market penetration strategies should be taken into account in establishing comparability.

7.2 Evaluation of Separate and Combined Transactions

This topic presents a difficult issue when harmonization of tax and customs transfer pricing rules is being sought. While no adverse consequence may result in the tax context if certain transactions are evaluated together, such an evaluation may, nevertheless, produce adverse consequences in the customs context (and vice versa).

The OECD Guidelines indicate that, "[i]deally, to arrive at the most precise approximation of the arm's length conditions, the arm's length principle should be applied on a transaction-by-transaction basis. However, there are often situations where separate transactions are so closely linked or continuous that they cannot be evaluated adequately on a separate basis."[119] The OECD Guidelines provide some examples of these situations:

- long-term contracts for the supply of commodities or services;
- rights to use intangible property; and
- pricing a range of closely linked products (e.g., in a product line).

115. *See* OECD Guidelines *supra* note 4, at 1.118. *See also* Hammer *supra* note 11, at 3.03.[5][a].
116. Hammer *ibid.*, at 3.03[5][a][ii].
117. *Ibid.*
118. *See* Note to GVC Article 1.1(b).
119. *See* OECD Guidelines *supra* note 4, at 3.9.

Under the GVC, the valuation analysis appears, at first glance, to be clearly focused on single import transactions.[120] However, this is only apparent as nothing in the GVC prevents Customs administrations from examining groups of transactions together. In fact, this is what normally happens in the case of ex-post examinations or audits. The provisions of GVC Article 1.2(a) also appear to be designed to determine whether the transaction value of a transaction is acceptable for customs purposes. However, nothing in the GVC prevents a customs administration from examining a number of separate related-party transactions on a combined basis in order to determine whether the relationship influenced the price. Each of these transactions may be regarded as a "circumstance surrounding the sale" vis-à-vis the other transactions.

Nevertheless, the combined analysis of separately contracted transactions should be made only for comparability purposes (e.g., in order to undertake a more accurate functional analysis or to better understand the economic circumstances or the business strategies of the enterprises). The combined analysis cannot, however, be used to determine whether a number of transactions – as a whole – are arm's length (regardless of whether or not the price of each individual transaction is arm's length), since this may not be consistent with GVC Article 1 or with the general objectives and principles of Customs law. Such inconsistency is illustrated in the following example:
When sold for export, two different goods (classified in different tariff headings and subject to different duty rates) are invoiced at individual prices which are individually non-arm's-length:

Invoice No. 001 for product A	100 c.u.
Invoice No. 002 for product B	400 c.u.

The arm's length values of the products are the following:

arm's length value of product A	200 c.u.
arm's length value of product B	300 c.u.

Consequently, tax and customs administrations determine that the total price invoiced for the goods (when considered together – i.e. 500 c.u.) is actually arm's length.

From a tax standpoint, assuming that the goods are imported for resale in the country of importation, there would probably be no adverse tax consequence derived from a combined analysis of the transactions.[121] In effect, if product A is sold at a price of 300 c.u. and product B is sold at a price of 500 c.u., the gross profit realized by the

120. *See* our comments to the publication issued by the U.S. Customs and Border Protection in 2007 in Section 3.1 above.
121. However, if the imported goods are capital assets of the importer, differences in the rate of depreciation of the assets may, nevertheless, produce adverse tax consequences.

importer would be equal to 300 c.u.[122] The gross profit would have been the same had the importer declared the individual arm's length value of each product.

From a customs standpoint, the result might be dramatically different. Assuming that product A is subject to a customs duty rate of 30% and product B is subject to a customs duty rate of 1%, the results would be the following:

customs duties on transaction values	34 c.u.
customs duties on arm's length values	63 c.u.

In our view, this is the type of "difference" observed by the TCCV in Commentary 23.1. It is not actually a difference in "methodologies", as neither Article 1.2(a) nor its interpretative note have methodologies. It is really a difference in the aggregation or disaggregation of the financial information about the transactions of the importer. The Customs administration may require disaggregated information where the tax administration would not require so. This, however, is not a reason to argument that the OECD Guidelines may not be used for purposes of the GVC's Circumstances-of-Sale Test, or that the information of an OECD-type transfer pricing study may or may not be used for customs purposes. This just means that the importer may be required to provide the Customs administration with additional disaggregated financial information in the context of the Circumstances-of-Sale Test. This additional "segmented" financial information should be supplied to Customs for applying a methodology in a manner consistent with the principles of the OECD Guidelines. For such purposes, useful guidance may be found in paragraph 2.109 of the OECD Guidelines, in particular with respect to the use of non-transactional third-party data in the transactional net margin method:

> While it is not specific to the transactional net margin method, the issue of the use of non-transactional third party data is in practice more acute when applying this method due to the heavy reliance on external comparables. The problem arises because there are often insufficient public data to allow for third party net profit indicators to be determined at transactional level. This is why there needs to be sufficient comparability between the controlled transaction and the comparable uncontrolled transactions. Given that often the only data available for the third parties are company-wide data, the functions performed by the third party in its total operations must be closely aligned to those functions performed by the tested party with respect to its controlled transactions in order to allow the former to be used to determine an arm's length outcome for the latter. The overall objective is to determine a level of segmentation that provides reliable comparables for the controlled transaction, based on the facts and circumstances of the particular case. In case it is impossible in practice to achieve the transactional level set out as the ideal by these Guidelines, it is still important to try to find the most reliable comparables as discussed at paragraph 3.2, through making suitable adjustments based on the evidence that is available.

122. For the purposes of the example: Gross Profit = Resale Price COGS. Other factors or elements are not included for simplicity purposes.

Therefore, segmentation of the financial information of the importer/taxpayer is key not only to find reliable comparables for the controlled transaction but also to avoid an aggregation of transactions that may be inappropriate for customs purposes.

While some separately contracted transactions between associated enterprises may need to be evaluated together in order to determine whether the conditions are arm's length, other transactions contracted between such enterprises as a package may need to be evaluated separately. In some cases, it may not be feasible to evaluate the package as a whole so that the elements of the package must be segregated. If such is the case, after determining separate transfer pricing for the separate elements, tax administrations should consider whether in total the transfer pricing for the entire package is arm's length.[123]

The Technical Committee on Customs Valuation, in Commentary 8.1[124] defines "package deal" as an agreement to pay a lump sum for a correlated group of goods, or a group of goods sold together, the price of the goods sold constituting the only consideration. Note that the OECD refers mainly to those situations where an MNE establishes a single price for a number of benefits such as licenses for patents, know-how and trademarks, the provisions of technical and administrative services and the lease of production facilities. The OECD remarks that such comprehensive packages would be unlikely to include sales of goods (although the price charged for sales of goods may cover some accompanying services.)[125] As one can see, the OECD Guidelines do not appear to focus on sales of goods.

Although paragraph 5 and 6 of Commentary 8.1 do not refer to package deals including services or intangibles, the principles underlying such paragraphs suggest that, where such elements are involved in a package deal that includes the sale of goods, the transaction value would not be acceptable under GVC Article 1.[126] Therefore, the application of GVC Articles 2, 3, 5, 6 and 7 may make difficult the achievement of harmonized results under tax and customs transfer pricing rules.

Where different goods are sold and invoiced at a single overall price, the fact of such single overall price for different goods does not constitute an impediment to establishing transaction value provided that the other conditions of GVC Article 1 are met.[127] Commentary 8.1 indicates that, in those instances where the goods are

123. *See* OECD Guidelines *supra* note 4, at 3.11.
124. *See* CVC *supra* note 39, at Com8.1/1. Note that Commentary 8.1 does not refer specifically to related-party transactions but, generally, to any kind of package deal.
125. *See* OECD Guidelines *supra* note 4, at 3.11.
126. Paragraphs 5 and 6 read: "(B) Goods of different quality sold and invoiced at a single overall price are only partially declared for home use in the country of importation – 5. In this situation, the nature of the problem is different and can be illustrated by the following example: A consignment comprising goods of three different qualities (top quality A, average quality B and low quality C) is purchased at an overall unit price of 100 currency units per kilo. In the country of importation, the buyer declares quality A for home use at 100 currency units per kilo but assigns the other qualities to some other procedure – 6. Since the overall price actually paid or payable has been agreed for a set of goods of various qualities there is no selling price for the goods declared for home use and Article 1 of the Agreement is therefore not applicable in this instance."
127. *See* CVC *supra* note 39, at Com8.1/1 (paragraph 3 of Commentary 8.1).

classifiable under separate tariff headings at different rates of duty, the overall price – which has been negotiated as part of a package deal – should not be rejected when applying GVC Article 1, solely for the purposes of tariff classification.

The Technical Committee on Customs Valuation recognizes that the proper apportionment of the overall price among the goods which are classifiable in different headings constitutes a practical problem. It suggests that "[s]everal methods are possible including, for example, the use of prices or values of identical or similar goods in previous importations, if such methods can provide a valid indication of the price of the various goods covered by the package deal."[128] Note that these recommendations are similar to those provided by paragraph 3.12 of the OECD Guidelines. The relevant part of such paragraph provides:

> Even in uncontrolled transactions, package deals may combine elements that are subject to different tax treatment under domestic law or an income tax convention ... In such circumstances, it may be still appropriate to determine transfer pricing on a package basis, and the tax administration could then determine whether for other tax reasons it is necessary to allocate the price to the elements of the package. In making this determination, tax administrations should examine the package deal between associated enterprises in the same way that they would analyze similar deals between independent enterprises. Taxpayers should be prepared to show that the package deal reflects appropriate transfer pricing.

7.3 Use of an Arm's Length Range

The OECD Guidelines explain that it will sometimes be possible to apply the arm's length principle to arrive at a specific price or profit margin that is the most reliable to establish whether the conditions of the transaction are arm's length. However, they indicate that the application of the most appropriate method or methods often produces a range of figures all of which are equally reliable.[129] The arm's length principle only produces an approximation of conditions that would have been established between independent enterprises. This fact may cause the differences in the figures that comprise the range. The Guidelines indicate that the different points in a range may simply represent the fact that independent enterprises engaged in comparable transactions under comparable circumstances may not establish exactly the same price.[130]

Nothing in GVC Article 1.2 or its Note prevents the importer or customs administrations from using an arm's length range in order to produce an approximation of conditions that would have been established between independent enterprises and, therefore, to produce a range of figures that – being all of equal reliability – would be acceptable for the purposes of GVC Article 1. An analysis of the provisions of the Note to GVC Article 1.2 suggests that the use of an arm's length range may be appropriate under certain circumstances. In effect, where the examination of the normal pricing practices of the industry, or of the way the seller settles prices for sales to unrelated

128. CVC *supra* note 39, at Com8.1/1 (paragraph 4 of Commentary 8.1).
129. *See* OECD Guidelines *supra* note 4, at 3.55.
130. *Ibid.*

buyers, produces a range of figures of equal reliability, the use of an arm's length range appears to be in accordance with the text of the Note.[131] In relation to this issue, the principles underlying the provisions of the GVC seem to be similar to those stated in the OECD Guidelines.

Commentary 15.1 of the Technical Committee on Customs Valuation[132] – regarding the application of the deductive value method – provides guidance to interpret the meaning of the expression "additions usually made for profit and general expenses in connection with sales in such country of imported goods of the same class or kind" in the context of GVC Article 5. This guidance may also be helpful in interpreting the second example of the Note to GVC Article 1.2, since the wording of such example has several points in common with the expression quoted above.[133]

Paragraph 11 of Commentary 15.1 indicates that "the usual amount for commission or profit and general expenses could constitute a range of amounts which probably would vary according to the class or kind of the goods being valued. In order for a range to be acceptable, it should be neither too wide nor too deficient in population. The range should be obvious and easily discernible in order for it to be the 'usual' amount."[134] As one can see, the Technical Committee on Customs Valuation understood that ranges could be used for the purposes of determining the appropriate "usual amount for profit and general expenses" under GVC Article 5. On the basis of such understanding, one can suggest that arm's length ranges could also be used for the purposes of examining profit margins under the Note to GVC Article 1.2. (i.e., for producing an approximation of conditions that would have been established between independent parties and, thus, for determining whether the relationship influenced the price).

Moreover, GVC Article 1.2(a), unlike Articles 2, 3, 5, 6 and 7, does not establish a strict sequential order of application of arm's length methods. In determining whether the relationship influenced the transaction value, the methods can be applied in any order[135] or even simultaneously. (GVC Article 1.2(a) only provides examples to illustrate situations where the relationship did not influence the price, but it does not

131. It should be taken into account that the harmonization of customs and tax rules becomes easier where the OECD Guidelines are integrated in the GVC through an appropriate construction of the provisions of the latter. Needless to say that such construction must respect not only the provisions of the GVC and their Notes, but also the general principles and objectives underlying them. If neither GVC Article 1.2 nor the GVC's general principles preclude the application of the OECD Guidelines in examining related-party transactions, such Guidelines should be used to interpret and implement the provisions of Article 1.2.

132. *See* CVC *supra* note 39, at Com15.1/1.

133. In effect, the second example provided by the Note reads: "where it is shown that the price is adequate to ensure recovery of all costs plus a profit which is representative of the firm's overall profit realized ... in sales of goods of the same class or kind, this would demonstrate that the price had not been influenced." Both the example and the expression quoted above, require the examination of profit margins realized in sales of goods of the same class or kind.

134. *See* CVC *supra* note 39, at Com15.1/2.

135. Note that, although there is no sequential order of application, under certain circumstances some methods are preferred over others. Further discussion of this issue will be found in Section 11.1. below.

set out the methods to be used or the order in which those methods must be applied. Note also that GVC Article 1.2(b) does not provide for a sequential order of application of its test values.). In this respect, the OECD Guidelines indicate that "a range of figures may also result when more than one method is applied to evaluate a controlled transaction." The use of arm's length ranges under GVC Article 1.2(a) is, therefore, consistent with the absence of strict sequential order of application and with the possible application of more than one method under such article.

The OECD Guidelines provide further guidance in relation to the use of arm's length ranges:

> Where the application of the most appropriate method ... produces a range of figures, a substantial deviation among the points in that range may indicate that the data used in establishing some of the points may not be as reliable as the data used to establish the other points in the range or that the deviation may result from features of the comparable data that require adjustments. In such cases, further analysis of those points may be necessary to evaluate their suitability for inclusion in any arm's length range.[136]

These guidelines may be complemented by those provided by the Technical Committee on Customs Valuation in paragraph 11 of Commentary 15.1 (quoted above). Where the importer submits information based on more than one method, customs administrations should be prepared to use arm's length ranges in order to arrive at more accurate results.[137]

7.4 Use of Multiple-Year Data

The main purpose of customs valuation is to determine the customs value of the goods when they enter the customs territory, avoiding arbitrary or fictitious values. The customs value of the goods constitutes the tax base of the customs duties. Unlike income tax, customs duties are not intended to tax the income of the taxpayer. Customs duties are indirect taxes.[138] The importation of goods evidences the existence of the ability to pay (either that of the importer, or that of the final consumer who finally bears the tax burden), and the customs value of the good is the basis that has been chosen (usually by the legislative branch of the state) to measure such ability.

One can suggest that, what is important for customs valuation purposes is the customs value of the good at a certain and specific point in time (e.g., the importation, the sale for export to the country of importation, etc.).

For income tax purposes, the point of departure is quite different. The tax base is the income of the taxpayer (as defined under each legislation). For tax calculation

136. *See supra* note 4, at 3.59.
137. Note that GVC Article 7.2 only prevents the Customs administrations from using a system which provides the acceptance for customs purposes of the higher of two values. The use of arm's length ranges does not fall within the provisions of Article 7.2, since it is not a method for determining substitute values. The transaction values declared by the importer are accepted under Article 1, if they are within the arm's length range.
138. *See* Levey *supra* note 3, at 8.05[1]. *See also* Finanzas *supra* note 24, at 757–804 (Jarach includes customs duties among the taxes on consumption).

purposes, the business lifetime must be divided in arbitrary segments (what gives rise to most problems of accurate income calculation). A taxpayer's lifetime is segmented into annual periods and the income realized during such period constitutes the tax base. However, the ascertainment of business profits at fixed intervals of 12 months is so arbitrary a process, considering the continuous nature of business operation, that methods of carryforward (and, sometimes, carryback) of loss are considered to be "an obvious concession to common sense"[139] and, thus, usually included in most of the income tax laws. The period over which benefits are received from any given expenditure may be long, and a liberal carryforward of losses is essential to overcome this limitation of the annual period of measurement.[140]

As one can see, income measurement tends to be based on yearly data or, even, on multiple-year data.

This seems to be a major difference between the customs and tax systems. However, this difference is only apparent. Even though income tax is calculated through a period of time (unlike customs duties that are calculated at a specific point in time), and that such calculation is made on income rather than on the value of the goods, this latter element must always be determined for income calculation purposes. (In effect, the determination of sales price and cost of goods sold is necessary to determine profits or losses.) The analysis of the present work aims at this specific element (value of the goods) and not to the whole process of income calculation.

One must distinguish two different sources of multiple-year data:

(i) Multiple-year data related to income calculation: among others, we can mention carryforward and carryback data which will affect the calculation of income for a specific period. It is irrelevant for customs valuation and transfer pricing purposes.

(ii) Multiple-year data used for comparability purposes: this kind of data (e.g., results of business activities, etc.) is used as a guide for applying the arm's length principle. The OECD Guidelines provide that "[t]o obtain a complete understanding of the facts and circumstances surrounding the controlled transaction, it might generally be useful to examine data from both the year under examination and prior years."[141] There is nothing in the GVC preventing an importer or a customs administration from using such kind of information in determining whether the relationship influenced the price. GVC Article 1.2 and its Note refer broadly to the examination of "the circumstances surrounding the sales" and the "relevant aspects of the transaction." Nothing seems to prevent the taxpayer from submitting, and

139. Ellis, J., "Aggregation of Income and Losses from Various Sources" in *Canadian Taxation* (Toronto: Richard de Boo, 1981) at 446.

140. Canada, *Report of the Royal Commission on Taxation* (Carter Report), Vol. 4 (Ottawa: Queen's Printer, 1966) at 252–255.

141. *See* OECD Guidelines *supra* note 4, at 3.76.

the customs administration from examining, multiple-year data for comparability purposes.

There are other problems caused by differences in timing between tax and customs laws which derive mainly from limitations in the procedure of valuation and liquidation of customs duties. We will analyze these problems in Chapter 5.

CHAPTER 3

Determining Whether the Relationship Influenced the Price: Arm's Length Prices

8 THE OECD ARM'S LENGTH METHODS AND THE METHODS LAID DOWN IN GVC ARTICLES 2, 3, 5 AND 6

The transfer pricing methods in the OECD Guidelines establish whether the conditions imposed in commercial and financial relations between associated enterprises are consistent with the arm's length principle. It must be noted that no one method is suitable in every possible situation.[142] Although in some cases the choice of a method may sometimes not be straightforward and more than one method may have to be initially considered, it should ultimately be possible to select one method that is apt to provide the best estimation of an arm's length price. However, there are many types of difficult situations where no one approach is conclusive. In these situations, a flexible approach allows various methods to be used in conjunction. Here, an attempt should be made to reach a conclusion consistent with the arm's length principle that is satisfactory from a practical viewpoint to all parties, taking into account the facts and circumstances of the case, the mix of evidence available, and the relative reliability of the various methods under consideration.[143]

The methods set forth in GVC Articles 2, 3, 5 and 6 of the GVC are not equivalent to those recommended by the OECD Guidelines. The former are not designed to provide the importer with guidance as to how its transfer prices should be set. Rather, they must be used where the transaction value (transfer price), if any, is not acceptable because there is no sale for export or the conditions of paragraphs (a), (b), (c) and (d) of Article 1.1 are not met. These methods must be used by the Customs authorities to determine substitute values. Even though they require a certain degree of comparability between the transaction being valued and the transactions the prices (or profit

142. *See* Hammer *supra* note 11, at 3.03[14].
143. *See* OECD Guidelines *supra* note 4, at 2.12.

margins) of which will be used to assess the substitute value, such requirement is far less important than that of the OECD Guidelines. In respect of the TVI[144] and TVS[145] methods, Sherman said that:

> [t]here is a flow in the logic of TVI and TVS which should be pointed out at once. The other transaction may not be truly comparable for any of several reasons which are not taken into account by the Code. The most important is that the other transaction may not have been entered into at the same time. Assume, for example, that prices have been steadily rising and that one importer purchases pursuant to a 5-year fixed-price supply contract, while the other importer buys on a spot basis and pays today's far higher spot price. Either one of these importers may find his goods being valued for customs purposes on the basis of the other's very different price if, for any reason, his own TV [transaction value] is rejected or does not exist. The low price importer can end up with a high customs value, or vice versa ... There is also some danger that an importer who has, for example, carefully excluded advertising costs or warranty costs or constructing and erection costs from his pricing will find his goods being valued on the basis of a price set by others who were not as careful.[146]

The importer will not use them to set its prices, nor are the Customs authorities permitted to use them to evaluate whether the relationship influenced the price. Even though this is not expressly established by the GVC, the wording of the Note to GVC Article 1.2(a) allows such an interpretation. In effect, no reference to the valuation methods of Articles 2, 3, 5 and 6 is made in such Note. Furthermore, none of the examples provided by the Note is strictly equivalent to any of those methods (although some of the examples might imply an application thereof). Finally, the methods laid down in GVC Articles 2, 3, 5 and 6 are to be used for the purpose of determining substitute values[147] if (and only if) the transaction value under GVC Article 1 is rejected or cannot be applied.[148] When examining whether the relationship influenced the price under GVC Article 1.2, the transaction value has not yet been rejected. Rather, this process of examination is the one that will determine whether the related-party transaction value is acceptable or has to be rejected.[149]

---

144. "Transaction value of identical goods" under GVC Article 2.
145. "Transaction value of similar goods" under GVC Article 3.
146. Sherman *supra* note 23, at 200. This author noted that, in his view, the Code should be interpreted to exclude such applications, but that it may not be interpreted in this way.
147. *See*, generally, Musso de Zunino, C., *Valoración aduanera en las importaciones. Problemas que se suscitan en relación a la aplicación del actual régimen de valor* (Derecho Tributario, 9, 227). *See also ESSO S.A.P.A.* v. *A.N.A. s/recurso de apelacion*, (7 October 1993) Tribunal Fiscal de la Nacion, Sala G, File No. 6872-A (Argentina).
148. *See* General Introductory Commentary to the GVC. *See also* Sherman *supra* note 23, at 200.
149. *See* Note to paragraph 2 of Article 1. *See* Sherman *supra* note 23, at 189 (... "relationship is not even presumptively a ground for departing from TV [transaction value]. It is only a reason for further inquiry or scrutiny. Departure from TV is not permitted unless justified on the basis of the results of the inquiry).

9 TEST VALUES

It should be noted that the application of test values under GVC Article 1.2(b) is also not equivalent to the application of the methods of GVC Articles 2, 3, 5 and 6.

GVC Article 1.2(b)(i) generally requires a higher degree of comparability between the transaction being examined and the test transaction than that required by GVC Articles 2 and 3. In effect, even though GVC Articles 2 and 3 require certain comparability criteria to be met (e.g., goods identical or similar, same country of importation, same commercial level and same quantity - or, otherwise, appropriate adjustments), they do not provide, unlike GVC Article 1.2(b), that "the elements enumerated in Article 8 and costs incurred by the seller in sales in which the seller and the buyer are not related that are not incurred by the seller in sales in which the seller and the buyer are related" must be taken into account in applying the test values. This clause prevents the importer from using test values that do not comply with the minimum standards of comparability. In other words, it authorizes Customs administrations to reject test values supplied by the importer when they are not comparable to the transaction in question. It should also be noted that the test value of GVC Article 1.2(b)(i) involves transaction values that are not controlled (i.e., transaction values in sales to unrelated buyers). This is not required under GVC Articles 2 and 3.

The test values laid down in GVC Articles 1.2(b)(ii) and (iii) require previous determinations of values of identical or similar goods under GVC Articles 5 or 6, which must have been accepted by the Customs administration. Therefore, these test values do not consist of a determination of value through the methods of GVC Articles 5 and 6, or of a comparison of the transaction value with a theoretical value arrived at through the application of those methods. Rather, they provide for the use - as a basis of comparison - of an actual customs value already accepted by the customs administration.[150]

10 CONSIDERATIONS REGARDING THE OECD ARM'S LENGTH METHODS

In the following sections we will analyze the application of the OECD arm's length methods for the purpose of determining whether the relationship influenced the price under GVC Article 1.2(a). This approach was the one that we suggested to the TCCV in the 20th Session, later on, in the two WCO-OECD joint transfer pricing and customs valuation conferences held in 2006 and 2007, and also in the 26th Session of the TCCV. This was the approach that we also suggested in the 11 draft case studies submitted to the Focus Group on Customs Valuation and Transfer Pricing in 2007 and it was accepted by the TCCV in its 27th Session when the item of the TCCV's agenda was shifted to the Agenda Item V "Specific technical questions" for the next sessions and presented under the title: "Related party transactions under the Agreement and Transfer Pricing". Being the methods set forth in GVC Articles 2, 3, 5 and 6 not directly

150. *See* paragraph 4 of the Note to GVC Article 1.2. *See also* Sherman *supra* note 23, at 194. *See* CVC *supra* note 39 at AO7.1/1 (Advisory Opinion 7.1). *See also* CVE *supra* note 45 at chapter XXXIV (Ruling 543568 (30 May 1986)).

applicable under GVC Article 1.2, there is no point in comparing them with the OECD arm's length methods. Where appropriate, we will make reference to the provisions of such articles and Article 7 since they contain general principles that are present in all the provisions of the GVC. Where appropriate, we will also make reference to the relationship between GVC Article 1.2(a) and GVC Article 1.2(b).

Finally, it should be noted that the OECD Guidelines should be used not only by importers (to ensure the arm's length character of their related-party transactions) but also by Customs administrations for the purposes of protecting the tax base and performing their functions of control on foreign trade. If the Note to GVC Article 1.2 were interpreted too broadly, wide acceptance of transaction values in controlled transactions might erode the tax base of customs duties and be harmful to the country of importation (not only in connection with its revenue but also in relation to its right to control foreign trade in its jurisdiction). This appears to be contrary to the general objectives of the GVC, especially after the adoption of the "Decision regarding cases where customs administrations have reasons to doubt the truth or accuracy of the declared value" by the Committee on Customs Valuation.[151] The OECD arm's length methods provide the Customs administrations with adequate instruments to protect the tax base of customs duties.

11 TRADITIONAL TRANSACTION METHODS

11.1 Comparable Uncontrolled Price Method ("CUP")

Under the OECD Guidelines, the CUP method compares the price charged for property or services transferred in a controlled transaction with the price charged for property or services transferred in a comparable uncontrolled transaction in comparable circumstances. Any difference between the two prices may indicate that some or all of the commercial and financial relations between the associated enterprises are not arm's length[152] and, therefore, that the relationship did influence the price for the purposes of GVC Article 1.2.

The Note to GVC Article 1.2 provides an example of application of this method: As an example of this, if the price had been settled in a manner consistent with the way the seller settles prices for sales to buyers who are not related to the seller, this would demonstrate that the price had not been influenced by the relationship.

The example of the Note to GVC Article 1.2, quoted above, seems to recommend the application of the CUP method using internal comparables (i.e., a comparison between the prices charged by the related seller to the related buyer and the price charged by the same seller to independent buyers). The OECD Guidelines provide a similar example in paragraph 2.26. As indicated above, it is important to bear in mind

151. WTO Doc. G/Val/1 (27 April 1995). This decision appears to address cases where the requisites mentioned in Article 1.1(i), (ii), (iii) and (iv) are met. However, it also provides a general rule applicable to all the cases where the Customs administrations have to examine transaction value (what also includes related-party transactions).
152. *See* OECD Guidelines *supra* note 4, at 2.14.

that the examples of the Note to GVC Article 1.2 are only illustrative. Therefore, they should only be taken as a starting point.[153] Nothing in the GVC prevents the importers or customs administrations from considering external comparables (i.e., prices charged by other sellers to independent buyers) for determining whether the relationship influenced the price.

In applying the CUP method, the OECD Guidelines suggest that an uncontrolled transaction is comparable to a controlled transaction if one of two conditions is met: (1) none of the differences (if any) between the transactions being compared or between the enterprises undertaking those transactions could materially affect the price in the open market; or (2) reasonably accurate adjustments can be made to eliminate the material effects of such differences.[154] As indicated in Chapter 2, the criteria of comparability are extremely important to determine whether the relationship influenced the price, and thus wholly applicable under GVC Article 1.2(a). The OECD Guidelines provide that, where it is possible to locate comparable uncontrolled transactions, the CUP method is the most direct and reliable way to apply the arm's length principle. Consequently, they recommend that, in such cases, the CUP method is preferable over all other methods.[155] The Note to GVC Article 1.2 neither sets out any particular order of application of the methods nor does it reveal preference for any of them.[156] However, we understand that the preference for the CUP method, where it is possible to locate comparable uncontrolled transactions, could be found in the structure of the GVC and in the general principles underlying its provisions. In effect, the methods of GVC Articles 2 and 3, although not equivalent, are similar to the CUP method. In effect, they are based on the transaction prices of comparable transactions (identical or similar goods, same commercial level and quantity, etc.). The sequential order of application of the methods establishes the preference for such methods over the others, where such comparable transaction values are available and where – existing differences of commercial levels or quantities – an appropriate adjustment on the basis of demonstrated evidence can be made.[157] Even though such sequential order is not applicable to GVC Article 1.2 (as indicated in Section 7.3), such order reflects a general principle or understanding vis-à-vis the degree of reliability of each of the methods. This indicates a preference that should be observed in interpreting and applying GVC Article 1.2.

In effect, the hierarchical order of application of the methods has been identified by the Technical Committee on Customs Valuation as a principle or general provision of the Agreement. To the question as to whether it is necessary to follow the hierarchical order with respect to the methods of valuation in GVC Articles 1–6, when applying GVC Article 7, the Technical Committee replied:

153. *See* Sherman *supra* note 23, at 193.
154. *See supra* note 4, at 2.15.
155. *Ibid.*
156. Note that it does not even mention which are those methods. It only provides examples where one can discern the application thereof.
157. General Interpretative Note of the GVC.

> There is no provision in the Agreement that specifically provides that the hierarchical order of Articles 1 to 6 should be followed when Article 7 is applied. However, Article 7 requires the use of reasonable means consistent with the principles and general provisions of the Agreement and this indicates that where reasonably possible, the hierarchical order should be followed. Thus, where several acceptable methods can be used to determine Customs value under Article 7, the hierarchy should be maintained.[158]

The specific comparability criteria for applying the CUP method provided by paragraph 2.17 of the OECD Guidelines should also be taken into account in the context of GVC Article 1.2. paragraph 2.17 states:

> In considering whether controlled and uncontrolled transactions are comparable, regard should be had to the effect on price of broader business functions other than just product comparability (i.e. factors relevant to determining comparability under Chapter 1). Where differences exist between the controlled and uncontrolled transactions or between the enterprises undertaking those transactions, it may be difficult to determine reasonably accurate adjustments to eliminate the effect on price. The difficulties that arise in attempting to make reasonably accurate adjustments should not routinely preclude the possible application of the CUP method. Practical considerations dictate a more flexible approach to enable the CUP method to be used and supplemented as necessary by other appropriate methods, all of which should be evaluated according to their relative accuracy ... .

It is interesting to analyze, from a customs perspective, the example provided in paragraph 2.24 of the OECD Guidelines. The first part of the example reads as follows:

> The CUP method is a particularly reliable method where an independent enterprise sells the same product as is sold between two associated enterprises. For example, an independent enterprise sells unbranded Colombian coffee beans of a similar type, quality, and quantity as those sold between two associated enterprises, assuming that the controlled and uncontrolled transactions occur at about the same time, at the same stage in the production/distribution chain, and under similar conditions ... .

In this part of the example, the OECD Guidelines follow criteria that are clearly consistent with those underlying the GVC. (Even though such comparability criteria are not expressly included in GVC Article 1.2(a), they are present in other provisions of the code, such as GVC Articles 1.2(b), 2 and 3.) In effect, the transactions being compared in the example involve similar goods, sold in similar quantities and at the same commercial level. The example continues as follows:

> ... If the only available uncontrolled transaction involved unbranded Brazilian coffee beans, it would be appropriate to inquire whether the difference in the coffee beans has a material effect on the price. For example, it could be asked whether the source of coffee beans commands a premium or requires a discount

158. Note that, as indicated above, the principle of hierarchical order, in the context of GVC Article 1.2, would only indicate a preference for the methods of Articles 2 and 3 over the other methods. It does not prevent the importer or customs administrations from combining methods or altering the order where the application of the CUP method does not produce reliable outcome (e.g., problems of comparability, existence of unique intangibles, etc.).

> generally in the open market. Such information may be obtainable from commodity markets or may be deduced from dealer prices. If this difference does have a material effect on price, some adjustments would be appropriate. If a reasonably accurate adjustment cannot be made, the reliability of the CUP Method would be reduced, and it might be necessary to combine the CUP method with other less direct methods, or to use such methods instead.

The use of an uncontrolled transaction involving goods of different origins would not be, in principle, contrary to the principles reflected by GVC Article 7 or to the criteria provided by the Note to GVC Article 1.2. However, goods cannot be regarded as "identical goods" or "similar goods" unless they were produced in the same country as the goods being valued. Thus, it could be argued that, not being useful for the purposes of GVC Articles 1.2(b), 2 or 3, transactions involving such goods should not be used for the purposes of the CUP method under GVC Article 1.2(a).

We do not believe that GVC Article 1.2(a) prevents the importer or the Customs administrations from comparing transactions involving goods of different origins. As indicated above, GVC Article 7 does not preclude the use of transactions involving goods of different origins. In fact, paragraph 3 of the Interpretative Note to Article 7, when it gives some examples of reasonable flexibility in applying the methods of Articles 1 through 6, provides:

> 3. Some examples of reasonable flexibility are as follows:
>
> (a) Identical goods - the requirement that the identical goods should be exported at or about the same time as the goods being valued could be flexibly interpreted; identical imported goods produced in a country other than the country of exportation of the goods being valued could be the basis for customs valuation; customs values of identical imported goods already determined under the provisions of Articles 5 and 6 could be used.
>
> (b) Similar goods - the requirement that the similar goods should be exported at or about the same time as the goods being valued could be flexibly interpreted; similar imported goods produced in a country other than the country of exportation of the goods being valued could be the basis for customs valuation; customs values of similar imported goods already determined under the provisions of Articles 5 and 6 could be used.

Sherman explains that "[i]n principle, and in practice as well, there should be no limit set to the exercise of persuasive intelligence to support the acceptability of a transfer price."[159] The Note to GVC Article 1.2 makes no reference to "identical goods" or "similar goods". It makes reference only to goods of the same class or kind in one of its examples of situations where the relationship did not influence the price. GVC Articles 2 and 3 describe a method of valuation that is similar but not equivalent to the CUP method. A major difference is the fact that GVC Articles 2 and 3 are not designed to evaluate whether a related-party transaction value is arm's length, but only to determine substitute values once the transaction value has been rejected. Therefore, in interpreting or applying the provisions of GVC Article 1.2(a), the provisions of GVC Articles 2 and 3 should not be regarded as strict rules to be complied with, but only as

159. *See* Sherman *supra* note 23, at 193.

guidance which reflects certain understandings and principles under the GVC. Likewise, paragraph 3 of the Interpretative Note to Article 7 should also be considered.[160] Taking into account such guidance, we can conclude that the comparison of transactions involving goods of different origin - although not precluded - should be minimized as much as possible for the purposes of the CUP method under GVC Article 1.2(a). In other words, transactions involving goods produced in different countries should only exceptionally be regarded as comparables.

It is also interesting to address the solution suggested by the OECD Guidelines to situations where there is a difference between the controlled and the uncontrolled prices, which indicates that the conditions of the commercial and financial relations of the related parties are not at arm's length. The OECD Guidelines indicate that, in such a case, the price in the uncontrolled transaction may need to be substituted for the price in the controlled transaction.[161] This solution would not be consistent, in principle, with the GVC. Under the GVC, such a difference between prices would indicate that:

(i) the relationship did influence the price;
(ii) the transaction value is not acceptable; and
(iii) the value cannot be determined under the provisions of GVC Article 1.

In this case, neither the importer nor the Customs administrations can substitute the price in the uncontrolled transaction for the price in the controlled transaction. In effect, GVC Article 1.2 does not authorize such a substitution. Where the transaction value is rejected, the customs value must be determined through the sequential application of the methods laid down in GVC Articles 2, 3, 5, 6 and 7.[162]

This could produce certain inconsistencies between the results derived from the application of tax and customs rules. For example, if during the examination of the circumstances surrounding the sale, the Customs and tax administrations based their analyses on the cost-plus method, and such method demonstrated that the price had been influenced by the relationship (i.e., the price was not arm's length), then the tax administration (on the basis of the OECD Guidelines) would try to substitute the cost-plus price arrived at, for the transaction value. At the same time, the Customs administration would be obliged to go sequentially through the methods of GVC Articles 2 through 6. As indicated above,[163] the degree of comparability required under the methods of GVC Articles 2 and 3 is lower than that required under the OECD Guidelines. Thus, the Customs administration may find a transaction involving similar

160. In 2016, Ecuador submitted a technical question to the TCCV about this issue. Jazmin Gonzalez Aguirre, delegate of Ecuador, expressed Ecuador's view in document VT1019S1a, with solid and consistent technical arguments.
161. *See supra* note 4 at 2.14.
162. Note that this is expressly established for the purposes of GVC Article 1.2(b). GVC Article 1.2(c) provides: "Substitute values may not be established under the provisions of paragraph 2(b)." The General Note to the GVC states: "Where the customs value cannot be determined under the provisions of Article 1, it is to be determined by proceeding sequentially through the succeeding Articles to the first such Article under which the customs value can be determined." The Technical Committee on Customs Valuation provides an example in Case Study 10.1 which shows the functioning of this principle (See CVC *supra* note 39, at CS10.1/3 (paragraph 15)).
163. *See* Section 8.

goods, at a similar commercial level and in the same quantities, but with an allocation of functions that is substantially different from that of the transaction in question. While the Customs administration will determine the Customs value on the basis of such transaction, the tax administration will simply substitute the cost-plus value for the transaction value. In effect, the tax administration would not be forced to duplicate the transfer pricing analysis or to accept the value of a transaction which does not comply with the OECD Guidelines' standards of comparability.[164]

The most consistent results can be achieved where the importer undertakes a thorough transfer pricing analysis. In effect, the application of the OECD Guidelines is possible under GVC Article 1.2(a), i.e., in examining the circumstances surrounding the sale and in determining whether the relationship influenced the price. However, the application of the OECD Guidelines is difficult (or even impossible) once the transaction value has been rejected, since the Customs administrations are forced to apply sequentially the methods of GVC Articles 2 through 6.[165]

11.1.1 Examples of Application of the CUP Method under GVC Article 1.2(a)

The US Customs Service has often applied this method in the context of GVC Article 1.2(a). We can mention Rulings 543984 (22 February 1988), 544809 (1 June 1994), 546285 (7 June 1996), among others.[166]

11.1.2 Test Values under GVC Article 1.2(b)(i)

The application of this test value at the initiative of the importer could also produce results that would not be consistent with those derived from the application of the OECD Guidelines. However, inconsistencies could be eliminated (or, at least, reduced), through an adequate interpretation of the provisions of GVC Article 1.2(b).

In effect, the comparability factors to be examined under GVC Article 1.2(b) include not only similar commercial levels and quantities but also "the elements enumerated in Article 8" and "costs incurred by the seller in sales in which the seller and the buyer are not related that are not incurred by the seller in sales in which the seller and the buyer are related." This would authorize the Customs administration to require the importer to apply actually comparable test values.

11.1.3 Case Study

The following case study was submitted by the author of this book to the Focus Group on Customs Valuation and Transfer Pricing, in the sidelines of the TCCV's 25th Session.

164. Bear in mind that, under GVC Articles 2 and 3, the transaction used for the purposes of determining the customs value may be another controlled transaction.
165. Nonetheless, an appropriate interpretation of such Articles could help reduce such inconsistencies. (However, an inquiry into this issue would exceed the purposes of this work.).
166. *See* CVE *supra* note 45, at 35.

It was intended to provide to the Focus Group and, later on, to the TCCV, an example on how the OECD CUP Method could be used in the context of the Circumstances-of-Sale Test.

Case Study 1

APPLICATION OF ARTICLE 1.2

Facts of transaction

1. Same facts as in Case Study 10.1 of the TCCV[167] with respect to ingredients in category (a), except that, in this case, ICO and XCO provided the following additional information to explain the difference in prices:

167. *See* CVC, *supra* note 39, at CS10.1/1. The facts of Case Study 10.1 of the TCCV are as follows:

Facts of transaction

1. ICO of country I purchased and imported two categories of ingredients used in the production of food flavourings from XCO of country X.
2. At the time of clearing the goods, ICO declared to Customs in country I that it was related to XCO as:
   (a) XCO held 22 % of the shares of ICO; and
   (b) officers and directors of XCO were also represented on the Board of Directors of ICO.
3. After importation, Customs in country I decided to conduct a review of the circumstances surrounding the sale of goods between XCO and ICO, pursuant to Article 1.2 of the Agreement, because it had doubts about the acceptability of the price. To this end, Customs forwarded a questionnaire to ICO which sought information regarding the sale of products by XCO to other buyers in country I and, if necessary, justification of any price difference as well as information relating to XCO's cost of production and profit. At the request of ICO, Customs also forwarded a questionnaire to XCO. From the responses received, facts as set out below were established.
4. ICO purchased many of the ingredients required for the production of food flavourings from XCO. The ingredients sold by XCO to ICO fall into two categories:
   (a) ingredients manufactured by XCO; and
   (b) ingredients stocked by XCO which have been acquired from other manufacturers and suppliers. Ingredients in this category are not manufactured or processed by XCO. Some of these ingredients may, however, be packaged for resale by XCO.
5. In terms of Article 15.2 of the Agreement, ingredients in category (a) are not identical or similar goods to the ingredients in category (b).
6. Ingredients in category (a) are also sold to other unrelated buyers in country I. The prices charged by XCO in respect of category (a) ingredients are:
   (i) Sold to ICO: 92 c.u. f.o.b.
   (ii) Sold to unrelated buyers: 100 c.u. f.o.b.
7. In respect of the ingredients in category (a) Customs found that:
   (i) unrelated buyers purchased the ingredients at the same commercial level and in similar quantities as ICO and used the ingredients for the same purpose. Importations of these ingredients by unrelated buyers were appraised with a transaction value of 100 c.u.; and
   (ii) the costs incurred by XCO were the same in relation to sales to ICO and unrelated buyers in country I.
8. Customs also established that there was no seasonal influence on the price of ingredients which might explain the 8 % difference in prices set out in paragraph 6.

(i) ICO and XCO provided Customs with a functional analysis which showed that the number of functions performed by ICO, in connection with the ingredients in category (a), was substantially larger than that of the unrelated buyers. The functions performed by ICO were also more significant than those performed by unrelated buyers in terms of their frequency, nature and value.

(ii) The functional analysis also identified and compared the assets employed by ICO and by the unrelated buyers. While the unrelated buyers have no inventories of ingredients in category (a) and an insignificant level of fixed assets, ICO had significant levels of inventories of ingredients in category (a), a warehouse and an industrial plant where it manufactures the food flavourings. The unrelated buyers have no plant and hire contract manufacturers to manufacture the food flavourings.

(iii) The functional analysis also showed that the risks assumed by XCO when selling to ICO were substantially lower than those assumed when selling to unrelated buyers. ICO's equity is 20 times greater than the unrelated buyers' average equity. Securities and stock issued by ICO have a credit rating substantially better than those issued by the unrelated buyers, what demonstrated that the credit rating of the unrelated buyers was significantly lower than that of ICO. In addition, ICO provided Customs with data showing that the average (uncontrolled) interest rate paid by the unrelated buyers on their current debts was 18% while the one paid by ICO was 6%.

(iv) XCO provided Customs with information about contractual terms in transactions with unrelated buyers and with ICO. The information indicated that the average term of payment in transactions with unrelated buyers was 190 days, while the average term of payment in transactions with ICO was 30 days. In transactions with unrelated buyers, no interest charges were distinguished from the price paid or payable for the goods.

(v) XCO and ICO informed to Customs that ICO was in a market penetration scheme. ICO was seeking to penetrate country I's market of food flavourings and, consequently, had to temporarily charge a price for its product that was lower than the price charged for comparable products in such market. The market penetration scheme was expected to increase ICO's market share in a term of 1 year and to produce a return sufficient to justify its costs. XCO and ICO showed that the expected return and the period of time would be acceptable in an arm's length arrangement. The expected outcome of the strategy would benefit both ICO and XCO and, therefore, the nature of the relationship between the parties would be consistent with both ICO and XCO bearing the costs of the business strategy.

Suggested determination of Customs value

2. Under Article 1.2 of the Agreement the responsibility for demonstrating that relationship has not influenced price lies with the importer. While the Agreement

Furthermore, after being asked to do so by Customs, ICO and XCO provided no additional information to explain the difference in prices.

9. Ingredients in category (b) are sold only to ICO in country I and there are no importations of identical or similar goods into country I.

10. In respect of the ingredients in category (b), Customs established that the prices charged to ICO were adequate to recover all XCO's costs, including the costs of acquisition plus the costs of repacking, handling and freight charges, as well as to recover a profit that was representative of the firm's overall profit over a representative period of time.

requires Customs to provide reasonable opportunity to the importer to provide information that would indicate that prices are not influenced by relationship, it does not require the Customs administration to conduct an exhaustive enquiry for the purpose of justifying the price difference. Thus, any decision in this regard must, to a significant degree, be based on the information provided by the importer.

3. The Interpretative Note to Article 1.2 provides that "the customs administrations should be prepared to examine relevant aspects of the transaction, including the way in which the buyer and seller organize their commercial relations and the way in which the price in question was arrived at, in order to determine whether the relationship influenced the price". This involves a complete analysis of the transaction in question and uncontrolled transactions in order to determine whether the relationship influenced the price. The examination of those aspects must always have a comparability purpose, since this is the only mechanism authorized by the Agreement for determining whether the relationship influenced the price. The language of the Interpretative Note to Article 1.2 is broad enough to permit a functional analysis and a comparison of contractual terms, economic circumstances and business strategies (in the context of a comprehensive transfer pricing study) under the more detailed rules of the Transfer Pricing Guidelines for Multinational Enterprises and Tax Administrations of the Organization for the Economic Cooperation and Development (hereinafter "OECD Guidelines") in determining whether the relationship influenced the transaction value.

4. The Interpretative Note to Article 1.2 gives some guidance in relation to the circumstances that Customs should examine and to the information that importers should submit. However, such guidance is very general. Customs administrations and importers cannot be expected to solve complex transfer pricing problems solely on the basis of such general provisions.

5. Furthermore, the Interpretative Note to Article 1.2 only provides examples of circumstances or aspects of the transactions which could be examined by Customs. Such examples do not constitute the only circumstances or aspects that Customs might explore and should be taken only as a starting point and as illustrative.[168]

6. The OECD Guidelines indicate that "[i]t may also be relevant and useful in comparing the functions performed to consider the risks assumed by the respective parties. In the open market, the assumptions of increased risk will also be compensated by an increase in the expected return. Therefore, controlled and uncontrolled transactions and entities are not comparable if there are significant differences in the risks assumed for which appropriate adjustments cannot be made .... The types of risks to consider include market risks, such as input cost and output price fluctuations; risks of loss associated with the investment in and use of property, plant, and equipment; risks of the success or failure of investment in research and development; financial risks such as those caused by currency exchange rate and interest variability; credit risk; and so forth."

168. Sherman and Glashoff explain that Agreement "does not confine itself to the facts regarding the sale – it deals with the broader concept of an inquiry into 'the circumstances surrounding' the sale. This language plainly speaks of the entire context of the transaction and not just of the transaction itself." [Sherman, S. and Glashoff, H., *Customs Valuation. Commentary on the GATT Customs Valuation Code* (New York, Kluwer Law and Taxation Publishers, 1988) at 193].

7. From the information submitted by ICO, it is possible to assess the risks assumed by XCO when selling to ICO and to unrelated buyers, and to make adjustments to account for the different risk levels and, thus, increase comparability.

8. The information submitted by XCO indicates that the unrelated buyers have the following terms of payment:

(i) unrelated buyer 1 210 days
(ii) unrelated buyer 2 200 days
(iii) unrelated buyer 3 190 days
(iv) unrelated buyer 4 180 days
(v) unrelated buyer 5 170 days

9. Such information also indicates that the interest rate paid by the unrelated buyers is, in average, 12 percent points greater than that of ICO. Taking into account the interest rate differential and the terms of payment, it is possible to make the following adjustments to increase comparability:

	Unit Price	Δ Annual Interest Rate U.B.-ICO	Interest Rate 30 days	Δ Days U.B. - ICO	Unrelated Buyer's Interest Rate	Interest Rate on Δ Days	Adjusted Unit Price
U.B. 1	92	12%	0.99%	180	18%	8.88%	101.07
U.B. 2	92	12%	0.99%	170	18%	8.38%	100.62
U.B. 3	92	12%	0.99%	160	18%	7.89%	100.17
U.B. 4	92	12%	0.99%	150	18%	7.40%	99.71
U.B. 5	92	12%	0.99%	140	18%	6.90%	99.26

10. The Agreement makes it clear that the significance of any price difference should be considered on the basis of the nature of the goods and industry in the case in question.

11. The OECD Guidelines indicate that "...because transfer pricing is not an exact science, there will also be many occasions when the application of the most appropriate method or methods produces a range of figures all of which are relatively equally reliable. In these cases, differences in the figures that comprise the range may be caused by the fact that in general the application of the arm's length principle only produces an approximation of conditions that would have been established between independent enterprises. It is also possible that the different points in a range represent the fact that independent enterprises engaged in comparable transactions under comparable circumstances may not establish exactly the same price for the transaction. However, in some cases, not all comparable transactions examined will have a relatively equal degree of comparability."

12. The price between ICO and XCO falls within the range of figures resulting from the application of adjustments to the prices of unrelated buyers. Furthermore, such price closely approximates to the median of the range. This shows that the price differences are not significant on the basis of the nature of the goods and industry in the particular case.

13. Other circumstances surrounding the sale indicate that it is not possible to compare the price between ICO and XCO with the prices charged by XCO to unrelated buyers. Differences in functions performed by ICO and by unrelated buyers and in business strategies are significant enough to justify price differentials.

14. Even though ICO has not been able to quantify such price differentials through economic adjustments, it is clear that ICO's price would not be below an otherwise adjusted range of prices. ICO performs more functions than the unrelated buyers what indicates that the compensation earned by ICO should reflect such higher level of functions.

15. The OECD Guidelines indicate that "[b]usiness strategies must also be examined in determining comparability for transfer pricing purposes. Business strategies would take into account many aspects of an enterprise, such as innovation and new product development, degree of diversification, risk aversion, assessment of political changes, input of existing and planned labor laws, and other factors bearing upon the daily conduct of business... Business strategies also could include market penetration schemes. A taxpayer seeking to penetrate a market or to increase its market share might temporarily charge a price for its product that is lower than the price charged for otherwise comparable products in the same market. Furthermore, a taxpayer seeking to enter a new market or expand (or defend) its market share might temporarily incur higher costs (e.g. due to start-up costs or increased marketing efforts) and hence achieve lower profit levels than other taxpayers operating in the same market... When evaluating a taxpayer's claim that it was following a business strategy that temporarily decreased profits in return for higher long-run profits, several factors should be considered. Tax administrations should examine the conduct of the parties to determine if it is consistent with the professed business strategy. For example, if a manufacturer charges its related distributor a below market price as part of a market penetration strategy, the cost savings to the distributor may be reflected in the price charged to the distributor's customers or in greater market penetration expenses incurred by the distributor...An additional consideration is whether there is a plausible expectation that following the business strategy will produce a return sufficient to justify its costs within a period of time that would be acceptable in an arm's length arrangement."

16. XCO and ICO submitted information that was sufficient to demonstrate that they were in a market penetration scheme and that ICO had to temporarily charge a price for its food flavourings that was lower then the price charged for comparable products in country I. On the basis of the data presented by ICO, the market penetration scheme was expected to increase ICO's market share in a reasonable period of time and to produce a return sufficient to justify its costs and acceptable in an arm's length arrangement. Since the expected outcome of the strategy would benefit both ICO and XCO, it would be consistent with XCO bearing a portion of the costs of the business strategy what, in turn, would justify a price differential in transactions with ICO and with unrelated buyers.

17. Therefore, in respect of ingredients in category (a), the examination of the circumstances of the sale shows that the price has been settled in a manner consistent with the way the seller settles prices for sales to buyers who are not related to the seller, once adjustments for contractual terms and financial risks were made. In addition, the examination of the relevant aspects of the transaction, including business strategies and functions performed by the importer, indicates that there is no reason to believe that the prices have not been settled in a manner consistent with the normal pricing practices of the industry in question.

11.2 Resale Price Method

The OECD Guidelines provide that "the resale price method begins with the price at which a product that has been purchased from an associated enterprise is resold to an independent enterprise. The price (the resale price) is then reduced by an appropriate gross margin on this price (the "resale price margin") representing the amount out of which the re-seller would seek to cover its selling and other operating expenses and, in the light of the functions performed (taking into account assets used and risks assumed), make an appropriate profit. What is left after subtracting the gross margin can be regarded, after adjustment for other costs associated with the purchase of the product (e.g. customs duties), as an arm's length price for the original transfer of property between the associated enterprises."[169] The OECD Guidelines suggest that this method is most useful where it is applied to marketing operations.

None of the examples of the Note to GVC Article 1.2 seems to be derived from the application of this method. In Ruling 545800 (28 June 1996), the US Customs Service analyzed certain information submitted by a related importer to demonstrate that the relationship did not influence the price. Among others, the importer provided information concerning costs and profits involved with its reselling the imported merchandise in the United States. The US Customs Service indicated that:

> [e]ven if the general expenses and profit realized by Tundra [the importer] are within the range of what constitutes the usual general expenses and profits of the relevant industry, this would not show that the price between Standard [the exporter] and Tundra was settled in a manner consistent with normal pricing practice in the industry ... In addition, the evidence submitted by counsel is not sufficient to show that the price of the imported merchandise was sufficient to recover all cost-plus a profit equivalent to the firm's overall profit realized over a representative period [of] time. Counsel has provided information regarding costs that Tundra incurs in selling the merchandise to its customers. However, this cost information does not indicate whether the price charged by Standard is sufficient to cover all its costs and earn a profit equal to its overall profit over a representative period of time. In other words, the relevant consideration would be Standard's [the exporter's] costs in producing the imported sweaters not Tundra's [the importer's] costs in reselling the sweaters in the United States. Since no evidence has been submitted on how much it costs for Standard to produce the imported sweaters, we

169. *See* OECD Guidelines *supra* note 4, at 2.27.

> cannot ascertain whether it has been able to recover all its costs plus earn a profit equal [to] its overall profit over a representative period of time through its pricing practices with Tundra.

It is clear that the US Customs Service interpreted the second example of the Note to GVC Article 1.2 as only allowing the use of the cost-plus (or computed value) method. Note that the US Customs Service rejected the information submitted by the importer on the grounds that such information relates to a resale price method, and not to the methods from which the examples of the Note to GVC Article 1.2 are derived. In other words, the US Customs Service interpreted the Note as preventing the importer from using a resale price method in demonstrating that the relationship had not influenced the price.

This interpretation ignores the fact that the examples of the Note are only illustrative. The importers are forced to base their analyses on the narrow situations described in such examples. This is inconsistent not only with the text, but also with the principles and objectives of GVC Article 1.2. On the one hand, the Note to GVC Article 1.2 does not establish "methodologies," which would be the logical instrument for determining whether the transaction value is at arm's length.[170] It only provides simple examples designed to give some guidance as to which methodologies can be used in determining whether the relationship influenced the price. Being illustrative in character (as most examples are), they do not authorize Customs administrations to limit the methodologies that the importer can avail himself of to those strictly used in the examples. The Customs administrations may reject a methodology that is contrary to the purposes of the examples or inconsistent with the general principles and objectives of the GVC. For example, the Customs administrations could reject a methodology which is based on arbitrary formulae of allocation of profits or fictitious values.

On the other hand, the second example of the Note might also be regarded as an application of the resale price method if flexibly interpreted.[171]

As indicated above, since the examples are only illustrative, the methods of the OECD Guidelines should be accepted in the context of GVC Article 1.2, as long as they are useful and reliable in determining whether the relationship influenced the price. On these grounds, importers and Customs administrations would be authorized – where

170. Note that the other provisions of the GVC, which are designed to determine customs values, laid down methodologies and not simple examples.

171. In effect, the example says: "Where it is shown that the price [it does not state whether it refers to sales or purchase price] is adequate to ensure recovery of all costs plus a profit which is representative of the firm's overall profit realized over a representative period of time ... in sales of goods of the same class or kind." The reference to the firm's overall profit in *sales* of goods of the same class appears to be connected with the price mentioned at the beginning of the sentence, what gives the idea that the price, that ensures a gross margin comparable to the firm's overall margin, is the sales price and not the purchase price. However, since not only a controlled sales price but also a controlled purchase price can affect the gross profit margin, a flexible interpretation may suggest that the example also refers to the resale price method.

appropriate – to use this method in examining the circumstances surrounding the sale. We believe that this was the approach taken by the U.S. CBP in more recent rulings.[172]

This is also the understanding of Revenue Canada, in Memorandum D13-4-5. As indicated above, the Canadian Customs Service (CBSA) will accept a price paid or payable which is derived from one of the methods set out by the OECD, unless there is information on prices available which is more directly related to the specific importations.[173]

11.2.1 Internal and External Comparables

The OECD Guidelines provide that the resale price margin of the re-seller in the controlled transaction may be determined by reference to the resale price margin that the same re-seller earns on items purchased and sold in comparable uncontrolled transactions.[174] The examples of the Note to GVC Article 1.2 appear to refer, generally, to this kind of comparables (i.e., internal comparables).

The Guidelines add that "[a]lso, the resale price margin earned by an independent enterprise in comparable uncontrolled transactions [i.e. *external comparables*] may serve as a guide."[175] As indicated above, the examples of the Note are illustrative and should not be interpreted as precluding the examination of comparable transactions different from those described thereby. The question that arises is whether the use of external comparables is consistent with GVC Article 1.2 or with the general principles of the GVC. For this purpose, one can find some guidance in paragraph 6 of

172. *See*, for instance, Ruling HQ H219515 (11 October 2012), where the U.S. CBP had the opportunity to examine transfer pricing documentation submitted by the importer in the context of the Circumstances-of-Sale Test. Even though the transfer pricing study was prepared using the Comparable Profits Method, the profit level indicator was the gross margin, which would produce a result similar to the Resale Price Method. The U.S. CBP said: "We also reviewed the comparable companies selected by the Importer's transfer pricing study and conclude that the products sold by the comparable companies are not of the same class or kind as the imported merchandise. The comparable companies distribute a range of goods, from medical products and supplies to notebooks and desktops. Under these circumstances, the comparison between the Importer and these other companies cannot be considered consistent with the market as a whole. However, even though the Importer's transfer pricing study by itself is not sufficient to show that a related party transaction value is acceptable for Customs purposes, the underlying facts and the conclusions reached in this transfer pricing study contain relevant information in examining the circumstances of the sale, since this transfer pricing study confirms the gross profit margins of the Importer, as set by the Importer and verified through the independent review of the analytical instruments industry and quantitative data of the Importer's direct competitors.

    Accordingly, even though none of the information provided strictly falls under the three illustrative examples under 19 CFR §152.103(l)(1)(i)-(iii), we find that the sales price will not be considered influenced by the relationship for purposes of the circumstances of the sale test, based on the totality of the information considered and our review and examination of all relevant aspects of the transaction, including the way in which the Importer and the related manufacturers organize their commercial relations and the way in which the price in question was arrived at. As a result, we determine that transaction value is the proper method of appraisement for the related-party import transactions."
173. *See* Memorandum *supra* note 44 (paragraph 15).
174. *See* OECD Guidelines *supra* note 4, at 2.28.
175. OECD Guidelines *supra* note 4, at 2.28.

the Note to GVC Article 5 which sets out rules for applying the deductive value method - which is similar to the resale price method. The relevant part of paragraph 6 provides:

> The figure for the purposes of this deduction should be determined on the basis of information supplied by or on behalf of the importer unless the importer's figures are inconsistent with those obtained in sales in the country of importation of imported goods of the same class or kind. Where the importer's figures are inconsistent with such figures, the amount for profit and general expenses may be based upon relevant information other than that supplied by or on behalf of the importer.

In this respect, the Technical Committee on Customs Valuation said:

> As a practical matter, it would not appear useful that the data necessary for ascertaining the usual amounts for commissions or profit and general expenses be obtained and maintained on an ongoing basis. In many instances, practical application will require Customs to consider situations involving multi-product companies, small industries with a limited number of importers, industries with a large number of related party transactions, etc. on a case by case basis. In this context, Customs could have recourse to its own records. The data could also be obtained from trade organizations, *other importers*, accounting firms, government agencies ... or any other reliable source[176] [emphasis added].

As one can see, the Technical Committee understands that external comparables could be used - in certain circumstances - in the context of GVC Article 5. Sherman confirms this understanding as follows:

> Still another application [of the deductive value method] will come in a related party situation (e.g. an export sale to a subsidiary) in which the transfer price is rejected as a basis for TV [transaction value]. Here, since the price at which the subsidiary purchases is thought to be distorted, the difference between the price and the resale price is presumably also distorted. In such a situation, the usual mark up must be found in the experience of other companies ...[177]

In the context of GVC Article 1.2(a), the transaction value has not yet been rejected. However, the purpose of paragraph 6 of the Note to GVC Article 5 and that of the resale price method - when applied for the purposes of GVC Article 1.2 - are similar:

- Paragraph 6 seeks to determine an appropriate mark up, since the price at which a related-party purchases is thought to be distorted and thus, the difference between such price and the resale price (mark up) is presumably also distorted.
- The resale price method - when applied for the purposes of GVC Article 1.2 - seeks to determine whether the price at which a related-party purchases has actually been distorted. For such purposes, the resale price method seeks to determine whether the mark up (i.e., the difference between the purchase price and the resale price) has been the appropriate one.

176. *See* CVC *supra* note 39, at Com15.1/2 (Commentary 15.1).
177. Sherman *supra* note 23, at 215.

Where the purposes of two provisions (i.e., determining (i) the appropriate mark up or (ii) whether the mark up has been the appropriate one) are similar, arguably the guidance provided by one of such provisions could be used in interpreting and applying the other. Therefore, since paragraph 6 of the Note to GVC Article 5 authorizes the use of external comparables to determine the appropriate mark up, one can conclude that external comparables appear also to be acceptable, in determining whether the mark up in a related-party transaction has been the appropriate one for the purposes of GVC Article 1.2(a). This conclusion is consistent with the position adopted by the TCCV in Case Study 14.1.[178]

Needless to say that, in the context of GVC Article 1.2(a), external comparables should comply with appropriate comparability standards.

The OECD Guidelines also state that, where the re-seller is carrying on a brokerage business, the resale price margin may be related to a brokerage fee, which is usually calculated as a percentage of the sales price of the product sold. The determination of the resale price margin in such a case should take into account whether the broker is acting as an agent or a principal.[179] Note that this is consistent with the general structure of GVC Article 5, which properly distinguishes between deductions usually made for commission and those usually made for profits and general expenses.[180] This is reflected by the following paragraph of Commentary 15.1 of the Technical Committee on Customs Valuation - which also provides additional guidance:

> Article 5 merely stipulates that the deduction will be for either commission or for profit and general expenses but it does not establish the criteria for determining which of these is to be deducted. In dealing with this issue and having regard to the General Introductory Commentary of the Agreement which recognizes that Customs value should be based on simple and equitable criteria consistent with commercial practices, a deduction for commission would normally occur where the sale in the country of importation of the goods being valued was or is to be made on an agency/commission basis. The deduction for profit and general expenses would normally be resorted to in transactions which do not involve commissions.[181]

11.2.2 Application of the Method

11.2.2.1 Product Comparability

Under the principles of the OECD Guidelines, an uncontrolled transaction can be regarded as comparable to a controlled transaction for purposes of the resale price method if one of the following conditions is met:

---

178. In Case Study 14.1, it was confirmed that the importer's operating margin was arm's length because it fell within the arm's length range of eight functionally comparable independent distributors (external comparables).
179. *See* OECD Guidelines *supra* note 4, at 2.28.
180. *See* GVC Article 5.1(a)(i).
181. *See* CVC *supra* note 39, at Com15.1/2 (Commentary 15.1).

(1) None of the differences between the transactions being compared or between the enterprises undertaking those transactions could materially affect the resale price margin in the open market; or
(2) Reasonably accurate adjustments can be made to eliminate the material effects of such differences.

The Guidelines also explain that, in making comparisons for purposes of the resale price method, fewer adjustments are normally needed than under the CUP method, due to the fact that minor product differences are less likely to have as material effect on profit margins as they do on price.[182] This is clearly implied in GVC Article 5, when it is read together with GVC Articles 2 and 3. In effect the latter two Articles – the methods of which are based on a direct comparison of prices – require a high degree of product comparability (i.e., identical or similar products, respectively). In determining profit margins, the degree of product comparability required under GVC Article 5 is significantly lower than that required under GVC Articles 2 and 3. GVC Article 5 refers to "commissions usually paid ... or additions usually made for profit and general expenses in connection with sales ... of *imported goods of the same class or kind*" [emphasis added]. GVC Article 15 defines "*goods of the same class or kind*" as "... goods which fall within a group or range of goods produced by a particular industry or industry sector ..."

Sherman explains that the GVC seems to make some assumptions, especially as regards profit and general expenses:

- that importers of goods of the same class or kind in any one country of importation will have one mark up or a narrow range of markups for goods which might be regarded as being of the same class or kind;
- that the same mark up or close range of markups can be obtained on goods within a class or kind irrespective of the country from which they are imported.[183]

Sherman suggests that none of the above assumptions is necessarily true. He considers that, sometimes, market conditions are volatile and trade must react to market changes from day to day.[184] In this respect, it is interesting to consider paragraphs 2.30 and 2.31 of the OECD Guidelines. The relevant part of paragraph 2.30 provides that:

> [i]n a market economy, the compensation for performing similar functions would tend to be equalized across different activities. In contrast, prices for different products would tend to equalize only to the extent that those products were substitutes for one another. Because gross profit margins represent gross compensation, after the cost of sales for specific functions performed ..., product differences are less significant. For example, the facts may indicate that a distribution company performs the same functions (taking into account assets used and risks

182. *See* OECD Guidelines *supra* note 4, at 2.29.
183. *See* Sherman *supra* note 23, at 219.
184. *Ibid.* at 220.

assumed) selling toasters as it would selling blenders, and hence in a market economy there should be a similar level of compensation for the two activities.

However, the last sentence of paragraph 2.30 and paragraph 2.31 address the issue pointed out by Sherman:

> However, consumers would not consider toasters and blenders to be particularly close substitutes, and hence there would be no reason to expect their prices to be the same.
>
> Although broader product differences can be allowed in the resale price method, the property transferred in the controlled transaction must still be compared to that being transferred in the uncontrolled transaction. Broader differences are more likely to be reflected in differences in functions performed between the parties to the controlled and uncontrolled transactions. While less product comparability may be required in using the resale price method, it remains the case that closer comparability of products will produce a better result.[185]

The principles derived from the provisions of GVC Articles 2–7 should be used to inform the application of GVC Article 1.2(a) while respecting certain comparability standards. The paragraphs of the OECD Guidelines quoted above provide guidance for determining such standards.

11.2.2.2 Functions

Where all the characteristics – other than the product itself – of two transactions are comparable, the resale price method might produce a more reliable measure of arm's length conditions than the CUP method.[186]

The resale price method depends on comparability of functions performed (taking into account assets used and risks assumed) since the amount of the resale price margin will be often influenced by the level of activities performed by the re-seller.[187] The resale price margin could, in light of functions performed, be a small one, if the re-seller in the controlled transaction does not carry on a substantial commercial activity but only transfers the goods to a third party. In contrast, where the seller bears special risks or contributes substantially to the creation or maintenance of intangible property associated with the product, it should be expected that the resale price margin will be higher.[188]

---

185. The last sentence of paragraph 2.31 gives the following example: "Where there is a high-value or relatively unique intangible involved in the transaction, product similarity may assume greater importance and particular attention should be paid to it to ensure that the comparison is valid."
186. *See* OECD Guidelines *supra* note 4, at 2.232.
187. In this respect, it is interesting the analysis of functions and risks made by Sherman regarding distributors and agents in the context of GVC Article 5. *See* Sherman *supra* note 23, at 215.
188. *See* OECD Guidelines *supra* note 4, at 2.37. Paragraph 2.37 of the Guidelines also explains that the "level of activities can range widely from the case where the reseller performs only minimal services as a forwarding agent to the case where the reseller takes on the full risk of ownership together with the full responsibility for and the risks involved in advertising, marketing, distributing and guaranteeing the goods, financing stocks, and other connected services."

Using an unadjusted resale price margin derived from uncontrolled transactions may be inappropriate in certain circumstances. This might occur, for example, if the re-seller employs valuable and possible unique assets, such as intangible property. The Guidelines indicate that, in such a case, the resale price margin in the uncontrolled transaction may underestimate the profit to which the re-seller in the controlled transaction is entitled, unless the comparable uncontrolled transaction involves the same re-seller or a re-seller with similarly valuable marketing intangibles.[189] This appears to be consistent with the examples of the Note to GVC Article 1.2 which show a preference for internal comparables.

11.2.3 Superdeductive Value Method

The OECD Guidelines indicate that an appropriate resale price is easiest to determine where the re-seller does not add substantially to the value of the product. In contrast, it may be more difficult to use the resale price method to arrive at an arm's length result where, before resale, the imported products are further processed or incorporated into a more complicated product so that their identity is lost or transformed.[190] This is expressly recognized under the GVC in the context of GVC Article 5. The Guidelines, read together with GVC Article 5.2, provide grounds to support the adoption of this principle in the context of GVC Article 1.2(a).

GVC Article 5.2 provides that:

> [i]f neither the imported goods nor identical nor similar imported goods are sold in the country of importation in the condition as imported, then, if the importer so requests, the customs value shall be based on the unit price at which the imported goods, after processing, are sold in the greatest aggregate quantity to persons in the country of importation who are not related to the persons from whom they buy such goods, due allowance being made for the value added by such processing and the deductions provided for in paragraph 1(a).

This provision is usually referred to as the "superdeductive value method." The following should be noted:

(1) It applies only where neither the goods being valued nor identical nor similar goods are sold in the condition as imported (i.e., it operates as a last resort method).
(2) It applies only if the importer elects to have it applied.
(3) It is based only on the resale price after further processing of the imported goods being valued, and not on the resale price of other goods similarly processed.[191]
(4) The Note to GVC Article 5.2 recognizes that the superdeductive value method would normally not be applicable when, as a result of further processing, the imported goods lose their identity.

189. *Ibid.* at 2.38.
190. *Ibid.* at 2.35.
191. *See* Sherman *supra* note 23 at 224.

As one can see, when regulating the superdeductive value method, the OECD Guidelines and the GVC are governed by similar principles.

11.2.4 Considerations Regarding Intangible Property

The examination of the resale price margin requires particular care where the re-seller contributes substantially to the creation or maintenance of intangible property associated with the product (e.g., trademarks or trade names) which is owned by a related party. In such cases, the contribution of the goods originally transferred to the value of the final product cannot be easily evaluated.[192]

As indicated above, even though customs administrations usually focus on transfers of tangible property, the examination of transfers, licenses, ownership and/or development and maintenance of intangible property plays a fundamental role where profit margins have to be compared. Therefore, in determining whether the relationship influenced the price, Customs administrations should be prepared to examine such circumstances as part of the circumstances surrounding the sale.

11.2.5 Time Elapsed Between Purchase and Resale

The OECD Guidelines provide that:

> [a] resale price margin is more accurate where it is realized within a short time of the reseller's purchase of the goods. The more time that elapses between the original purchase and resale the more likely it is that other facts – changes in the market, in rates of exchange, in costs, etc. – will need to be taken into account in any comparison.[193]

In the context of the deductive value method, GVC Article 5.1(b) addresses this problem, providing that:

> [i]f neither the imported goods nor identical nor similar imported goods are sold at or about the time of importation of the goods being valued, the customs value shall be, subject otherwise to the provisions of paragraph 1(a), be based on the unit price at which the imported goods or identical or similar goods are sold in the condition as imported at the earliest date after the importation of the goods being valued but before the expiration of 90 days after such importation.

Although this provision is to be applied in determining substitute values under GVC Article 5, it provides a general rule for applying the deductive value method which, as indicated above, is similar to the resale price method. Therefore, it could reasonably be followed for applying the resale price method in the context of GVC Article 1.2(a).[194]

192. *See* OECD Guidelines *supra* note 4, at 2.35.
193. *Ibid.* at 2.36.
194. Note, however, that the 90-day period should not be interpreted strictly in the context of Article 1.2(a). Bear in mind that a flexible administration of this requirement is not precluded under Article 7 for the purposes of the fall-back method.

11.2.6 Case Study

The following case study was submitted by the author of this book to the Focus Group on Customs Valuation and Transfer Pricing, in the sidelines of the TCCV's 25th Session. It was intended to provide to the Focus Group and, later on, to the TCCV, an example on how the OECD Resale Price Method could be used in the context of the Circumstances-of-Sale Test.

Case Study 5

APPLICATION OF ARTICLE 1.2

Facts of transaction

1. ICO, a distributor of country I, purchased and imported toasters from XCO, a related company of country X.

2. After importation, Customs in country I decided to conduct a review of the circumstances surrounding the sale of goods between XCO and ICO, pursuant to Article 1.2 of the Agreement, because it had doubts about the acceptability of the price. To this end, Customs forwarded a questionnaire to ICO which sought information regarding the sale of products by XCO to other buyers in country I and, if necessary, justification of any price difference as well as information relating to XCO's cost of production and profit. At the request of ICO, Customs also forwarded a questionnaire to XCO. From the responses received, facts as set out below were established.

3. ICO did not purchase toasters or any other product from unrelated sellers. XCO did not sell toasters or goods of the same class or kind to unrelated buyers.

4. There is no available financial information about sellers of goods of the same class or kind in country X.

5. There is available financial information about 2 distributors of blenders and rice cookers and 3 distributors of coffee makers and waffle makers in country I.

6. ICO provided Customs with a transfer pricing study which was prepared on the basis of a resale price method, as described in Subchapter C of Part II of Chapter II of the OECD Guidelines.

7. Since ICO does not buy the toasters from unrelated sellers, then the gross profit margin was established by reference to the gross profit margin that would have been earned in comparable transactions by independent enterprises.

8. ICO provided information showing that the gross profit margins on the resale of toasters, blenders, rice cookers, coffee makers and waffle makers are generally the same in the small home appliances distribution industry.

9. The functional analysis showed that the number of functions performed by ICO, in connection with the toasters, was substantially similar to that of the five unrelated buyers. ICO and the five unrelated buyers distribute the small home appliances. ICO and the five unrelated buyers have similar levels of inventories and fixed assets. The functional analysis showed that the risks assumed by ICO were substantially similar to those assumed by the five unrelated buyers.

10. In the relevant fiscal year, the gross profit margin of ICO when reselling the toasters was 33 %. In the same fiscal year, the gross profit margins of the five

unrelated buyers when reselling their small home appliances were:

Buyer 1	33 %
Buyer 2	31 %
Buyer 3	27 %
Buyer 4	25 %
Buyer 5	23 %

11. The median is 27 % and the upper limit of the range is 33%.

12. In order to calculate the gross profit margin realized by ICO in the particular sale under examination, ICO had to use its financial statements for the relevant fiscal year because it did not prepare financial statements for sub-periods within a fiscal year (e.g., quarterly financial statements). Likewise, the calculation of cost of goods sold was made on an annual basis, taking into account initial inventories, purchases during the year and final inventories. Consequently, the calculation of the gross profit margin in each particular transaction had to be made with reference to the gross profit margin calculated for the complete fiscal year.

13. In addition, ICO provided information to Customs showing that the purchase prices of the toasters have not changed during the relevant fiscal year.[195]

14. ICO and the five unrelated buyers offer a warranty with respect to all products so that the downstream price is uniform. Buyer 1 performs the warranty function but is, in fact, compensated by its unrelated seller (Seller 1) through a lower price. The other buyers (Other Buyers) and ICO do not perform the warranty function which is performed by their respective unrelated sellers (Other Sellers) and by XCO (products are sent back to the factory). However, XCO and the Other Sellers charge ICO and the Other Buyers a price higher than the one charged by Seller 1 to Buyer 1. Buyer 1 accounts for the warranty expenses as operating expenses, and there is no detailed financial information, at an operating expense level, in order to identify and re-classify such warranty expenses.

Suggested determination of Customs value

15. The OECD Guidelines provide that "the resale price method begins with the price at which a product that has been purchased from an associated enterprise is resold to an independent enterprise. The price (the resale price) is then reduced by an appropriate gross margin (the "resale price margin") representing the amount out of which the reseller would seek to cover its selling and other operating expenses and, in the light of the functions performed (taking into account assets used and risks assumed), make an appropriate profit. What is left after adjustment for other costs associated with the purchase of the product (e.g. customs duties), is an arm's length price for the original transfer of property between the associated enterprises". The OECD Guidelines suggest that this method is most useful where it is applied to marketing operations.

16. None of the examples of the Interpretative Note to Article 1.2 seem to be derived from the application of this method. However, if those examples were interpreted as preventing the importer from using other possible methods in

195. Therefore, the gross profit margin calculated for any particular transaction during the fiscal year would necessarily be the same.

demonstrating that the relationship did not influence the price, then such examples would prescribe the only applicable methods, what would be contrary to their purpose and to the ordinary meaning of the term "example" in its context. Such an interpretation would ignore the fact that the examples of the Interpretative Note are only illustrative. Nothing in the Agreement suggests that the examination of the circumstances of sale should be based on the narrow situations described in such examples.

17. The Interpretative Note to Article 1.2 does not create "methodologies".[196] In contrast, the Interpretative Note to Article 1.2 only provides simple examples designed to give guidance as to which methodologies can be used in determining whether the relationship influenced the price. Being illustrative in character (as examples generally are), they do not authorize Customs to limit the methodologies that the importer can avail himself of to those strictly used in the examples. Customs may reject a methodology that is contrary to the purposes of the examples or inconsistent with the purpose and objectives of the Agreement. For example, Customs could reject a methodology which is based on arbitrary formulae of allocation of profits or fictitious values.

18. In addition, the second example of the Interpretative Note might also be regarded as an application of the resale price method if flexibly interpreted. In effect, the example says: "Where it is shown that the price [it does not state whether it refers to sales or purchase price] is adequate to ensure recovery of all costs plus a profit which is representative of the firm's overall profit realized over a representative period of time ... in sales of goods of the same class or kind". The reference to the firm's overall profit in sales of goods of the same class appears to be connected with the price mentioned at the beginning of the sentence, what gives the idea that the price, that ensures a gross margin comparable to the firm's overall margin, is the sales price and not the purchase price. However, since not only a controlled sales price but also a controlled purchase price can affect the gross profit margin, a flexible interpretation may suggest that the example also refers to the resale price method.

19. The methods of the OECD Guidelines should be accepted in the context of Article 1.2, as long as they are useful and reliable in determining whether the relationship influenced the price. On these grounds, importers and Customs administrations would be authorized – where appropriate – to use the resale price method in examining the circumstances surrounding the sale.

20. The functional analysis showed that there were no significant differences in functions, risks and assets between ICO and the five unrelated buyers.

21. In addition, an adequate level of product comparability – as required under the resale price method – is observed between the transactions of the five unrelated buyers and those of ICO. In effect, toasters, blenders, rice cookers, coffee makers and waffle makers may be regarded as goods of the same class or kind and the gross profit margins on the sale of this type of goods are generally the same in the small home appliances distribution industry.

22. Customs established that the prices charged to ICO were adequate to recover all ICO's costs. ICO's transfer pricing documentation shows that ICO's gross profit margin (33%) was above the median and equal to the upper limit of the range of

196. Where the Agreement wanted to create methodologies, it did so through clear prescriptive rules (Articles 2, 3, 5 and 6).

gross profit margins realized by the five unrelated buyers. This would indicate, in principle, that the prices charged by XCO to ICO allowed ICO to recover a gross profit margin that was representative of the gross profit margin realized by unrelated distributors in sales of goods of the same class or kind over the relevant period of time. Consequently, this would also indicate that the prices charged by XCO to ICO were not influenced by the relationship.

23. However, since Buyer 1 accounts for the warranty expenses as operating expenses, there is a distortion in the gross profit margins which must be corrected. If Seller 1 performed the warranty itself, it would increase the transfer price, and therefore, Buyer 1's gross profit margin would be lower. Therefore, the margins of ICO and Buyer 1 are not comparable until an adjustment is made to account for that difference. Since there is no detailed financial information, at an operating expense level, in order to identify and re-classify such warranty expenses, an adjustment cannot be made. Consequently, Buyer 1's margin must be excluded from the range because it does not comply with an adequate comparability standard.

24. The new range of comparable gross profit margins has a median of 26% and an upper limit of 31%. Now, ICO's gross profit margin is above the upper limit of the range. This indicates that the gross profit margin realized by ICO in sales of toasters is above the comparable unrelated buyers' profits realized over a representative period of time in sales of goods of the same class or kind and, therefore, that the price charged by XCO to ICO would be influenced by the relationship. Consequently, the transaction value method would not be applicable. Recourse to an alternative method for determining the Customs value of the toasters would be necessary.

11.2.7 Case Study Submitted by China to the TCCV

In the 38th Session of the TCCV, China submitted a draft case study to illustrate the application of the Resale Price Method in examining the circumstances of the sale under Article 1.2(a). This case study is the result of China's concerns regarding certain distortions that the use of the Transactional Net Margin Method - as originally proposed during the debates that preceded the adoption of Case Study 14.1 - could produce if the operating expenses of the buyer included services supplied by the seller or by companies related to the seller.[197] This concern was finally also addressed in paragraph 21 of Case Study 14.1 as follows:

21. Based on the information provided in paragraph 8:

- The Sales figure can be accepted since ICO is selling only to unrelated parties (and it is assumed ICO is rationally seeking to maximize its profits in its dealings with unrelated parties).
- The Operating expenses amount has been examined and accepted as reliable since it is determined that these expenses are paid by ICO to unrelated parties, with ICO seeking to minimize its costs and these expenses have not been paid for the benefit of the seller.

197. *See* Annex VI to Document VT0935E1b of the TCCV.

11.3 Cost-Plus Method

The application of the cost-plus method starts with the computation of the costs incurred by the supplier of property in a related-party transaction for property transferred to a related purchaser and continues with the computation of an appropriate cost-plus mark up, to make an appropriate profit in light of the functions performed and the market conditions.[198] The definition of the OECD Guidelines is similar (although not identical) to the definition of the computed value method under GVC Article 6. Interestingly, the Note to GVC Article 6 indicates that the use of this method will generally be limited to those cases where the buyer and seller are related. It seems for this reason that the Note includes detailed guidance for determining the "amount for profit and general expenses" to be added.

Although not directly applicable in the context of GVC Article 1.2(a), the provisions of GVC Article 6 and its Note provide guidance for interpreting and applying the cost-plus method in such a context. Therefore, reference to the provisions of GVC Article 6 and its Note will be made throughout this section.

The OECD Guidelines explain that the cost-plus method probably is most useful where semifinished goods are sold between associated parties, where related parties have concluded joint facility agreements or long-term buy-and-supply arrangements.[199]

What is arrived at after adding the cost-plus mark up to the costs may be regarded as an arm's length price of the original controlled transaction.[200] The comparison of this price with the transaction value originally agreed upon between the related parties would determine whether the relationship influenced the price. This understanding can be derived from the Note to GVC Article 1.2(a), which states:

> As a further example, where it is shown that the price is adequate to ensure recovery of all costs plus a profit which is representative of the firm's overall profit realized over a representative period of time ... in sales of goods of the same class or kind, this would demonstrate that the price had not been influenced.

One could suggest that this example is an application of the cost-plus method. In effect, the example of the Note can be represented by the following formula:

$$C = A + B$$

where

A = All the costs.

B = Profit (representative of the firm's overall profit realized in sales of goods of the same class or kind).

C = Amount to be compared to the transaction value.

Then, if C were equal to (or less than) the transaction value agreed upon between the related parties, the latter would not be regarded as being influenced by the relationship.

198. *See* OECD Guidelines *supra* note 4, at 2.45.
199. *Ibid.*
200. *Ibid.*

In Ruling 546211, the acceptability of a related-party transaction value was at stake. The importer submitted information establishing that the transfer price had been calculated according to a formula of standard costplus [x] percent. The information detailed the allocation of costs between domestic sales and sales to the related importer in accordance with the formula agreed to by the related parties. The US Customs Service understood that such information established that the related exporter had intended to settle prices with the related importer in the same fashion that it settled prices with unrelated buyers since the same costs were reflected in both prices and the same return was anticipated. Thus, the US Custom Service decided that, based on the information provided, the transfer price was sufficient to recover all costs plus a profit that exceeded the exporter's overall profit based on the exporter's financial statements. Therefore, the transaction value was accepted as a basis of appraisement of the imported goods.[201]

As one can see, the US Customs Service (now, the U.S. CBP) accepted an analysis under the cost-plus method to demonstrate that the relationship had not influenced the related-party transaction value. Indeed, it framed such analysis not only in the second example provided by the Note to GVC Article 1.2, but also in the first example provided by such Note (i.e., that the exporter intended to settle prices with the related importer in the same fashion that it settled prices with unrelated buyers).

However, in applying the all costs plus a profit test, the U.S. CBP normally considers the "firm's" overall profit to be the profit of the parent company. Thus, if the seller of the imported goods is a subsidiary of the parent company, the price must be adequate to ensure recovery of all the seller's costs plus a profit that is equivalent to the parent company's overall profit.[202] The CBP understands that, if the profit of the seller is equal to or higher on the U.S. imports than the firm's overall profit, the purchase price would not be artificially low for Custom's purposes.[203]

According to Article 31 of the Vienna Convention on the Law of Treaties, treaties shall be interpreted in good faith in accordance with the ordinary meaning to be given to the terms of the treaty in their context and in the light of its object and purpose.[204] Nothing in the language of the Interpretative Note to Article 1.2(a) seems to indicate that, when it refers the "firm's overall profit", it actually means the parent company's profit.

201. *See* United States Customs Service, Ruling No. 546211 (10 June 1996), online: https://rulings.cbp.gov/index.asp?ru=546211&qu=546211&vw=det ail. In such Ruling, the US Customs Service said that "Company Y's related-party sales were ... the most profitable part of its operation. Thus, based on the information provided, the transfer price was sufficient to recover all costs plus a profit that exceeded Company Y's overall profit based on the company's 1993 financial statements. It is therefore our position that transaction value is an acceptable basis of appraisement."

202. *See* U.S. CBP, HQ 546998 (19 January 2000) and H238990 (7 April 2014).

203. *See* U.S. CBP, HQ H106603 (25 July 2011; HQ H065015 (14 April 2011); HQ H065024 (28 July 2011; and H238990 (7 April 2014).

204. United Nations, Treaty Series, vol. 1155, p. 331. Done at Vienna on 23 May 1969. Entered into force on 27 January 1980.

In addition, the U.S. CBP recognizes that the examples of the interpretative note are illustrative.[205] Therefore, there is no point in establishing strict or arbitrary limitations in the way in which the examples of the note may or may not be applied, because they are not methodologies.

On these grounds, it could be concluded that the cost-plus method is applicable in the context of GVC Article 1.2(a). The OECD Guidelines, read together with the provisions of GVC Article 6 and its Note, could provide useful guidance for applying such method in such a context.

11.3.1 Internal and External Comparables

The example of the Note to GVC Article 1.2, quoted above, clearly refers to the use of internal comparables. In this respect, the Guidelines provide that "[t]he cost plus mark up of the supplier in the controlled transaction should ideally be established by reference to the cost plus mark up that the same supplier earns in comparable uncontrolled transactions."[206]

Nevertheless, the Guidelines also state that "[i]n addition, the cost-plus mark up that would have been earned in comparable transactions by an independent enterprise may serve as a guide."[207]

This statement would not be inconsistent with the Note to GVC Article 1.2. As indicated above, the examples of the Notes are illustrative and do not preclude the use of methods which are consistent with the general principles of the GVC (as reflected by the Note to GVC Article 1.2 read together with the other provisions of the GVC). First, the use of external comparables is not arbitrary or fictitious, being, therefore, consistent with the Preamble of the GVC. Second, the examination of external comparables would be generally consistent with the process of examining the "normal pricing practices of the industry."[208] Note that this was the approach adopted in Case Study 14.1 by the TCCV. Third, the Note to GVC Article 6 allows the use of external comparables. In effect, where the producer's own figures for profit and general expenses are not consistent with those usually reflected in sales of goods of the same class or kind as the goods being valued which are made by producers in the country of exportation for export to the country of importation, the amount for profit and general expenses may be based upon relevant information other than that supplied by or on behalf of the producer of the goods.[209]

205. *See* U.S. CBP, HQ W548314 (16 May 2012) and H238990 (7 April 2014), among many others.
206. *See* OECD Guidelines *supra* note 4, at 2.46.
207. *Ibid.*
208. Even though the reference to "normal pricing practices of the industry" is made in another example, consistency with such practices would demonstrate consistency with the principles underlying the Note.
209. *See* paragraph 5 of the Note to GVC Article 6.

11.3.2 *Application of the Method*

11.3.2.1 Product Comparability

The comparability standards described in Section 7 should be observed in applying the cost-plus method. This is especially true when such method is used in the context of GVC Article 1.2(a). The OECD Guidelines explain that, for the purposes of the cost-plus method, an uncontrolled transaction is comparable to a controlled transaction if one of two conditions is met:

(1) None of the differences between the transactions being compared or between the enterprises undertaking those transactions materially affect the cost-plus mark up in the open market; or
(2) Reasonably accurate adjustments can be made to eliminate the material effects of such differences.[210]

The OECD Guidelines also indicate that "fewer adjustments may be necessary to account for product differences under the cost-plus method than the CUP method, and it may be appropriate to give more weight to other factors of comparability described in Chapter 1, some of which may have a more significant effect on the cost-plus mark up than they do on price ..."[211] In this respect, see the analysis made in sub section 11.2.2.1, which is also applicable in the context of the cost-plus method.

11.3.2.2 Economic Circumstances and Relative Efficiency

The OECD Guidelines state that the cost-plus method presents some difficulties in the determination of costs. The Guidelines indicate that "[a]lthough it is true that an enterprise must cover its costs over a period of time to remain in business, those costs may not be determinant of the appropriate profit in a specific case for any one year. While in many cases companies are driven by competition to scale down prices by reference to the cost of creating the relevant goods or providing the relevant service, there are other circumstances where there is no discernible link between the level of costs incurred and a market price (e.g. where a valuable discovery has been made and the owner has incurred only small research costs in making it)."[212]

All these circumstances should also be taken into account in applying the cost-plus method in the context of GVC Article 1.2(a). Grounds to support this argument can be found in paragraph 5 of the Note to GVC Article 6, which also provides further guidance in this respect. The relevant part of such paragraph indicates that:

> ... "[t]he amount for profit and general expenses" has to be taken as a whole. It follows that if, in any particular case, the producer's profit figure is low and the

210. *See* OECD Guidelines *supra* note 4, at 2.47.
211. *Ibid.*
212. OECD Guidelines *supra* note 4, at 2.49.

> producer's general expenses are high, the producer's profit and general expenses taken together may nevertheless be consistent with that usually reflected in sales of goods of the same class or kind. Such a situation might occur, for example, if a product were being launched in the country of importation and the producer accepted a nil or low profit to offset high general expenses associated with the launch. Where the producer can demonstrate a low profit on sales of the imported goods because of particular commercial circumstances, the producer's actual profit figures should be taken into account provided that the producer's pricing policy reflects usual pricing policies in the branch of industry concerned. Such a situation might occur, for example, where producers have been forced to lower prices temporarily because of an unforeseeable drop in demand, or where they sell goods to complement a range of goods being produced in the country of importation and accept a low profit to maintain competitivity.

Sherman explains that this attitude under the GVC is in sharp contrast to the prevailing views under the old US valuation system. Under the latter a price yielding little or no profit would in practice generally be rejected because it was "lacking an element of value." Under the GVC, it is sufficient for the manufacturer to show good commercial reasons for his making little or no profit. Such reasons need not apply to all competing producers, so long as they reflect usual policies for the branch of industry.[213] This author also indicates that "[a]ll of this is one of the clearest indications of the powerful conviction underlying the Code, that valuation should be based on commercial reality - even to the extent of recognizing that commercial reality sometimes includes selling at little or no profit."[214]

In this context, another interesting issue is that of the relative efficiency of the enterprises being compared. Levey explains that an unrelated party probably would not accept paying a higher price resulting from the other party's inefficiency. Likewise, if the other party is more efficient than can be expected under normal circumstances, it should benefit from that advantage.[215] The OECD Guidelines indicate that, in these circumstances, unless it is possible to adjust for the effect of differences in profit margins, the application of the cost-plus method would not be wholly reliable.[216] This should also be taken into account in the context of GVC Article 1.2(a). It should be examined as part of the producer's valid commercial reasons to justify the producer's actual profit figures[217] and as part of the circumstances surrounding the sale under GVC Article 1.2(a).

11.3.2.3 *Functions Performed*

In applying the cost-plus method, it is particularly important to consider differences in the level and types of expenses associated with functions performed and risks assumed by the parties for the transactions being compared. Differences in these expenses may indicate the following:

213. *See* Sherman *supra* note 23, at 232.
214. Sherman *supra* note 23, at 232.
215. *See* Hammer *supra* note 11, at 4.04[2][g].
216. *See* OECD Guidelines *supra* note 4, at 2.48.
217. *See* paragraph 5 of the Note to GVC Article 6.

- An adjustment to the cost-plus mark up may be required if the expenses reflect a functional difference which has not been taken into account in applying the method;
- If the expenses reflect additional functions that are distinct from the activities tested by the method, separate compensation for those functions may need to be determined.
- No adjustment to the gross margin may be appropriate if differences in the expenses of the parties being compared merely reflect efficiencies or inefficiencies of the enterprises (as would often be the case for supervisory, general and administrative expenses).[218]

The Guidelines also indicate that, in any of the above circumstances, it may be appropriate to supplement the cost-plus method by considering the results obtained from applying other methods.[219] As indicated in Section 7.3, this combined application of methods is possible under GVC Article 1.2.

11.3.2.4 Accounting Consistency

The General Note to the GVC states that:

> [f]or the purposes of this Agreement, the Customs administrations of each Member shall utilize information prepared in a manner consistent with generally accepted accounting principles in the country which is appropriate for the Article in question. For example, the determination of usual profit and general expenses under the provisions of Article 5 would be carried out utilizing information prepared in a manner consistent with generally accepted accounting principles of the country of importation. On the other hand, the determination of usual profit and general expenses under the provisions of Article 6 would be carried out utilizing information prepared in a manner consistent with generally accepted accounting principles of the country of production. As a further example, the determination of an element provided for in paragraph 1(b)(ii) or Article 8 undertaken in the country of importation would be carried out utilizing information in a manner consistent with the generally accepted accounting principles of that country.

Accounting consistency is a relevant concern under the OECD Guidelines. Where the accounting practices are different in the controlled transaction and the uncontrolled transaction, the Guidelines indicate that appropriate adjustments should be made to the data used, to ensure that the same kind of costs are used in each case to ensure consistency.[220] As indicated by the General Note, generally accepted accounting principles of different countries could be involved in determining customs values under the GVC. Thus – since accounting inconsistencies might occur – importers and Customs administrations should pay special attention to ensure accounting

218. *See* OECD Guidelines *supra* note 4, at 2.51.
219. *Ibid.*
220. *Ibid.* at 2.52.

consistency and be prepared to make appropriate adjustments to the data used in determining whether the relationship influenced the price.[221]

11.3.3 Case Studies

The following case studies were submitted by the author of this book to the Focus Group on Customs Valuation and Transfer Pricing, in the sidelines of the TCCV's 25th Session. They were intended to provide to the Focus Group and, later on, to the TCCV, examples on how the OECD Cost-Plus Method could be used in the context of the Circumstances-of-Sale Test.

CASE STUDY 2

APPLICATION OF ARTICLE 1.2

Facts of transaction

1. ICO of country I purchased and imported a natural ingredient used in the production of food flavourings from XCO of country X.

2. At the time of clearing the goods, ICO declared to Customs in country I that it was related to XCO.

3. After importation, Customs in country I decided to conduct a review of the circumstances surrounding the sale of goods between XCO and ICO, pursuant to Article 1.2 of the Agreement, because it had doubts about the acceptability of the price. To this end, Customs forwarded a questionnaire to ICO which sought information regarding the sale of products by XCO to other buyers in country I and, if necessary, justification of any price difference as well as information relating to XCO's cost of production and profit. At the request of ICO, Customs also forwarded a questionnaire to XCO. From the responses received, facts as set out below were established.

4. ICO purchased the natural ingredient from XCO for the production of food flavourings. The natural ingredient has been acquired by XCO from other manufacturers. It is not manufactured or processed by XCO.

5. The ingredient is sold only to ICO in country I and there are no importations of identical or similar goods into country I.

6. XCO does not sell other goods.

7. Five sellers in country X sell synthetic ingredients to unrelated buyers in country I. The synthetic ingredients have been acquired by the sellers from other

221. The Guidelines also provide that the gross profit markups must be measured consistently between the associated enterprise and the independent enterprise. *See* OECD Guidelines *supra* note 4, at 2.52. In this respect, it is interesting to note that, under the Guidelines, the cost-plus method will use margins computed after direct and indirect cost of production (a net margin method will use margins computed after operating expenses as well – *see* OECD Guidelines *supra* note 4, at 2.54). The Note to GVC Article 6, in a manner consistent with the Guidelines, provides that "general expenses" include "the direct and indirect costs of producing and selling the goods for export which are not included under paragraph 1(a) of Article 6" (the cost included under paragraph 1(a) is the cost or value of materials and fabrication or other processing employed in producing the imported goods).

manufacturers. They are not manufactured or processed by the sellers. The unrelated buyers purchased the synthetic ingredients from the sellers also for the production of food flavourings.

8. The natural ingredient and the synthetic ingredients fall within the range of goods produced by the ingredients sector of the food flavouring industry. Therefore, they may be regarded as "goods of the same class or kind".

9. ICO provided Customs with a transfer pricing study which was prepared on the basis of a cost plus method, as described in Subchapter D of Part II of Chapter II of the OECD Guidelines.

10. Since XCO does not sell the natural ingredients to unrelated buyers, then the cost plus mark up was established by reference to the cost plus mark up that would have been earned in comparable transactions by independent enterprises.

11. ICO provided information showing that the profit margins on the sale of synthetic and natural ingredients are generally the same in the food flavouring industry.

12. The functional analysis showed that the number of functions performed by XCO, in connection with the natural ingredients, was substantially similar to that of the five unrelated sellers. The functions performed by XCO were as significant as those performed by the five unrelated sellers in terms of their frequency, nature and value. The functional analysis also identified and compared the assets employed by XCO and by the five unrelated sellers. Both XCO and the five unrelated sellers have no inventories of ingredients and insignificant levels of fixed assets. The functional analysis also showed that the risks assumed by XCO when selling to ICO were substantially similar to those assumed by the five sellers when selling to the unrelated buyers.

13. ICO provided Customs with information showing that the contractual terms in transactions between the five sellers and the unrelated buyers were substantially similar to those in transactions between XCO and ICO.

14. In the relevant fiscal year, the cost plus mark up of XCO in its transactions with ICO was 30%. In the same fiscal year, the cost plus mark ups of the five sellers in transactions with unrelated buyers in country I were:

Seller 1	33 %
Seller 2	30 %
Seller 3	27 %[222]
Seller 4	25 %
Seller 5	23 %

15. The median of the range is 27 %. The first and third quartiles are 25 % and 30 %, respectively.

222. Seller 3 sold synthetic ingredients to country I and to countries J, K and L. The financial information of Seller 3 did not show separately the cost, expense and profit figures in respect of exports to different countries. However, ICO had information showing that the prices at which Seller 3 was selling to countries I, J, K and L were the same.

16. Customs established that the prices charged to ICO were adequate to recover all XCO's costs, including the costs of acquisition plus the costs of repacking, handling and freight charges, but it could not establish whether such prices were adequate to recover a profit that was representative of the firm's overall profit over a representative period of time, because 100 % of the firm's overall profits were the profits from the sale of the natural ingredient to ICO in country I.

Suggested determination of Customs value

17. The Interpretative Note to Article 1.2 provides that "the customs administrations should be prepared to examine relevant aspects of the transaction, including the way in which the buyer and seller organize their commercial relations and the way in which the price in question was arrived at, in order to determine whether the relationship influenced the price". This involves a complete analysis of the transaction in question and uncontrolled transactions in order to determine whether the relationship influenced the price. The examination of those aspects must always have a comparability purpose, since this is the only mechanism authorized by the Agreement for determining whether the relationship influenced the price. The language of the Interpretative Note to Article 1.2 is broad enough to permit a functional analysis and a comparison of contractual terms, economic circumstances and business strategies (in the context of a comprehensive transfer pricing study) under the more detailed rules of the Transfer Pricing Guidelines for Multinational Enterprises and Tax Administrations of the Organization for the Economic Cooperation and Development (hereinafter "OECD Guidelines") in determining whether the relationship influenced the transaction value.

18. The Interpretative Note to Article 1.2 gives some guidance in relation to the circumstances that Customs should examine and to the information that importers should submit. However, such guidance is very general. Customs administrations and importers cannot be expected to solve complex transfer pricing problems solely on the basis of such general provisions.

19. Furthermore, the Interpretative Note to Article 1.2 only provides examples of circumstances or aspects of the transactions which could be examined by Customs. Such examples do not constitute the only circumstances or aspects that Customs might explore and should be taken only as a starting point and as illustrative.[223]

20. The second example of the Interpretative Note to Article 1.2 provides guidance on the type of examination of the circumstances of sale required by the Agreement. It does not require that the methodology used by the importer in the examination of the circumstances of the sale be identical to the one used for purposes of the example. Otherwise, the Interpretative Note would not have used the words "as an example" and "as a further example" but, rather, a more prescriptive language.

21. In this context, the use of the cost plus method, as described in the OECD Guidelines, is consistent with the examples of the Interpretative Note and with the objective and purpose of the Agreement. Furthermore, the use of external comparables (i.e., the use of cost plus mark ups of unrelated sellers in the absence of sales by XCO to unrelated buyers) is also consistent with such examples and with the

223. Sherman and Glashoff explain that Agreement "does not confine itself to the facts regarding the sale – it deals with the broader concept of an inquiry into 'the circumstances surrounding' the sale. This language plainly speaks of the entire context of the transaction and not just of the transaction itself." *See supra* note 23 at 193].

objective and the purpose of the Agreement. Firstly, the use of external comparables is not arbitrary or fictitious, being, therefore, consistent with the Preamble of the Agreement. Secondly, the examination of external comparables would be generally consistent with the process of examining the "normal pricing practices of the industry."[224] Thirdly, although not directly applicable in the context of paragraph (a) of Article 1.2, the Interpretative Note to Article 6 allows the use of external comparables. In effect, where the producer's own figures for profit and general expenses are not consistent with those usually reflected in sales of goods of the same class or kind as the goods being valued which are made by producers in the country of exportation for export to the country of importation, the amount for profit and general expenses may be based upon relevant information other than that supplied by or on behalf of the producer of the goods. Taking into account that a treaty shall be interpreted in accordance with the ordinary meaning to be given to the terms of the treaty in their context, the provisions of Article 6 and its Interpretative Note are part of such context and, therefore, provide guidance for interpreting and applying Article 1.2.

22. The OECD Guidelines indicate that "the cost plus method begins with the costs incurred by the supplier of property (or services) in a controlled transaction for property transferred or services provided to a related purchaser. An appropriate cost plus mark up is then added to this cost, to make an appropriate profit in light of the functions performed and the market conditions. What is arrived at after adding the cost plus mark up to the above costs may be regarded as an arm's length price of the original controlled transaction. This method probably is most useful where semifinished goods are sold between related parties, where related parties have concluded joint facility agreements or long-term buy-and-supply arrangements, or where the controlled transaction is the provision of services... The cost plus mark up of the supplier in the controlled transaction should ideally be established by reference to the cost plus mark up that the same supplier earns in comparable uncontrolled transactions. In addition, the cost plus mark up that would have been earned in comparable transactions by an independent enterprise may serve as a guide."

23. The OECD Guidelines also provide that an uncontrolled transaction is comparable to a controlled transaction (i.e., it is a comparable uncontrolled transaction) for purposes of the cost plus method if one of two conditions is met:

1. none of the differences (if any) between the transactions being compared or between the enterprises undertaking those transactions materially affect the cost plus mark up in the open market; or
2. reasonably accurate adjustments can be made to eliminate the material effects of such differences.

24. In making comparisons for purposes of the cost plus method, fewer adjustments are normally needed to achieve comparability, because minor product differences are less likely to have as material an effect on profit margins as they do on price. These comparability standards are also observed in the Agreement. In effect, the product comparability standard is less rigid in the second example of the Interpretative Note to Article 1.2 (goods of the same class or kind) where a profit margin comparison is required, than in its first example or in Article 1.2(b)(i) where a price comparison is required. The same logic is followed throughout the

224. Even though the reference to "normal pricing practices of the industry" is made in another example, consistency with such practices would demonstrate consistency with the principles underlying the Note.

other Articles of the Agreement (Articles 1.2(b)(i), 2 and 3 require identical or similar goods, while Articles 1.2(b)(ii), 1.2(b)(iii), 5 and 6 require goods of the same class or kind).

25. The functional analysis showed that there were no significant differences in functions, risks and assets between XCO and the five unrelated sellers. Also, ICO demonstrated that the contractual terms in sales made by the five unrelated sellers and by XCO were substantially similar.

26. In addition, an adequate level of product comparability – as required under the cost plus method – is observed between the transactions of the five unrelated sellers and those of XCO. In effect, synthetic and natural ingredients may be regarded as goods of the same class or kind and the profit margins on the sale of those ingredients are generally the same in the food flavouring industry.

27. Customs established that the prices charged to ICO were adequate to recover all XCO's costs, including the costs of acquisition plus the costs of repacking, handling and freight charges. XCO's cost plus mark up (30%) is above the median of the range of cost plus mark ups charged by the five unrelated sellers. In fact, it is equal to the third quartile of the range.[225]

28. Therefore, XCO's prices are adequate to recover a profit that is representative of the comparable unrelated sellers' profit realized over a representative period of time (i.e., the relevant fiscal year) in sales of goods of the same class or kind. In accordance with paragraph 3 of the Interpretative Note to Article 1.2, transaction values in respect of the natural ingredients may be acceptable for Customs purposes.

Case Study 3

APPLICATION OF ARTICLE 1.2

Facts of transaction

1. ICO of country I purchased and imported a natural ingredient (NI) and a natural flavour modifier (NFM) used in the production of food flavourings from XCO of country X.

2. At the time of clearing the goods, ICO declared to Customs in country I that it was related to XCO.

3. After importation, Customs in country I decided to conduct a review of the circumstances surrounding the sale of goods between XCO and ICO, pursuant to Article 1.2 of the Agreement, because it had doubts about the acceptability of the price. To this end, Customs forwarded a questionnaire to ICO which sought information regarding the sale of products by XCO to other buyers in country I and, if necessary, justification of any price difference as well as information relating to XCO's cost of production and profit. At the request of ICO, Customs also forwarded a questionnaire to XCO. From the responses received, facts as set out below were established.

225. If we exclude Seller 3 from the arm's length range, then the first quartile, the median and the third quartile of the range would be 24.5, 27.5 and 30.75. XCO's cost-plus mark up would be within the interquartile range and still above the median.

4. ICO purchased the NI and the NFM from XCO for the production of food flavourings. The NI and NFM have been acquired by XCO from other manufacturers. They are not manufactured or processed by XCO.

5. The NI and NFM are sold only to ICO in country I and there are no importations of identical or similar goods into country I.

6. XCO does not sell other goods.

7. NIs and NFMs are classifiable under separate tariff headings at different rates of duty. The import duty rates applicable to NIs and NFMs are 20 % and 2 %, respectively.

8. Five sellers in country X sell synthetic ingredients (SI) and synthetic flavour modifiers (SFM) to unrelated buyers in country I. The SIs and SFMs have been acquired by the sellers from other manufacturers. They are not manufactured or processed by the sellers. The unrelated buyers purchased the SIs and SFMs from the sellers also for the production of food flavourings.

9. The NIs and SIs fall within the range of goods produced by the ingredients sector of the food flavouring industry. Likewise, the NFMs and SFMs fall within the range of goods produced by the flavour modifiers sector of the food flavouring industry.

10. ICO provided Customs with a transfer pricing study which was prepared on the basis of a cost plus method, as described in Subchapter C of Part II of Chapter II of the OECD Guidelines.

11. Since XCO sells neither the NI nor the NFM to unrelated buyers, then the cost plus mark up was established by reference to the cost plus mark up that would have been earned in comparable transactions by independent enterprises.

12. ICO understood that the sales of NI and NFM by XCO were so closely linked that they should not be evaluated on a separate basis. Also, it believed that it was impractical to determine pricing for NI and NFM separately and that it was more reasonable to assess the arm's length terms for the two items together.

13. ICO provided information showing that the profit margins on the sale of SIs and NIs are generally the same in the food flavouring industry. It also provided information showing that the profit margins on the sale of NFMs and SFMs are generally the same in such industry.

14. The functional analysis showed that the number of functions performed by XCO, in connection with the NI and NFM, was substantially similar to that of the five unrelated sellers in connection with the SIs and SFMs. The functions performed by XCO were as significant as those performed by the five unrelated sellers in terms of their frequency, nature and value. The functional analysis also identified and compared the assets employed by XCO and by the five unrelated sellers. Both XCO and the five unrelated sellers have no inventories of ingredients or flavour modifiers and insignificant levels of fixed assets. The functional analysis also showed that the risks assumed by XCO when selling to ICO were substantially similar to those assumed by the five sellers when selling to the unrelated buyers.

15. ICO provided Customs with information showing that the contractual terms in transactions between the five sellers and the unrelated buyers were substantially similar to those in transactions between XCO and ICO.

16. In the relevant fiscal year, the overall cost plus mark up of XCO in its transactions with ICO was 30%. In the same fiscal year, the overall cost plus mark ups of the five sellers in transactions with unrelated buyers in country I were:

Seller 1	33 %
Seller 2	30 %
Seller 3	27 %
Seller 4	25 %
Seller 5	23 %

17. The median of the range is 27 %. The first and third quartiles are 25 % and 30 %, respectively.

18. Customs established that the prices charged to ICO were adequate to recover all XCO's costs, including the costs of acquisition plus the costs of repacking, handling and freight charges, but it could not establish whether such prices were adequate to recover a profit that was representative of the firm's overall profit over a representative period of time, because 100 % of the firm's overall profits were the profits from the sale of the NI and NFM to ICO in country I.

Suggested determination of Customs value

19. The functional analysis showed that there were no significant differences in functions, risks and assets between XCO and the five unrelated sellers. Also, ICO demonstrated that the contractual terms in sales made by the five unrelated sellers and by XCO were substantially similar.

20. In addition, an adequate level of product comparability – as required under the cost plus method – is observed between the transactions of the five unrelated sellers and those of XCO. In effect, SIs and NIs may be regarded as goods of the same class or kind and the profit margins on the sale of those ingredients are generally the same in the food flavouring industry. Likewise, SFMs and NFMs may also be regarded as goods of the same class or kind and the profit margins on the sale of those modifiers are generally the same in such industry.

21. Customs established that the prices charged to ICO were adequate to recover all XCO's costs, including the costs of acquisition plus the costs of re-packing, handling and freight charges. XCO's cost plus mark up (30%) is above the median of the range of cost plus mark ups charged by the five unrelated sellers. In fact, it is equal to the third quartile of the range.

22. However, on the basis of the combined analysis made in the transfer pricing study, Customs may not determine whether XCO's prices in sales of NIs and NFMs are separately adequate to recover a profit that is representative of the comparable unrelated sellers' profit realized, separately, in sales of SIs and SFMs. Since NIs and NFMs are classifiable in different headings at different duty rates, if the cost plus mark up realized in sales of NFMs is above the profit realized by unrelated sellers in sales of SFMs and the cost plus mark up realized in sales of NIs is below the profit realized by unrelated sellers in sales of SIs, then XCO's prices could reduce the total liability of the importer for Customs duties, without altering the result of the combined analysis (because, on a combined basis, the overall cost plus mark up realized in sales of NIs and NFMs may be equal to the overall cost plus mark up realized in sales of SIs and SFMs).

23. Therefore, the transfer pricing study is not enough to demonstrate that the transaction values of the NI and NFM are acceptable for Customs purposes under paragraph 3 of the Interpretative Note to Article 1.2. In this type of situation, the importer would have to evaluate the transactions of NI and NFM on a separate basis when preparing the transfer pricing studies for Customs purposes. In addition, the methods described in paragraph 4 of Commentary 8.1 may be used in order to make the proper apportionment of the overall cost plus mark up among the goods which are classifiable in different headings.

Case Study 4

APPLICATION OF ARTICLE 1.2

Facts of transaction

1. Same facts as in Case Study 3, except that:

(a) Even if ICO understood that, for income tax purposes, it was impractical to determine pricing for the NI and NFM separately and that it was more reasonable to assess the arm's length terms for the two items together, it has nevertheless segmented its financial statements in order to analyze separately the cost plus mark ups realized in transactions of NI and NFM.

(b) In the relevant fiscal year, the cost plus mark up of XCO in sales of NFM was 31%, and in sales of NI, 22%.

(c) Five sellers (XSIs) in country X sell synthetic ingredients to unrelated buyers in country I. The synthetic ingredients have been acquired by the XSIs from other manufacturers. They are not manufactured or processed by the XSIs. The unrelated buyers purchased the synthetic ingredients from the sellers also for the production of food flavourings.

(d) Five other sellers (XSMs) in country X sell synthetic flavour modifiers to unrelated buyers in country I. The synthetic flavour modifiers have been acquired by the XSMs from other manufacturers. They are not manufactured or processed by the XSMs. The unrelated buyers purchased the synthetic flavour modifiers from the XSMs also for the production of food flavourings.

(e) The functional analysis showed that the number of functions performed by XCO, in connection with the natural ingredients and flavour modifiers, was substantially similar to that of the ten unrelated sellers (i.e. the XSIs and the XSMs). The functions performed by XCO were as significant as those performed by the ten unrelated sellers in terms of their frequency, nature and value. The functional analysis also identified and compared the assets employed by XCO and by the ten unrelated sellers. XCO and the ten unrelated sellers have no inventories of ingredients or flavour modifiers and an insignificant level of fixed assets. The functional analysis also showed that the risks assumed by XCO when selling to ICO were substantially similar to those assumed by the ten unrelated sellers when selling to the unrelated buyers.

2. ICO provided Customs with information showing that the contractual terms in transactions between the ten sellers and their unrelated buyers were substantially similar to those in transactions between XCO and ICO.

3. In the same fiscal year, the cost plus mark ups of the five XSIs in transactions with unrelated buyers in country I were:

Seller 1	30 %
Seller 2	26 %
Seller 3	25 %
Seller 4	24 %
Seller 5	23 %

4. The median of the range is 25 %. The first and third quartiles are 24 % and 26 %, respectively.

5. In such fiscal year, the cost plus mark ups of the five XSMs in transactions with unrelated buyers in country I were:

Seller 1	33 %
Seller 2	31 %
Seller 3	27 %
Seller 4	25 %
Seller 5	23 %

6. The median of the range is 27 %. The first and third quartiles are 25 % and 31 %, respectively.

Suggested determination of Customs value

7. The functional analysis showed that there were no significant differences in functions, risks and assets between XCO and the unrelated sellers. Also, ICO demonstrated that the contractual terms in sales made by the unrelated sellers and by XCO were substantially similar.

8. In addition, an adequate level of product comparability – as required under the cost plus method – is observed between the transactions of the unrelated sellers and those of XCO. In effect, SIs and NIs may be regarded as goods of the same class or kind and the profit margins on the sale of those ingredients are generally the same in the food flavouring industry. Likewise, SFMs and NFMs may also be regarded as goods of the same class or kind and the profit margins on the sale of those flavour modifiers are generally the same in such industry.

9. Customs established that the prices charged to ICO were adequate to recover all XCO's costs, including the costs of acquisition plus the costs of repacking, handling and freight charges. In addition, XCO's cost plus mark up (i.e. 31%) in sales of NFM is above the median of the range of cost plus mark ups charged by the five XSMs in sales of SFMs in the relevant period of time. In fact, it is equal to the third quartile of the range.

10. Therefore, XCO's prices in sales of NFMs are adequate to recover a profit that is representative of the comparable unrelated sellers' profit realized over a representative period of time (i.e. the relevant fiscal year) in sales of goods of the same class or kind. In accordance with paragraph 3 of the Interpretative Note to Article 1.2, transaction values in respect of the NFM may be acceptable for Customs purposes.

11. With respect to the NI, Customs established that the prices charged to ICO were not adequate to recover a profit that is representative of the profit realized by unrelated sellers in sales of goods of the same class or kind (i.e. the SIs) over the relevant period of time. In effect, XCO's cost plus mark up (i.e. 22%) is below the bottom of the range. In respect of the NI, therefore, the transaction value method would not be applicable. Recourse to an alternative method for determining Customs value of the NI would be necessary.

12 TRANSACTIONAL PROFIT METHODS

The OECD Guidelines describe two transactional profit methods: the transactional profit split method and the transactional net margin method. They examine the profits that arise from particular controlled transactions and, therefore, we can affirm that they are transactional in character, what is especially relevant for customs valuation purposes. Profit arising from a controlled transaction can be a relevant indicator of whether the transaction was affected by conditions that differ from those that would have been made by independent enterprises in otherwise comparable circumstances[226] or, in other words, whether the relationship between buyer and seller influenced the price.

12.1 Transactional Net Margin Method

The OECD Guidelines define this method in the following words:

> The transactional net margin method examines the net profit margin relative to an appropriate base (e.g. costs, sales, assets) that a taxpayer realises from a controlled transaction (or transactions that are appropriate to aggregate under the principles of paragraphs 3.9–3.12). Thus, a transactional net margin method operates in a manner similar to the cost-plus and resale price methods. This similarity means that in order to be applied reliably, the transactional net margin method must be applied in a manner consistent with the manner in which the resale price or cost-plus method is applied. This means that the net profit indicator of the taxpayer from the controlled transaction ... should ideally be established by reference to the net profit indicator that the same taxpayer earns in comparable uncontrolled transactions.[227]

The transactional net margin method appears to be consistent with the example provided by the Note to GVC Article 1.2. In effect, such example compares the profit of the controlled transaction ("price" minus "all costs") and a profit which is representative of the firm's overall profit realized in sales of goods of the same class or kind. The WCO Guide to Customs Valuation and Transfer Pricing explains that "...[t]he example does not define whether 'profit' is 'gross' or 'operating' profit, but this gives Customs the flexibility to review both kinds of profits, depending on what is considered to be useful. Normally, operating profit is a better measure of real profitability because it

226. *See supra* note 4, at 2.63.
227. OECD Guidelines *supra* note 4, at 2.64.

shows what is earned after all expenses have been paid. Also it is the measure for which information concerning independent parties will most often be available. Operating profit is also the most common Profit Level Indicator when the CPM/TNMM method is used..."[228]

In Case Study 14.1, the TCCV explains how the information supplied by the importer in a transfer pricing study, which applied the Transactional Net Margin Method, may be used to prove that the prices were not influenced by the relationship between buyer and seller. This confirms that the Transactional Net Margin Method may be used in the context of the Circumstances-of-Sale Test of Article 1.2(a), as it was proposed in the first edition of this book in 2002 and in the paper and draft case studies that we submitted to the TCCV and the Focus Group on Customs Valuation and Transfer Pricing between 2005 and 2010. Needless to say that the use of a transfer pricing study for examining the circumstances surrounding the sale must be considered on a case-by-case basis, as proposed by the TCCV in Commentary 23.1.

The OECD Guidelines indicate that, where it is not possible to establish the net margin of the taxpayer from the controlled transaction by reference to the net margin that the same taxpayer earns in comparable uncontrolled transactions, the net margin that would have been earned in comparable transactions by an independent enterprise may serve as a guide. In this case, a functional analysis of the controlled and uncontrolled transactions is required to determine whether the transactions are comparable and what adjustments may be necessary to obtain reliable results.[229]

One strength of this method is that the net profit indicators (e.g., return on assets, operating income to sales,) are less affected by transactional differences than in the case with price, as used in the CUP method.[230] Also, net profit indicators are usually more tolerant to some functional differences between the controlled and uncontrolled transactions than gross profit margins. Another practical strength is that, as with any one-sided method, it is necessary to examine a financial indicator for only one of the related parties (the "tested party"). The Guidelines indicate that this can be practically advantageous when one of the parties to the transaction is complex and has many interrelated activities or when it is difficult to obtain reliable information about one of the parties.[231] This is especially important in the customs context, where it is generally

228. The U.S. CBP seems to agree with this proposition. For instance, in Ruling HQ H238990 (7 April 2014), the U.S. CBP said: "...CBP Regulations do not define what profit we are to consider – gross profit or operating profit. However, CBP is of the view that the operating profit margin is a more accurate measure of a company's real profitability because it reveals what the company actually earns on its sales once all associated expenses have been paid. Nevertheless, in certain circumstances, gross profit can be considered. *See* HQ H037375, dated December 11, 2009..." *See also* U.S. CBP Ruling HQ H258447 (19 January 2016).

229. *See* OECD Guidelines *supra* note 4, at 2.64.

230. *Ibid* at 2.68.

231. *Ibid* at 2.69.

recognized that the customs value should be (i) based on simple and equitable criteria[232] and (ii) determined on the basis of information readily available in the country of importation.[233]

In paragraphs 2.74 through 2.81, the OECD Guidelines provide detailed and specific guidance on establishing comparability for the transactional net margin method. This guidance is as important in a tax transfer pricing study as it is in the Circumstances-of-Sale Test of GVC Article 1.2(a).

As explained above, the transactional net margin method examines a "net profit indicator" which is defined by the OECD Guidelines as the ratio of net profit to an appropriate base (e.g., costs, sales, assets). The transactional net margin method relies on a comparison of an appropriate net profit indicator for the controlled transaction with the same net profit indicator in comparable uncontrolled transactions. The OECD Guidelines address in particular the cases where (i) the net profit is weighted to sales (net profit margin or "NPM"), (ii) the net profit is weighted to costs, and (iii) the net profit is weighted to assets (return on assets or return on capital employed). They also include a discussion on other possible net profit indicators and on the Berry ratios (the ratio of gross profit to operating expenses). Below we will see that, in Case Study 14.1, the TCCV examined a case where the transfer pricing study of the importer used the net profit margin (operating profit margin) as the net profit indicator, as it was proposed by us in Case Study No. 6 submitted to the Focus Group on Customs Valuation and Transfer Pricing in 2007 and to the TCCV in its 27th Session.

The OECD Guidelines explain that the net profit margin is frequently used to determine the arm's length price of purchases from an associated enterprise for resale to independent customers and that, in such cases, the sales figure at the denominator should be the resales of items purchased in the controlled transaction under review. The way in which an NPM-based TNMM is applied resembles that of the deductive value method of GVC Article 5 and, as it is to be generally used in the case of imports of goods for resale in the country of importation, it appears to be the net profit indicator that will be most often considered by Customs administrations.

Paragraph 2.77 of the OECD Guidelines explain that net profit indicators may be directly affected by such forces operating in the industry as follows: threat of new entrants, competitive positions, management efficiency and individual strategies, threat of substitute products, varying costs structures, differences in the cost of capital and the degree of business experience and that, in turn, each of these factors can be influenced by numerous other elements. As an example, they suggest that the level of the threat of new entrants may be determined by such elements as product differentiation, capital requirements and government subsidies and regulations. All these factors may be regarded as circumstances of the sale which generally have an impact on the way in which the prices in question are arrived at, and which normally determine the pricing practices of the industry in question.

---

232. *See* Preamble of the GVC.
233. *See* Note to GVC Article 6. Note that the first sentence of such note provides a "general rule" applicable under the whole agreement.

In paragraph 2.97, the OECD Guidelines address the particular problem of how to account for rebates and discounts that may be granted to customers by the taxpayer/importer or the comparables when applying an NPM-based TNMM. We have observed this problem in practice particularly where the rebates and discounts are granted by the importer to its customers on a global basis and not on the basis of particular transactions. This type of global rebates or discounts certainly have an impact on the resale price of the imported goods and need to be duly considered by the Customs administrations when using transfer pricing documentation and by the importers in supplying segmented financial information for the purposes of GVC Article 1.2(a). The OECD Guidelines suggest that, depending on the accounting standards, rebates and discounts may be treated as a reduction of sales revenue or as an expense and that, consequently, where such items materially affect the comparison, the key is to follow the same accounting principles for the taxpayer and for the comparables.

12.1.1 Case Studies

In 2007, we submitted to the Focus Group on Customs Valuation and Transfer Pricing and, later on, to the TCCV, a draft case study illustrating the application of the TNMM in the context of the Circumstances-of-Sale Test.[234] Such case study is transcribed below in Subchapter 19 of Chapter 5. It was intended to provide an example on how the OECD Transactional Net Margin Method could be used in the context of the Circumstances-of-Sale Test. A similar example was used by the WCO in Subchapter 5.2.2 of the Guide to Customs Valuation and Transfer Pricing in approaching the issue of whether or not transfer pricing data referring to a product range can be used for customs valuation purposes.

12.1.2 Case Study 14.1 of the Technical Committee on Customs Valuation

For the author of this book, Case Study 14.1 of the TCCV is not just a simple case study. It is the result of a long process that started in 2005, which involved hundreds of hours preparing papers, draft case studies and presentations for meetings at the WCO. It was a whole new subject, and most Customs administrations did not know much about transfer pricing. In fact, there was some prejudice towards the term "transfer pricing", as it was associated with the inappropriate manipulation of prices by large MNEs, and it was not really understood that this subject was, in essence, a set of economic principles, procedures and guidelines to help both tax administrations and MNEs to fix arm's length prices. There was a long learning curve. At the very beginning, it was the private sector and the OECD that explained transfer pricing principles to customs delegates. Later on, when the delegates got a better understanding of the subject, the discussions became richer. Most of the principles and proposals suggested in the first edition of this book back in 2002 have been followed in Case Study 14.1:

234. Case Study Nbr. 6 of the 11 draft case studies submitted to the Focus Group on Customs Valuation and Transfer pricing in 2007.

- in order to use the TNMM in the context of the Circumstances-of-Sale Test, the TCCV found support in the first example contained in the Interpretative Note to Article 1.2(a), saying that "since all the comparable companies sell goods of the same class or kind, the transfer pricing study supports the finding that the price between ICO and XCO was settled in a manner consistent with the normal pricing practices of the industry". We had suggested that the use of the TNMM under Article 1.2(a) could find support in the last example of its Interpretative Note. The position of the TCCV may have been influenced by the particular interpretation of the third example of the Interpretative Note that has traditionally been applied by the US Customs Service (the so-called "all cost plus profit method");
- product comparability under the TNMM was interpreted in the light of the GVC's product comparability standards. In Case Study 14.1, the comparable distributors sell goods of the same class or kind as those imported by ICO. We had pointed out that the third example of Interpretative Note to Article 1.2(a) contained this product comparability standard and was consistent with the comparability standards of the OECD Guidelines;
- the use of arm's length ranges of operating margins was accepted. In 2002, we indicated that nothing in Article 1.2 or its Interpretative Note prevents the importer or Customs administrations from using an arm's length range in order to produce an approximation of the conditions that would have been established between independent enterprises and, therefore, to produce a range of figures that – being all of equal reliability – would be acceptable for the purposes of the Circumstances-of-Sale Test; and
- the functional analysis was used as a relevant source of information to determine comparability when examining the circumstances of sale. In 2002, we indicated that, in dealings between two independent enterprises, compensation usually reflects the functions that each enterprise performs, and that such functions were clearly among those circumstances surrounding the sale that should be examined by the Customs administrations under Article 1.2(a). Also, in the draft case studies submitted to the Focus Group and, later on, to the TCCV, we indicated "[t]he language of the Interpretative Note to Article 1.2 is broad enough to permit a functional analysis and a comparison of contractual terms, economic circumstances and business strategies (in the context of a comprehensive transfer pricing study) under the more detailed rules of the Transfer Pricing Guidelines for Multinational Enterprises and Tax Administrations of the Organization for the Economic Cooperation and Development ... in determining whether the relationship influenced the transaction value."

In Case Study 14.1, like in its previous draft versions, the transfer pricing study submitted by the importer was reviewed by the tax authorities of countries I and X in the context of an APA. In our view, this does not appear to provide any relevant information to solve the case. Rather, it appears to be an attempt to restrict the scope of application of the case study. In real life, it would be very difficult to find cases where an importer would be able to submit to Customs a transfer pricing study approved in a bilateral APA. However, the principles underlying this case study are that the economic information contained in a transfer pricing study is relevant in examining the circumstances of the sale and that the TNMM may be an acceptable methodology under Article 1.2(a). The existence of an APA is not really a relevant fact. If a transfer pricing study is complete and accurate, then it is irrelevant whether or not it was approved by the tax administrations of the importing and exporting countries.

Case Study 14.1 also addresses one specific concern with respect to the TNMM that was raised by a number of countries: where inter-company expenses form part of the operating expenses figure as contained in the financial statements and the distortions that such inter-company expenses may cause when using the TNMM for Customs purposes. For this reason, Case Study 14.1 indicates that the operating expenses amount was examined and accepted as reliable since it was determined that it had been paid by ICO to unrelated parties, with ICO seeking to minimize its costs, and it had not been for the benefit of the seller. This concern was not raised in the draft case studies that we submitted to the TCCV at the 27th Session, nor in the draft case studies submitted by the United States.

Case Study 14.1

USE OF TRANSFER PRICING DOCUMENTATION WHEN EXAMINING RELATED PARTY TRANSACTIONS UNDER ARTICLE 1.2 (a) OF THE AGREEMENT

Introduction

1. This document describes a case where Customs took into account information provided in a company's transfer pricing study based on the Transactional Net Margin Method (TNMM) when examining whether or not the price of imported goods had been influenced by the relationship between buyer and seller in accordance with Article 1.2 (a).

This case study does not indicate, imply, or establish any obligation on Customs authorities to utilize the OECD Guidelines and the documentation resulting from the application of the OECD Guidelines in interpreting and applying the WTO Valuation Agreement.

Facts of Transaction

2. XCO, a manufacturer in country X sells relays to its wholly-owned subsidiary, ICO, a distributor of country I. ICO imports the relays and does not purchase any products from unrelated sellers. XCO does not sell relays or goods of the same class or kind to unrelated buyers.

3. In 2012, ICO entered its goods using the transaction value, based on the price stated on the commercial invoice, which was submitted to Customs of country I. There is no indication that special circumstances exist as set out in subparagraphs (a) to (c) of Article 1 of the Agreement that would prevent the use of transaction value.

4. After importation, Customs in country I decided to review the circumstances surrounding the sale of goods between ICO and XCO, pursuant to Article 1.2 (a) of the Agreement, because it had doubts about the acceptability of the price.

5. The importer did not provide test values in accordance with Article 1.2 (b) and (c), as a means of demonstrating that the relationship did not influence the price.

6. In response to Customs request for additional information, ICO presented a transfer pricing study for the period 2011, prepared by an independent firm on behalf of ICO.

7. The transfer pricing study used the Transactional Net Margin Method ("TNMM") that, in this case, compared ICO's operating margin with the operating margins of functionally comparable distributors of goods of the same class or kind, also located in Country I, that conducted comparable uncontrolled transactions in the same period of time. The transfer pricing study was prepared in order to comply with the requirements of Country I tax regulations and applied principles contained in the OECD Transfer Pricing Guidelines for Multinational Enterprises and Tax Administrations of the Organisation for Economic Cooperation and Development ("OECD Transfer Pricing Guidelines"). The transfer pricing study covered all relays purchased by ICO from XCO.

8. Relevant data for ICO, taken from the company's financial records:

- Sales 100.0
- Cost of Goods Sold (COGS) 82.0
- Gross profit 18.0
- Operating expenses 15.5
- Operating profit 2.5
- Operating profit margin (benchmarked) 2.5% of sales

9. The transfer pricing study, using data taken from ICO's company records, indicated that ICO's operating profit margin on the sale of relays purchased from XCO was 2.5 percent in 2011.

10. The study concludes that it is possible to find reliable comparables for ICO and, accordingly, ICO was selected as the tested party in the transfer pricing study.

11. ICO's transfer pricing study had been reviewed by the Tax authorities of countries I and X in the context of negotiating a bilateral Advance Pricing Agreement (APA). An APA was subsequently agreed between ICO, XCO and the Tax authorities of countries I and X with respect to all transactions between ICO and XCO. While in review by the Tax authorities of countries I and X, ICO provided information showing that the profit margins it earns on the sale of its relays are generally the same as those made by independent distributors in the electrical apparatus and electronic parts industries.

12. In the transfer pricing study, eight distributors, unrelated to their suppliers, were selected based on the substantial similarity of their functions, assets and risks, compared to ICO.

13. Information concerning these eight distributors was taken for fiscal year 2011 for purposes of the comparison. The range of operating profit margins earned by these unrelated distributors was 0.64 to 2.79 percent, with a median of 1.93 percent. In the context of the APA negotiations, this range was accepted by the Tax authorities as an arm's length range of operating profit margins for transactions comparable to ICO's transactions with XCO. This arm's length range was established using the operating profit margins of the eight comparable companies, using the financial records of these companies available in public databases. ICO's operating profit margin was 2.50 percent, thus falling within the range. The 2.50

percent margin achieved by the importer in the country of importation was a function of: a) the price actually paid or payable by ICO to XCO, b) ICO's own sales revenue, and c) ICO's own costs.

14. It was determined that no adjustments prescribed by Article 8 of the Agreement were required to be made to the price actually paid or payable. Additionally, ICO did not make compensating adjustments for tax purposes for the year 2011.

15. ICO sets its selling prices in order to allow the company to earn an operating profit that meets the target arm's length (interquartile) range as set out in the transfer pricing study. The price paid or payable to XCO has not undergone significant changes over the year.

Issues for Determination

16. Does the transfer pricing study supplied in this case, prepared on the basis of the OECD Transfer Pricing Guidelines and used as the basis of a bilateral APA, provide information which enables Customs to conclude whether or not the price actually paid or payable for the imported goods is influenced by the relationship of the parties under Article 1 of the Agreement?

Analysis

17. Under Article 1 of the Agreement, a transaction value is acceptable as the Customs value when the buyer and the seller are not related, or if related, the relationship does not influence the price. Where the buyer and seller are related, Article 1.2 of the Agreement provides two ways of establishing the acceptability of the transaction value when Customs have doubts concerning the price: (1) the circumstances surrounding the sale shall be examined to determine whether the relationship influenced the price (Article 1.2 (a)); or (2) the importer demonstrates that the value closely approximates one of three test values (Article 1.2 (b)). In this case, as indicated in paragraph 5, the importer did not provide test values therefore Customs examined the circumstances surrounding the sale.

18. The Interpretative Note to Article 1.2 of the Agreement provides that in examining the circumstances surrounding the sale, "the customs administrations should be prepared to examine relevant aspects of the transaction, including the way in which the buyer and the seller organize their commercial relations and the way in which the price in question was arrived at, in order to determine whether the relationship influenced the price."

19. Based on the information obtained from ICO, XCO does not sell the merchandise to unrelated buyers. Therefore, ICO is unable to demonstrate that the price was settled in the same manner as in sales to unrelated parties, specified in Note 1 to Article 1.2 (a) of the Agreement.

20. During its review of the circumstances surrounding the sale, Customs took into account the examination of information discussed in the transfer pricing study when determining whether the price had been settled in a manner consistent with the normal industry pricing practices under the Note to Article 1.2 (a). In this regard, the term "industry" includes the industry or industry sector that contains goods of the same class or kind (including identical or similar goods) as the imported goods.

21. Based on the information provided in Paragraph 8:

- The Sales figure can be accepted since ICO is selling only to unrelated parties (and it is assumed ICO is rationally seeking to maximize its profits in its dealings with unrelated parties)
- The Operating expenses amount has been examined and accepted as reliable since it is determined that these expenses are paid by ICO to unrelated parties, with ICO seeking to minimize its costs and these expenses have not been paid for the benefit of the seller
- The transfer pricing study confirms that ICO's operating profit margin is within the arm's length range (i.e., based on a study of comparable, but independent (unrelated) distributors)
- The Cost of Goods Sold of ICO reflects the price paid or payable to XCO and represents the transaction between ICO and its related party, XCO. This is the transfer price in question.

By working back from the arm's length range of operating profit margins and the other accepted information set out above, it could be deduced that the transfer price is an arm's length amount. This demonstrates that information relating to the transaction between ICO and unrelated distributors can be helpful and relevant to Customs when examining the circumstances surrounding the sale between XCO and ICO.

22. The functional analysis showed that there were no significant differences in functions, risks, and assets between ICO and the eight unrelated distributors. In addition, an adequate level of product comparability was observed. The comparable companies were chosen from the electrical apparatus, and electronic parts industries (companies that sell goods of the same class or kind as the imported goods). Thus, the operating profit margin on the resale of the imported goods was shown to be generally the same as in the electrical apparatus and electronic parts industries. Specifically, the transfer pricing study found that the arm's length range of the comparable companies' operating profit margins was 0.64 % to 2.79 %. As previously noted, ICO's operating profit margin was 2.50 %. Accordingly, since all the comparable companies sell goods of the same class or kind, the transfer pricing study supports a finding that the price between ICO and XCO was settled in a manner consistent with the normal pricing practices of the industry.

Conclusion

23. After examination of the circumstances surrounding the sale in respect of related party transactions between ICO and XCO, Customs concluded, including by analysis of a transfer pricing study based on the TNMM and additional information concerning operating expenses as deemed necessary, that under the provisions of Article 1.2 (a) of the Agreement, the relationship between the parties did not influence the price.

24. As indicated in Commentary 23.1, the use of a transfer pricing study for examining the circumstances surrounding the sale must be considered on a case-by-case basis.

12.2 Profit Split Method

The OECD Guidelines provide that "[t]he transactional profit split method seeks to *eliminate the effect on profits of special conditions made or imposed in a controlled transaction* ... by determining the division of profits that independent enterprises would have expected to realise from engaging in the transaction or transactions."[235] [emphasis added].

Thus, this method would be useful not only in the context of GVC Articles 1.1(d) and 1.2(a) (i.e., in determining whether the relationship influenced the price) but also in that of GVC Article 1.1(b), (i.e., in determining the value of *certain conditions or considerations – to which the sale or price is subject* – for which a value cannot, otherwise, be determined). The result of this would be that the rejection of the transaction value, under GVC Article 1.1(b), might be substantially reduced. This would be in accordance with one of the general purposes of the GVC, which is expressed in its Preamble as follows:

> ... the basis for valuation of goods for customs purposes should, to the greatest extent possible, be the transaction value of the goods being valued.

Sherman explains that this portion of the Preamble of the GVC makes clear the strong preference of the GVC's authors for the use of transaction value basis of valuation wherever appropriate.[236]

In this respect, it is interesting to examine Advisory Opinion 16.1 of the Technical Committee on Customs Valuation. The relevant part of such opinion states:

> According to clause (b) of Article 1.1 the Customs value of the imported goods cannot be established on the basis of the transaction value if the sale or price is subject to some condition or consideration for which a value cannot be determined with respect to the goods being valued.

The provision of clause (b) of Article 1.1 should be interpreted to mean that if the value of a condition or consideration can be determined with respect to the goods being valued, the Customs value of the imported goods should, subject to the other provisions and conditions of Article 1, be the transaction value as determined under that Article. Interpretative Notes to Article 1 and Annex III make it very clear that the price actually paid or payable is the total payment made by the buyer to or for the benefit of the seller, that the payment may be made directly or indirectly and that the price includes all payments actually made or to be made by the buyer to the seller, or by the buyer to a third party. Thus the value of the condition, when it is known and relates to the imported goods, is a part of the price actually paid or payable.

It should rest with individual administrations as to what they consider would be sufficient information to specifically determine the value of a condition or consideration.[237]

The last paragraph of this opinion is especially important. A narrow approach as to what is considered to be sufficient information could bar every transfer pricing analysis under the profit split method. This might produce major inconsistencies

235. *See* OECD Guidelines *supra* note 4, at 2.114.
236. *See* Sherman *supra* note 23, at 62.
237. CVC *supra* note 39, at AO16.1.

between customs and tax valuation results, since in the absence of an acceptable transaction value under GVC Article 1.1 (b), the methods of GVC Articles 2, 3, 5, 6 and 7 would be applicable, i.e., no transfer pricing analysis would need to be undertaken under GVC Article 1.2. In contrast, a flexible approach would eliminate most of these inconsistencies, since the price would be less likely to be rejected on the basis of GVC Article 1.1 (b). This approach would, therefore, enable customs administrations to undertake transfer pricing analyses - under GVC Article 1.2 - in cases where such analysis would otherwise be impossible.[238]

12.2.1 Functioning of the Method

The profit split method first identifies the profit to be split for the related enterprises from the controlled transactions in which the related enterprises are engaged. This method then splits those profits between the related enterprises on an economically valid basis that approximates the division of profits that would have been anticipated and reflected in an agreement made at arm's length.[239]

The Guidelines discuss two approaches for estimating the division of profits, based on either projected or actual profits which independent enterprises would have agreed. These approaches (the analysis of which exceeds the purposes of this work) are the contribution analysis and the residual analysis.[240] Under a contribution analysis, the combined profit (i.e., the total profits from the controlled transactions) would be divided between the related enterprises based upon a reasonable approximation of the division of profits that independent enterprises would have expected to realize from engaging in comparable transactions. This division can be supported by comparable data where available. In the absence thereof, it is often based on the relative value of the functions performed by each of the associated enterprises participating in the controlled transactions, taking account of their assets used and risks assumed.[241] A residual analysis divides the combined profit from the controlled transaction in two stages. In the first stage, each related enterprise is allocated - by applying one of the traditional transaction methods or a transactional net margin method - an arm's length remuneration for its non-unique contributions in relation to the controlled transactions in it is engaged.[242]

In the second stage, any residual profit (or loss) remaining after the first stage division would be allocated among the related parties based on the facts and circumstances of the case. The criteria of allocation used to split the profits should (a) be reasonably independent of transfer pricing policy formulation; and (b) be supported by comparables data, internal data, or both.[243]

238. In relation to the examples given by the Note to GVC Article 1.1 (b), Sherman explains that "loosely read or interpreted, they erroneously could be taken to imply that there can be no TV [transaction value] in any barter transaction" (Sherman *supra* note 23, at 181).
239. *See* OECD Guidelines *supra* note 4, at 2.114.
240. *Ibid.* at 2.124.
241. *Ibid.* at 2.125.
242. *Ibid.* at 2.127.
243. *Ibid.* at 2.138.

Bear in mind that, in the customs context, these methods - as well as the traditional transaction methods - are only to be used for the purposes of examining whether the relationship influenced the price (i.e., not to determine substitute values).

CHAPTER 4

Tax Bases: Customs Value and Tax Value of Imported Goods – Adjustments

13 INTRODUCTION

In the previous chapters, we proposed that the OECD Guidelines could be used, in the customs context, for the purposes of GVC Article 1.2(a). In other words, we suggested that the OECD Guidelines constitute a detailed body of rules that could not only supplement successfully the general provisions of GVC Article 1.2(a), but also help harmonize the customs and tax transfer pricing systems.

Ideally, our proposal intends to achieve a degree of harmonization such that transfer pricing for tax and customs purposes would be based on a single determination or examination of arm's length conditions. This single determination should be made using criteria that are acceptable under both tax and customs rules. In Chapters 2 and 3, our objective was to demonstrate that such criteria can be found in the OECD Guidelines.

However, we are conscious that most of the countries are far from achieving such degree of harmonization. Therefore, in most of the cases, the value of the imported goods will be first established or determined for the purposes of one of the systems (e.g., for customs purposes), and then for the purposes of the other (e.g., for tax purposes). Our goal would be, in such circumstances, that the transfer price established or determined under the rules of one system be acceptable under the rules of the other. This would be enough to avoid an unnecessary double determination (or examination) of transfer prices. However, this would only be possible where the criteria used to establish or determine the transfer prices are acceptable under both tax and customs rules. Hence, our objective in Chapters 2 and 3 (i.e., to demonstrate that such commonly accepted criteria could be found in the OECD Guidelines) is also valid in this more realistic context.

The fact that the OECD Guidelines should be accepted to establish or determine transfer prices under both tax and customs rules, does not mean that the transfer price established or determined under the rules of one system will constitute the tax base of duties or taxes under the rules of the other system. Rather, it only means that an arm's length transaction value established under the rules of one system can constitute a valid transaction value under the rules of the other system. This transaction value will be only one element among the many elements that make up the tax base of duties and taxes under each of the systems. In effect, the transaction value constitutes one of the elements of the customs value, which is the tax base of customs duties in those countries that adopted the GVC. Customs value includes some elements which may or may not be included in the transaction value. Where such elements have not been included in the transaction value, GVC Article 8 provides for its inclusion into customs value (i.e., in the tax base of customs duties). In the same way, customs value does not include some elements that may or may not be included in the transaction value. Where such elements have been included in transaction value, the GVC provides – subject to certain conditions – for their deduction from customs value. Likewise, transaction value constitutes one element of the tax base of income taxes (e.g., sales price), or even one specific part of a broader element of such tax base (e.g., cost of goods sold, inventory cost, etc.).

As indicated above, ideally, the importer/taxpayer should determine a single arm's length transaction value for both tax and customs purposes, and then calculate the tax bases of income tax and customs duties. Likewise, customs and tax authorities could examine whether transfer prices are arm's length, irrespective of whether such transfer prices have been declared for tax or customs purposes. However, importers and taxpayers usually determine and declare tax bases. The process of determination is sometimes undertaken first under the rules of one system and, afterwards, under the rules of the other. In other words, sometimes there is not merely one single determination of an arm's length transfer price (which is later included into the tax bases of income tax and customs duties), but rather two separate determinations (i.e., one for tax purposes and another for customs purposes) in which the determination of the arm's length transaction value and that of the tax base are not clearly distinguished.

If the importer/taxpayer wished to use the results of one of these determinations to establish the arm's length transaction value for the purposes of the other (thus, avoiding an unnecessary double determination of arm's length prices), the results would not be accurate unless the differences between the tax bases were properly identified and appropriate adjustments were made to account for such differences.

Likewise, if the Customs administration determined that the Customs values declared by the taxpayer/importer were acceptable under GVC Article 1.2(a), this information would not be useful for the tax administrations (e.g., to avoid double scrutiny of the taxpayer) unless the differences between the tax bases were properly identified.

If the taxpayer declared arm's length transaction values for tax and customs purposes, then the Customs value and the appropriate element of the tax base of income taxes (e.g., COGS) should be equivalent, once the differences between such tax bases have been identified and appropriate adjustments to account for such differences have been made. This argument could constitute a shield in the hands of a taxpayer to prevent Customs and tax administrations from taking inconsistent positions in determining the appropriate arm's length transaction value. In effect, if a tax administration had already decided that a transaction value declared by the importer/ taxpayer was arm's length, and the importer had demonstrated that the customs value - once the appropriate adjustments to account for the differences in the tax bases of customs duties and income tax have been made - is equivalent to such transaction value, then the Customs administration would not be entitled to reject such value on the basis of GVC Article 1.2(a), unless it demonstrated that the decision of the tax administration was incorrect.

We believe that a principle of consistency must guide the conduct of the tax and Customs administrations, either where they are departments of the same governmental agency or where they are agencies of the same Ministry or branch of the State.

Two departments of the same agency or two agencies of the same government should not have different views as to whether a transfer price is arm's length and, if they do have different views, the importer/taxpayer should not be forced to deal with such inconsistency or to struggle between these departments or agencies to find out how to satisfy both of them.

As indicated in Section 6, the example of Revenue Canada in its Memorandum D13-4-5 and that of the USCS in participating in the APA process, should be followed or even improved by the Customs and tax administrations of those countries which have adopted the GVC and transfer pricing provisions based on the OECD Guidelines. In this sense, Commentary 23.1 and Advisory Opinion 14.1 of the TCCV are in line with this position and more instruments from the TCCV would be recommendable and more than welcome by the trade community.

Accordingly, it could be necessary to clearly identify the differences between the tax bases of customs duties and income taxes, to avoid unnecessary double determinations or examinations of arm's length transfer prices.

The different elements of the taxable base of income taxes (e.g., cost of goods sold, inventory cost of property, etc.) are defined in the income tax statutes of the different countries. The analysis of multiple income tax statutes would exceed the purposes of this work. In contrast, the elements of the tax base of customs duties are defined in the GVC, which is applicable to most of the WTO members. Therefore, in this Chapter, we will analyze the rules of computation of customs value (i.e., the tax base of customs duties) under the GVC, in order to identify the most relevant additions to and deductions from the customs value of imported goods.[244] This will help undertake any subsequent comparison between the GVC and any particular income tax statute. We will also indicate which of these additions or deductions may generally have a different treatment for income tax purposes and, thus, when adjustments to account for such differences in treatment might be required.

Note that, throughout this chapter, we will refer to adjustments in computing either the tax base of customs duties or the elements of the tax base of income tax,

244. Note that this additions to and deduction from the transaction value have, in principle, no relationship with the process of determining whether the relationship influenced the price. The additions to and deductions from the price paid or payable (i.e., the transaction value) must be made under GVC Articles 1 and 8 irrespective of whether or not the transaction is controlled.

depending on the kind of adjustment and depending on whether the original determination (to be adjusted) was made under tax or customs rules.

14 IRC SECTION 1059A

Section 1059A of the Internal Revenue Code ("IRC") of the United States[245] could be viewed as an effort to harmonize tax and customs transfer pricing regimes. However, such an understanding might not be completely correct. Section 1059A provides that:

> If any property is imported into the United States in a transaction (directly or indirectly) between related persons (within the meaning of Section 482), the amount of any costs:
> (1) which are taken into account in computing the basis or inventory cost of such property by the purchaser; and
> (2) which are also taken into account in computing the customs value of such property;
>
> shall not, for purposes of computing such basis or inventory cost for purposes of this chapter [chapter 26 of the United States Code, which is the Internal Revenue Code in general], be greater than the amount of such cost taken into account in computing such customs value.

The specific concern that the US Congress addressed in introducing Section 1059A was the possibility that the "Brittingham case"[246] provided an incentive to US companies to declare one value for US Customs purposes and a different, presumably higher, value (as a COGS figure) for US tax purposes.[247] In such case, the price a US importer paid to a related Mexican seller was higher than the customs value (declared by the importer), and this price was used as the COGS figure for US tax purposes. The ("IRS") based its deficiency determination on the customs value. This resulted in a lower cost of goods sold and higher profit margins. The Tax Court found that, being the customs values based on inappropriate criteria for Section 482[248] purposes, such customs value was not indicative of an arm's length price. Thus, the Tax Court upheld the position of the importer.[249] In the GAO Report 94–61,[250] it was explained that "the legislative history indicates that Congress understood that Brittingham supported the proposition that some importers could claim a transfer price for income tax purposes that was higher than would be consistent with the transfer price claimed for customs purposes."

Section 1059A came to require certain consistency between customs and tax rules. In this respect, Section 1059A constitutes an actual application of some of the

245. *Internal Revenue Code*, 26 U.S.C. §1059A.
246. *Brittingham* v. *Commissioner*, 66 TC 373 (1976), aff'd [1979], 598 F2d 1375 (5th Cir. 1979).
247. *See* Lowell *et al. US International Transfer Pricing*, (WL, 2000) at 18.03[3][b]. On line: WL (Lowell, Burge & Brieger, US International Transfer Pricing) (date accessed: 28 May 2000) [hereinafter "USITP"].
248. *Internal Revenue Code*, 26 U.S.C. § 482.
249. *See* USITP *supra* note 248 at 18.03[2].
250. US, General Accounting Office, *International Taxation: IRS' Administration of Tax-Customs Valuation Rules in Tax Code Section 1059A.* (4 February 1994). GAO/GGD-94-61. [hereinafter, "GAO"] On line: http://www.gao.gov/products/GGD-94-61.

ideas and principles described in Chapters 1, 2 and 3 above and, consequently, a valuable legislative precedent to support them. However, the application of these ideas and principles under Section 1059A has not been complete. In effect, Section 1059A only prevents the use of higher values for tax than for customs declaration purposes.[251] The legislative history indicates that the US Congress did not express the view that valuation of property for customs purposes should always determine valuation of property for tax purposes.[252] Thus, the legislative history does not indicate whether Section 1059A may be used by the taxpayer to prevent tax and customs authorities from taking inconsistent positions in determining whether a controlled transaction is arm's length.[253]

Under the principles indicated in Section 13, a determination of the arm's length character of a transaction value which followed appropriate standards of comparability and methodologies (e.g., those of the OECD Guidelines) should be acceptable for both customs and tax purposes. Ideally, where a transaction value has been successfully defended by the importer in a customs procedure and such transaction value (subject to the adjustments indicated in Section 13 to account for differences in the tax bases of income tax and customs duties) has been declared to the tax administration for income tax purposes, internal legislation of the country should prevent the tax administration from re-examining such transaction value. This would also be true in the case of transaction values successfully defended by the importer/taxpayer in tax procedures, vis-à-vis re-examinations undertaken subsequently by the customs administration.

Nevertheless, the examination of Section 1059A and its regulation is especially useful for the purposes of this Chapter, since they address the adjustments to be made to customs value to account for differences in the tax bases of customs duties and income tax.[254] Taking into account the observations made above, we will make reference to them throughout this Chapter, since they could constitute a guide to analyze the tax base of customs duties and the adjustments that might be necessary to account for differences between such tax base and that of income taxes.

---

251. *See* USITP *supra* note 248, at 18.03[c].
252. *See* GAO *supra* note 251.
253. *See* USITP *supra* note 248, at 18.03[3][b].
254. The US Congress indicated that tax and customs valuation principles differ in several areas and appropriate adjustments would need to be made in order to accommodate the distinctions in the respective regimes. It also said that the IRS would provide rules for coordinating customs and tax valuation principles, including provisions for proper adjustments for amounts such as freight charges, where customs pricing rules may differ from appropriate tax valuation rules (*see* US, Staff of Joint Comm. on Taxation, General Explanation of the Tax Reform Act of 1986, 100th Cong., 1st Sess. 1062 (1987). *See also* USITP *supra* note 248, at 18.03[3][e]). In the context of related-party transactions (i.e., in determining whether the relationship influenced the price) one can argue that tax and customs valuation principles do not really differ (as indicated in Chapters II and III). The differences can be found in the rules for computing the taxable bases of customs duties and income taxes. This conceptual difference is extremely important to avoid unnecessary inconsistencies when tax and customs valuation systems are applied.

15 DEFINITION OF THE TERM "RELATED PARTIES"

Under GVC Article 15 and its Note[255] persons shall be deemed to be related only if:

(a) they are officers of one another's business;
(b) they are legally recognized partners in business;
(c) they are employer and employee;
(d) any person directly or indirectly owns, controls or holds 5% or more of the outstanding voting stock or shares of both of them;
(e) one of them directly or indirectly controls the other;
(f) both of them are directly or indirectly controlled by a third person;
(g) together they directly or indirectly control a third person; or
(h) they are members of the same family.

Persons who are associated in business with one another in that one is the sole agent, sole distributor or sole concessionaire, however described, of the other shall be deemed to be related for purposes of the GVC if they fall within the criteria of (a) to (h) above. To the question as to whether sole agents, sole distributors and sole concessionaires are "legally recognized partners in business" in terms of Article 15.4(b) of the Agreement, the Technical Committee on Customs Valuation answered the following:

> An association would be a partnership only where the national legal requirements for the creation of a partnership are satisfied. Thus, persons are not related under the Agreement simply because one person is the sole agent, sole distributor or sole concessionaire of the other.
>
> While it is true that sole agents, sole distributors, etc. may have a close association with their suppliers, this fact alone would provide no reason to treat them differently from any other unrelated party.
>
> For the purpose of clarification, a Member may choose to incorporate or refer to its national law of partnership in the valuation provisions of its Customs law. However, it would not be appropriate for a Member to devise a different definition of partnership specifically for the interpretation of the valuation provisions of its Customs law.[256]

In certain cases, it may be necessary to compare this definition of "related parties" with the one included in the relevant tax statutes or provided by case law. The scope of the definitions included in such tax statutes or provided by case law may differ from country to country.[257]

---

255. IRUCC Article 127, 19 U.S.C. 1401a(g)(1), Subsection 45(3) of the *Customs Act* of Canada.
256. CVC *supra* note 39, at AO21.1/1. It is interesting to compare this advisory opinion with the opinion of the USCS in HQ Ruling 545481 (14 September 1994). In such ruling, the USCS examined a distributorship agreement under which the importer exercised a substantial degree of influence or control over its distributors. The USCS indicated that "[b]y virtue of the "control" the importer exercised pursuant to the distributorship agreement, and by virtue of the market control the importer realized as the exclusive importer of certain vehicles, the importer was in fact related to the distributors. Consequently, the USCS found that sales between the importer and the distributors could not be used as the basis of deductive value.
257. In the United States, a fundamental definition to the coverage of Section 482 of the IRC (basic transfer pricing provision of such code) is the concept of the common control of the

In the OECD Guidelines, the term "associated enterprises" have the meaning set forth in Article 9 of the OECD MTC. Under Article 9, two enterprises are "associated enterprises" where (a) an enterprise of a Contracting State participates directly or indirectly in the management, control or capital of an enterprise of the other Contracting State, or the same persons participate directly or indirectly in the management, control or capital of an enterprise of a Contracting State and an enterprise of the other Contracting State.[258] This definition will be generally applicable in transfer pricing cases which involve enterprises residing in countries which have entered into OECD-type tax treaties.

16 TAX BASE OF CUSTOMS DUTIES

In the countries that adopted the GVC, the tax base of customs duties (and, sometimes, of other taxes applied on importation of goods) is the customs value of the imported goods. Under GVC Article 1,[259] this term is defined as "the transaction value ... adjusted in accordance with the provisions of Article 8." The Note to GVC Article 1 supplements this definition, excluding - under certain specific conditions - certain elements from transaction value.

Therefore, the tax base of customs duties (hereinafter "customs value") is equal to

A + B - C

where

A = Transaction value (hereinafter, also referred to as "price actually paid or payable").

B = Elements listed in GVC Article 8.

C = Elements listed in the Note to GVC Article 1.

"organizations, trades, or businesses," which concept represents the essential premise for the concern as to non-arm's length bargaining. In this respect, the Regulations (since 1935) define the term 'controlled' to include any kind of control, direct or indirect, whether legally enforceable, and however exercisable or exercised. It is the reality of the control which is decisive, not its form or the mode of its exercise. [*See* USITP *supra* note 248 at 3.0(3).].

Under Section 15 of the Argentine Income Tax Act (*see Ley de Impuesto a las Ganancias, supra* note 15), in order to identify the existence of economic relationship between enterprises, the following facts should be analyzed:

- whether the enterprises are controlled directly or indirectly by the same persons;
- whether any of the following circumstances permit any person or persons to influence or define the activities of the enterprises in question:
  (a) equity participation or ownership
  (b) debts
  (c) functional influence
  (d) any other kind of influence, either contractual or not.

258. The use of the term "associated enterprises" in the OECD Guidelines would be equivalent to that of the term "related parties" in the GVC. *See*, e.g., paragraph 4 of Commentary on Article 9 of the OECD MTC, at 115.
259. For the purposes of this chapter, we assume that the relationship did not influence the price and, therefore, that the price is acceptable under Article 1. Therefore, we will not analyze the definitions of customs value under Articles 2 through 7.

16.1 Transaction Value

Not every transaction value is acceptable for customs purposes. Transaction value is the price actually paid or payable for the goods when sold for export to the country of importation.[260] The price actually paid or payable is the total payment made or to be made by the buyer to or for the benefit of the seller for the imported goods.[261]

The payment need not necessarily take the form of a transfer of money. It may be made directly or indirectly.[262]

16.1.1 Existence of a Sale

The existence of a sale is a basic requisite under GVC Article 1. Where there is no sale, the value cannot be determined under Article 1 and, therefore, it should be determined under Articles 2 through 7. A clear understanding of this issue is extremely important for the purposes of this work since, where there is no sale for export to the country of importation, the results obtained through the sequential application of the methods of Articles 2 through 7 may not be consistent with those derived from the application of the OECD Guidelines.[263] Therefore, harmonization of the regimes applicable to these situations would require an amendment to either the customs or the tax rules.

The GVC contains no definition of sale. The Technical Committee on Customs Valuation, in Advisory Opinion 1.1 suggested that, in conformity with the basic intention of the GVC – i.e., that the transaction value of imported goods should be used to the greatest extent possible for customs valuation purposes – uniformity of interpretation and application can be achieved by taking the term "sale" in the widest sense, to be determined only under the provisions of Articles 1 and 8 read together.[264] The Technical Committee considered useful to prepare a list of cases which would not be deemed to constitute sales meeting the requirements and conditions of the GVC. Even though the list is not intended to be exhaustive, it provides useful guidance on this issue. Thus, free consignments, goods imported on consignment, goods imported by branches (in cases where a branch cannot be regarded as a separate legal entity under the legislation concerned), goods imported under a hire or a leasing contract (even if the contract includes an option to purchase the goods), goods supplied on loan (which remain property of the sender) or goods imported for destruction in the country of importation (with the sender paying the importer for his services) cannot be regarded as sales under the GVC.[265]

260. *See* GVC Article 1.1.
261. *See* Note to GVC Article 1.1.
262. *Ibid.*
263. *See* Sections 3.2 and 11.1.
264. *See* CVC *supra* note 39, at AO1.1/1.
265. *Ibid.*

16.1.2 Sale for Export

Many issues arise from the expression "when sold for export" of GVC Article 1.1. A first issue relates to the question of when a sale must be regarded as a "sale for export". In Advisory Opinion 14.1, the Technical Committee on Customs Valuation of the World Customs Organization expressed the following view:

> The Council's Glossary on Customs Valuation Terms defines the term importation as "the act of bringing any goods into the Customs territory" and the term exportation as "the act of taking any goods out of the Customs territory." Therefore, the fact that the goods are presented for valuation of itself establishes their importation which, in turn, establishes the fact of their exportation, The only remaining requirement then, is to identify the transaction relating thereto.

In this respect, there is no need that the sale takes place in a specific country of exportation. If the importer can demonstrate that the immediate sale under consideration took place with the view to export the goods to the country of importation, then Article 1 can apply. It follows that only transactions involving an actual international transfer of goods may be used in valuing merchandise under the transaction value method.

A second issue arises in the case of successive sales before valuation.

Paragraph 1 of Article 70 of the IRUCC provides:

> The transaction value of the goods sold for export to the customs territory of the Union shall be determined at the time of acceptance of the customs declaration on the basis of the sale occurring immediately before the goods were brought into that customs territory.[266]

The IRUCC repealed the "first sale" concept that, under certain circumstances, was acceptable under Article 147 of the Implementing Regulations of the European Customs Code. The position adopted by the European Commission seems to be in line with Commentary 22.1 of the Technical Committee on Customs Valuation in which the following view was expressed:

> The underlying assumption of Article 1 is that normally the buyer would be located in the country of importation and that the price actually paid or payable would be based on the price paid by this buyer. The Technical Committee concludes that in a series of sales situation, the price actually paid or payable for the imported goods when sold for export to the country of importation is the price paid in the last sale occurring prior to the introduction of the goods into the country of importation, instead of the first (or earlier) sale. This is consistent with the purpose and overall text of the Agreement.

In "*Nissho Iwai American Corporation* v. *United States*", the Court of Appeals for the Federal Circuit of the United States reversed the lower court's finding and held that it was the contract between a foreign manufacturer of certain subway cars and Nissho Iwai Corporation (the middleman), rather than the sale between Nissho Iwai American Corporation (a subsidiary of the middleman) and the New York City Metropolitan

266. *See supra* note 7.

Transportation Authority (the US purchaser), which served as the basis for determining transaction value. The Court stated that the Customs Service ruling which held that when there are two or more sales which could be used as a transaction value, then Customs looks to the sale which "most directly causes the merchandise to be exported to the United States," is "legally unsound." The Court overruled the requirement of "a weighing of the relative importance of two viable transactions."[267]

As one can see, the positions of the TCCV and the European Commission are inconsistent with that of the US Court of Appeals in "Nissho Iwai."

Sherman points out the special case where goods are sold from a customs (bonded) warehouse in the country of importation prior to clearance through Customs. This author correctly indicates that the solution reached by any one Customs administration may depend on the legal status of the warehouse. Under General Resolution 2793/2010 of the Argentine Federal Revenue Administration, it appears that, where the goods are sold from a customs warehouse in Argentina prior to clearance through Customs, such a sale shall constitute the relevant sale for export to Argentina.[268] We believe that this view is incorrect. Under Section 5 of the Argentine Customs Code,[269] customs warehouses are part of the general customs territory of Argentina. Those goods, which have been placed under the customs warehouse procedure (*destinación de depósito de almacenamiento*), have already been imported into the general customs territory of Argentina, even though they have not been released for free circulation. Therefore, a sale from a customs warehouse is a sale in the customs territory of Argentina (i.e., the country of importation) and cannot be regarded as a sale for export to Argentina. Thus, such a sale should not be used as a basis for transaction value.[270] The position of the Argentine Federal Revenue Administration seems to be similar to the position adopted by the European Commission in paragraph 2 of Article 70 of the IRUCC, which provides:

> 1. Where the goods are sold for export to the customs territory of the Union not before they were brought into that customs territory but while in temporary storage or while placed under a special procedure other than internal transit, end-use or outward processing, the transaction value will be determined on the basis of that sale.[271]

16.1.3 Cash or Kind: Direct or Indirect Payment

The Note to GVC Article 1 states that the payment need not necessarily take the form of a transfer of money and may be made directly or indirectly. Sherman explains that the only requirement is that the goods or services must have an agreed price.[272] This

267. 982 F.2d 505 (1992).["Nissho Iwai"]. *See* CVE *supra* note 45, at 320.
268. B.O., 8 March 2010.
269. Law 22,415, as amended, B.O., 23 March 1981.
270. This case is not similar to the case of sales from free zones, which are not part of the general customs territory under Article 3 of the Argentine Customs Code.
271. *See supra* note 7.
272. *See* Sherman *supra* note 23, at 73.

author also explains that there is one important exception, and that is where the buyer provides goods or services for use in connection with the production or sale for the export of the imported goods - without charging the full cost or value to the manufacturer - such items are to be added to the price only if they are listed in GVC Article 8.1(b). Otherwise, they should be regarded as non-dutiable contributions, rather than as payments for the goods forming part of the price and, thus, of the customs value.[273] This assertion implies that those goods or services - that are provided by the buyer without charging the full cost or value to the manufacturer but that do not qualify as assists under 8.1(b) - cannot be regarded as indirect payments. Some observations should be made in relation to this issue. The Technical Committee on Customs Valuation, in Advisory Opinion 16.1, has said that:

> Interpretative Notes to Article 1 and Annex III make it very clear that the price actually paid or payable is the total payment made by the buyer to or for the benefit of the seller, that the payment may be made directly or indirectly and that the price includes all payments actually made or to be made by the buyer to the seller, or by the buyer to a third party. Thus the value of the condition, when it is known and relates to the imported goods, is a part of the price actually paid or payable.[274]

Article 133 of the IRUCC[275] appears to follow such opinion. The relevant part of Article 133 reads:

> Where the sale or price of imported goods is subject to a condition or consideration the value of which can be determined with respect to the goods being valued, such value shall be regarded as part of the price actually paid or payable, unless those conditions or considerations relate to either of the following:
>
> (a) an activity to which Article 129(2) of this Regulation applies;
> (b) an element of the customs value under Article 71 of the Code.

GVC Article 8.4 provides that "[n]o additions shall be made to the price actually paid or payable in determining the customs value except as provided in this Article". However, the value of a condition or consideration - the value of which can be determined with respect to the goods being valued - constitutes an indirect payment and, therefore, part of the price paid or payable. Under this understanding, the value of the condition or consideration is not an "addition" to the price (in the meaning of GVC Article 8) but is the price itself (or a part of it). If such value is part of the price and not an addition to such price, then it is not within the scope of GVC Article 8.4 but, rather, under the scope of GVC Article 1.1 and its Note. Therefore, it would be part of the customs value.

273. *Ibid.*
274. *See* CVC *supra* note 38, at AO16.1/1.
275. *See supra* note 7. *See*, generally, Lasok, D., *The Trade and Customs Law of the European Union*, 3rd ed. (London, Kluwer Law International, 1998) at 279–83. *See*, generally, Inama, S. and Vermulst, E., *Customs and Trade Laws of the European Community* (London, Kluwer Law International, 1999) at 167.

However, this understanding seems to be inconsistent with other provisions of the GVC and with the interpretation made by the Technical Committee in Case Study 1.1. The Note to GVC Article 1.1(b) reads:

> ... the fact that the buyer furnishes the seller with engineering and plans undertaken in the country of importation shall not result in rejection of the transaction value for the purposes of Article 1. Likewise, if the buyer undertakes on the buyer's own account, even though by agreement with the seller, activities relating to the marketing of the imported goods, the value of these activities is not part of the customs value nor shall such activities result in rejection of the transaction value.

In paragraph 8 of Case Study 1.1, the Technical Committee did not add to the selling price certain services (graphs and drawings) provided within the country of importation to the seller. Nor did the Technical Committee add the cost of engineering services furnished by the buyer within the country of importation to the selling price. Moreover, the Technical Committee did not regard these services as indirect payments.

Therefore, the assertion made by Sherman appears to be correct, at least, with respect to the treatment of assists expressly excluded under GVC Article 8.2(iv).[276] However, it is not clear whether this principle also applies to other services supplied by the buyer free of charge which, although not included in the list of GVC Article 8.1, constitute a consideration the value of which is known and relates to the goods being valued. In effect, where it can be demonstrated that the value of the consideration relates to the goods being valued (i.e., the consideration is a payment for the goods and not for other concepts, such as financial services[277]) and such value is known, the value of such consideration might be regarded as an indirect payment and, thus, as part of the price paid or payable if Advisory Opinion 16.1 were followed. (Note that this understanding could also be inconsistent with paragraph 2 of the Note to GVC Article 1.1, which provides that "[a]ctivities undertaken by the buyer on the buyer's own account, other than those for which an adjustment is provided in Article 8, are not considered to be an indirect payment to the seller. The cost of such activities shall not, therefore, be added to the price actually paid or payable in determining the customs value.") The Technical Committee on Customs Valuation should clarify this issue and, especially, the meaning of paragraph 2 of the Note to Article 1.1 in this context.[278]

16.1.4 Activities Benefiting Both Buyer and Seller

As indicated above, paragraph 2 of the Note to GVC Article 1.1 provides that activities undertaken by the buyer on the buyer's account, other than those for which an adjustment is provided in GVC Article 8, are not considered to be an indirect payment

276. Paragraph (iv) of Article 8.1 reads: "engineering, development, artwork, design, work, and plans and sketches *undertaken elsewhere than in the country of importation* and necessary for the production of the imported goods." [emphasis added].
277. In relation to this, *see* paragraph 13 of Case Study 2.2. (*see* CVC *supra* note 39, at CS2.2/2).
278. Note that the Technical Committee on Customs Valuation did not address this specific issue in Commentary 9.1. *See* CVC *supra* note 39, at Com9.1/1.

to the seller, even though they might be regarded as of benefit of the seller. The cost of such activities should not, therefore, be added to the price actually paid or payable in determining the customs value.

The most important of such activities are advertising and warranty and other marketing and promotional efforts, which benefit both the exporter and the importer by increasing sales and by making the trademark - if there is one - more valuable.[279]

The Note also states that "if the buyer undertakes on his own account, even though by agreement with the seller, activities relating to the marketing of the imported goods, the value of these activities is not part of the customs value nor shall such activities result in rejection of the transaction value."

In this respect, IRUCC Article 1(2) provides that the term "marketing activities" means, in the context of customs valuation, all activities relating to advertising or marketing and promoting the sale of the goods in question and all activities relating to warranties or guarantees in respect of them.

Note that if the exporter pays the importer for advertising activities and recovers the expense through his pricing, the cost is included in his price and there is no provision in the GVC for excluding it from transaction value (A in our formula of customs value). The result is, therefore, more favorable from a customs perspective if the amount for advertising is deducted from the purchase price at the outset and the buyer is obliged to spend at least a corresponding amount on advertising.[280]

16.1.5 Discounts

A discount freely agreed upon after the date of valuation in principle does not affect the customs value retroactively.[281]

This kind of discounts generally affects the tax base of income taxes (e.g., they could affect the COGS or the inventory cost of imported property) and must usually be declared. Thus, the existence of this type of discounts should be taken into account when the customs value of imported goods and the elements of the tax base of income taxes are being compared. In other words, where this type of discounts has been effected, the customs value would not be equivalent to the transfer price for tax purposes, unless appropriate adjustments were made to account for such discounts.[282]

279. *See* Sherman *supra* note 23, at 75.

280. *Ibid.* at 76.

281. *Ibid.* at 78. In the United States, this principle is also stated in 19 U.S.C. 1401a(b)(4)(B), which provides: "Any rebate of, or decrease in, the price actually paid or payable that is made or otherwise effected between the buyer and seller *after* the date of importation of the merchandise into the United States shall be disregarded in determining the transaction value under paragraph (1)."

282. Bear in mind that, for the purposes of this work, we do not refer to "adjustments" as the procedure of adding elements to or deducting elements from the customs value to arrive at the value of the imported property for income tax purposes (or at a specific limit to inventory cost of imported property). Rather, the term "adjustments," in this work, is used in the context of a comparison between tax and customs results. This comparison is made for the purposes mentioned in Section 13.

A special case is presented where the seller allows a cash discount for prompt payment. In such cases, there are in effect two (or more) agreed prices, depending on when the payment is made.[283] If payment has been made before the goods have arrived or are entered through customs, the actual amount paid must govern.[284] If payment has not been made before the goods have arrived or entered through customs, the solution of the GVC is not clear. The Technical Committee on Customs Valuation, in Advisory Opinion 5.3, has expressed the following view:

> When a cash discount is available but payment has not yet been made at the time of valuation, the amount the importer is to pay for the goods should be taken as the basis for transaction value under Article 1. Procedures for determining what is to be paid may vary: for example a statement on the invoice might be accepted as sufficient evidence or a declaration by the importer as to the amount he is to pay could be the basis for action, subject to verification and to possible application of Article 13 and 17 of the Agreement.[285]

IRUCC Article 144 reflects the position of the European Community in relation to this issue:

1. For the purposes of determining the customs value under Article 70(1) of the Code, discounts shall be taken into account if, at the time of acceptance of the customs declaration, the sales contract provides for their application and their amount.
2. Discounts for early payment shall be taken into account with regard to goods for which the price has not actually been paid at the time of acceptance of the customs declaration.
3. Discounts arising from amendments to the contract subsequent to the time of acceptance of the customs declaration shall not be taken into account.

GVC Article 13 has been interpreted by the Technical Committee to permit a delay in the final determination of the customs value.[286] Therefore, we can conclude that, where the legislation of the country adopts any of the procedures proposed above by the Technical Committee (or any other procedure to permit verification and acceptance of the discounted price), such discounts should be taken into account in determining the transaction value.[287]

283. *See* Sherman *supra* note 23, at 79.
284. *Ibid. See* CVC *supra* note 39, at AO5.1/1 (Advisory Opinion 5.1 of the Technical Committee on Customs Valuation).
285. *See* CVC *supra* note 39, at AO5.3/1.
286. *See* CVC *supra* note 39 at Com4.1/1 (Commentary 4.1).
287. Note that the United States Customs Service has taken a different position. In Ruling 546037 (31 January 1996), the USCS said that: "A discounted price must be agreed to and *effected prior to importation* in order for the discounted price to constitute the price actually paid or payable." [emphasis added] (CVE *supra* note 45, at chapter XIII).

16.1.6 Interest Charges

This issue was originally addressed by the Committee on Customs Valuation on 26 April 1984, through the adoption of Decision 3.1 "Treatment of Interest Charges in the Customs Value of Imported Goods"[288] This decision was also adopted by the World Trade Organization's Committee on Customs Valuation at its meeting of 12 May 1995.[289]

The decision expresses that charges for interest under a financing arrangement entered into by the buyer and relating to the purchase of imported goods shall not be regarded as part of the customs value provided that the following conditions are met:

(1) the charges are distinguished from the price actually paid or payable for the goods;
(2) the financing arrangement was made in writing;
(3) where required, the buyer can demonstrate that (a) the goods are actually sold at a price declared as the price actually paid or payable, and (b) the claimed rate of interest does not exceed the level for such transactions prevailing in the country where, and at the time when the finance was provided.

Despite its clear basic principle, the Decision introduced some vague terms and conditions which may be difficult to comply with in commercial practice.[290] Where such conditions are not met, the interest charges will be part of the price paid or payable (A in our formula of customs value). This inclusion should be taken into account when the customs value of imported goods and the elements of the tax base of income taxes are being compared. In effect, where - pursuant to Decision 3.1 - interest charges are to be included into transaction value in computing the customs value of the imported goods, the customs value might not be equivalent to the value of the imported goods for income tax purposes, unless appropriate adjustments were made to account for such charges. (Note that under the income tax legislation of some countries, interest payments made to non-resident persons are subject to income tax withholdings.[291] Thus, if the customs value included the interest charges, such charges might have to be identified and segregated from the price paid or payable for income tax purposes.)

288. GATT Doc. Val/M/9.
289. WTO Doc. Val/6/Rev.1. (WTO Doc. G/Val/5, 13 October 1995).
290. *See* Sherman *supra* note 23, at 95.
291. *See*, e.g., *Ley de Impuesto a las Ganancias, t.o. 1997 y sus modificaciones*, (Argentina), Article 93 (*supra* note 15).

16.2 GVC Article 8: Additions to the Price Paid or Payable

16.2.1 Commissions and Brokerage: Buying Commissions

GVC Article 8.1 requires the addition of "commissions and brokerage" - except buying commissions - to customs value, provided they have not been included in the price paid or payable.

For the purposes of this work, it is interesting to analyze the concept and treatment of "buying commissions" under the GVC, since their exclusion from customs value might need to be accounted for in comparing tax and customs valuation results.

The term "buying commissions" is defined as "fees paid by an importer to the importer's agent for the service of representing the importer abroad in the purchase of the goods being valued."[292] Sherman explains that these provisions deal with the compensation of middlemen.[293] Commentary 17.1 of the Technical Committee on Customs Valuation provides further guidance in relation to "buying commissions." Such commentary addressed the question of what evidence would be necessary to establish whether fees paid by the buyer to an intermediary are buying commissions. The Technical Committee mentioned, among other elements, the existence of an agency contract between the agent and the buyer, which should accurately reflect the terms of the Agreement between them. The Technical Committee also mentioned other documentary evidence, such as purchase orders, letters of credit, correspondence, etc. It also recommended the examination of a number of factors related to the nature of the activities of the so-called agent. One of these factors may be whether the buying agent assumes any risk or performs additional services other than those normally carried out by the buying agents. The extent of these additional services could affect the customs treatment of the buying commissions.[294]

In "*Rosenthal-Netter, Inc.* v. *United States*",[295] the US Court of International Trade indicated that the following factors should be examined in deciding whether a bona fide agency relationship exists:

- the right of the principal to control the agent's conduct;
- the transaction documents;
- whether the importer could have purchased directly from the manufacturers without employing an agent;
- whether the intermediary was operating an independent business, primarily for its own benefits; and
- the existence of a buying agency agreement.

The Court of International Trade added that although no single factor is determinative, the primary consideration is the right of the principal to control the agent's conduct with respect to the matters entrusted to him. In "*Jay-Arr Slimwear, Inc.* v.

292. Note to GVC Article 1(a)(i).
293. *See* Sherman *supra* note 23, at 109.
294. *See* CVC *supra* note 39, at Com17.1/1.
295. 12 CIT 77, 679 F.Supp. 21 (1988), aff'd 861 F.2d 261 (1988).

United States",[296] the Court of International Trade provides examples of services which are characteristic of those rendered by buying agents: compiling market information, gathering samples, translating, placing orders based on the buyer's instructions, procuring the merchandise, assisting in factory negotiation, inspecting and packing merchandise and arranging for shipment and payment.

In HQ Rulings 542141 (9/29/80), 542362 (3/18/81), 542176 (5/19/81) among others, the USCS indicated that where the payment made to the seller by the buyer for imported merchandise includes a buying commission, there is no authority to deduct the amount from the price actually paid or payable.[297] In HQ Ruling 547098 (2/2/99), the buyer included the buying agent's commission in the transaction value of the merchandise it imported from the seller. The USCS held that "the buying agent's commission is considered dutiable as part of the transaction value of the goods, because it constitutes a disbursement 'to, or for the benefit of, the seller' under section 402(b)(4)(A) of the TAA, regardless of whether the seller's billing invoice identified separately the buying commission from the per se value of the goods."[298] This is consistent with the decision of the US Court of International Trade in "*Moss Manufacturing Co. Inc.* v. *United States*",[299] where it was held that, if a payment for goods is made by the buyer to the seller with instructions to the seller to remit a portion of the payment to the buyer's agent, where the agent assisted in bringing about the sale, such a payment is a disbursement for the benefit of the seller within the meaning of 19 U.S.C. 1401a(b) and is properly part of the price actually paid or payable.

A condition for allowing the exclusion of certain elements - among which one can find the buying commissions - from customs value under the GVC is that such elements should be "distinguished" from the price actually paid or payable for the goods. The European Community Customs Code Committee expressed the following view:

> 4. For the purpose of satisfying the condition that an element is "distinguished", it is necessary not only to make a claim in the appropriate boxes of the DV1 declaration but also, where appropriate, to establish the nature of the element and its amount in monetary terms.
>
> 5. Any type of commercial documentation, including documents of long-term validity relating to more than one import transaction, (e.g., contract, invoice for the goods, or invoice for transport) relating to the goods being valued can in principle serve to establish this "nature" and "amount"...[300]

In "*Hauptzollamt Karlsruhe* v. *Gebrüder Hepp GmbH & Co. KG.*", Gebrüder Hepp GmbH & Co. KG ("Hepp") used the services of Novimex Fashion Ltd. ("Novimex"), a Swiss company with which Hepp had concluded an agreement in 1982 governed by Swiss law. Under that agreement, Novimex bought goods from a Korean undertaking

296. 12 CIT 133, 681 F.Supp. 875 (1988).
297. *See* CVE *supra* note 45 at 49.
298. *Ibid* at 52.
299. 13 CIT 420, 714 F.Supp. 1223 (1989). *See* CVE *supra* note 45 at 44.
300. E.C., European Commission, Directorate General XXI - Customs and Indirect Taxation, Customs Code Committee, Commentary No. 5, CCVT at 22.

in its own name but on behalf of Hepp. The goods were forwarded to Hepp against payment of a buying commission of 6–7 % and reimbursement of expenses. The prices fixed in the transactions concluded with the Korean supplier and the commissions were invoiced separately. In its customs declarations Hepp mentioned Novimex' name under the heading "seller" and submitted Novimex' invoices issued to it but did not mention the agreed commissions. The issue in the main proceedings was whether the buying commission invoiced separately by Novimex to Hepp had to be included in the customs value of the goods imported by Hepp. The European Court of Justice indicated that the objective of "a fair, uniform and neutral system of customs valuation excluding the use of arbitrary or fictitious customs values" would not be attained if no account were taken of a buying agent's actual function. The Court explained that since such agent acts on behalf of the importer, his function in relation to the purchase of goods is only one of representation and he bears no financial risks in the purchase.[301] The Court held:

> The transaction to which reference must be made in order to determine the customs value ... is accordingly the transaction between the manufacturer or supplier of the goods and the importer. The fact that the transaction is carried out through the medium of a buying agent is irrelevant in this regard since the financial risk connected with the transaction is assumed by the importer... It follows that the sums paid by the importer to the buying agent for the service of representing him in the purchase of the goods in question constitute a buying commission which ... must not be included in the customs value. The fact that the importer has entered the agent's name as "seller" in his customs value declaration and has declared the price of the goods invoiced by the agent does not affect the customs value ..."[302]

Buying commissions generally affect the tax base of income taxes (e.g., they could affect the COGS or the inventory cost of imported property – increasing such cost). Thus, the existence of this type of commissions should be taken into account when the customs value of imported goods and the elements of the tax base of income taxes are being compared. Where buying commissions (as defined under the GVC) have been paid, the customs value might not be equivalent to the value of the imported goods for income tax purposes (e.g., the value of the goods in computing COGS), unless appropriate adjustments were made to account for such buying commissions.

16.2.2 Containers and Packing

In determining the customs value, the cost of containers which are treated as being one for customs purposes with the imported goods and the cost of packing whether for

301. Compare this with HQ Ruling 544669 ([15 August 1991] – *see* CVE *supra* note 45 at 46), where the USCS accepted the existence of a buying agency relationship even though the agent was directed by the importer to retain the title and bear the risk of loss for the imported merchandise. *See*, however, HQ Ruling 546981 ([8 February 1999] – *see* CVE *supra* note 45 at 52).
302. Case C-299/90, 25 July 1991, European Court reports 1991 Page I-04301. *See also* Conclusion No. 14 of the EC Customs Code Committee ("Imports through contract agents"), CCVT at 55.

labor or materials, must be added to the customs value (B in our formula of customs value). However, such inclusion must be made only if:

(i) the costs are incurred by the buyer; and
(ii) they are not included in the price paid or payable.[303]

Sherman explains that these provisions are neither intended to include the cost of large commercial containers used for long-distance transport and then reused for other shipments, nor the cost of reusable containers. These "containers" constitute modes of transport which usually - due to classification rules - will not be treated as being one with the goods. The provisions are intended to cover only items which are generally classified under the tariff item of the goods packed in them. The provision refers to the cost (not the value) of the containers, which means the actual charge incurred by the buyer.[304]

16.2.3 Assists

Pursuant to GVC Article 8.1(b), another addition to the customs value is the value, apportioned as appropriate, of the following goods and services where supplied directly or indirectly by the buyer free of charge or at a reduced cost for use in connection with the production and sale for export of the imported goods, to the extent that such value has not been included in the price paid or payable:

(1) materials, components, parts and similar items incorporated in the imported goods;
(2) tools, dies, molds and similar items used in the production of the imported goods;
(3) materials consumed in the production of the imported goods;
(4) engineering, development, artwork, design work, and plan and sketches undertaken elsewhere than in the country of importation and necessary for the production of the imported goods.

These goods and services are usually referred to as "assists." Sherman explains that a number of conditions must be met before the assist addition provided for in GVC Article 8.1(b) is required.

These conditions are particularly important, in the context of this work, since the addition to or deduction from customs value of assists might be a factor of adjustment where tax and customs valuation results are to be compared. In effect, where the tax statutes require certain assists to be included in the value of the imported property for income tax purposes (e.g., in the inventory cost of such property) and such assists are not added to the customs value of the imported goods pursuant to GVC Article 8, a comparison between the tax and customs values of the goods would not be possible,

303. *See* GVC Article 8.1(a)(ii) and (iii).
304. *See* Sherman *supra* note 23, at 111.

since these tax bases would not be homogeneous. To achieve homogeneity, adjustments to account for the differences between the tax bases (in this case, the addition to or deduction from customs value or tax value of assists) should be made. The conditions that must be met before the assist addition to customs value is required, are the following:

(1) the goods or services must be supplied free of charge or at reduced cost;[305]
(2) the assist must be used in connection with the production or sale for export of the imported goods. Thus, services not related to production are not dutiable. Services in the nature of marketing or sales-related activities are not included in customs value;[306]
(3) the value of the assist must not be included in the price;
(4) the value of the assist must be "apportioned as appropriate" to determine the amount properly attributable to the particular goods being valued. (Differences in the methods of apportionment eventually used for tax and customs purposes might also result in differences in tax bases. Therefore, such differences should also be identified.).
(5) the assist must be of a category listed in GVC Article 8. Article 8.4 provides that no additions to price shall be made unless provided for in Article 8.[307] Sherman explains that certain categories of assistance sellers receive from buyers were deliberately not included in the list and are not part of the customs value.[308] The furnishing of financial assistance by the buyers to the seller has been held in the United States not to be a dutiable assist.[309] Neville provides a list of items of value furnished by a buyer to a seller that the US Customs Service has not characterized as dutiable assists:
    - management services (Ruling 543820 – 12 December 1986);
    - salaries of production foremen and production engineers if incidental to work undertaken in the United States (Ruling 542141 – 4 February 1981);
    - salaries of plant manager, plant engineer, production foremen and quality control personnel (Ruling 542696 – 22 February 1982);

305. The USCS said that "[p]ayments made to the seller for expenses incurred for research and development are part of the price actually paid or payable rather than added on as an assist." (CVE *supra* note 45, at chapter XX, Ruling 543324, 8 August 1984). It also said that "[p]ayments made by the buyer to the seller for tooling are indirect payments and part of the price actually paid or payable for the imported merchandise." (CVE *supra* note 45, at chapter XX, Ruling 543951, 23 September 1987).

306. *See* Neville, M., "Customs planning may avoid conflict with IRS transfer pricing rules" (1993) 4 J.Int'l Tax'n 70, online: LEXIS (date accessed: 5 July 2000).

307. For a discussion regarding whether or not some assists that are not included in the list of Article 8, might be regarded as being an indirect payment, *see* Section 16.1.3.

308. *See* Sherman *supra* note 23, at 113.

309. *Ibid. See also* USCS, *Customs Valuation Rulings under the Trade Agreement Act of 1979* (December 1984), Trade Agreement Act Decision 17. A similar understanding can be found in paragraph 13 of Case Study 2.1 of the Technical Committee on Customs Valuation (*see* CVC *supra* note 39, at CS2.1/2).

- costs associated with purchasing, receiving, inspection, warehouse, production control, design, engineering, accounting and sales functions (Ruling 542412 - 27 March 1981);
- machinery and equipment not used in actual production (Ruling 542302 - 27 February 1981); and
- management, accounting and legal services (Ruling 542122 - 4 September 1980).[310]

In this respect, it is interesting to refer to some adjustments allowed by the IRS under Section 1059A. The US Customs Service generally defined "assists" as various general purpose equipment expenses and direct manufacturing expenses.[311] In response to IRS's questions about what is included in customs value, customs advised IRS that general, administrative and overhead expenses were not assists. Customs advised IRS that the following related-party expenses were not assists: office equipment rental fees, business expenses, telephone bills, postage expenses, removal of trash, legal fees, classified advertising, executive development, travel and entertainment expenses, professional dues and subscriptions, charitable contributions and expenses attributable to conversion currencies.[312] The IRS recognized that - under tax law - these expenses were the kind of items that were properly includible in cost basis for federal tax purposes.[313] Therefore, in a technical advice memorandum, the IRS concluded that it could not apply Section 1059A to prevent the US taxpayer from including the expenses paid on behalf of its foreign-related party in its cost basis because the expenses were not subject to customs duty. In other words, in determining the limitation on claimed basis or inventory cost of property under Section 1059A, the taxpayer may increase the customs value of imported property by amounts corresponding to the referred expenses.[314] These amounts would fall within the fourth type of adjustment cited in the Regulations for Section 1059A[315] (i.e., "[a]ny other amounts which are not taken into account in determining the customs value, which are not properly includible in customs value, and which are appropriately included in the cost basis or inventory cost for income tax purposes").[316]

One can observe that the IRS required homogeneous tax bases (or elements of such tax bases) for comparing tax and customs values of imported property under the provisions of Section 1059A. Thus, the adjustments we examined in the foregoing paragraph constitute an example of those analyzed throughout this Chapter.[317] It

310. *See* Neville *supra* note 307.
311. *See* GAO *supra* note 251.
312. *Ibid.*
313. *Ibid.*
314. *Ibid.*
315. 26 CFR §1.1059A-1 (revised as of 1 April 2000). [hereinafter "Regulations for Section 1059A"].
316. *See* Neville *supra* note 326. *See also* USITP *supra* note 248, at 18.03[4][b].
317. In Private Ruling 9543048 (1 August 1995) the IRS said: "Application of Section 1059A, as impacted by Nissho Iwai, may be summarized as follows: 1. If a taxpayer reports different values to Customs and IRS, a reduction to the tax value reported to the IRS may be made under section 1059A if the value reported to Customs is lower than the value reported for income tax purposes. The potential adjustment to the tax value is the entire amount of the difference

should be noted that, under the income tax statutes of some countries, adjustments for these items might not be necessary. It will depend on how taxable income is computed under such statutes.

16.2.4 Royalties and License Fees

Pursuant to GVC Article 8.1(c), royalties and license fees related to the goods being valued that the buyer must pay, either directly or indirectly, as a condition of sale of the goods being valued, must be added to the customs value, to the extent that such royalties and fees are not included in the price actually paid or payable (A in our formula of customs value).

There is no definition of the terms "royalties" and "licence fees" in the GVC. Sherman explains that:

> ... there is no part of the Code where so much is left to interpretation and implementation, and so little can be derived from a literal reading of the words used. Some critics have thought the authors of the Code did not explore this subject sufficiently, and it is true that the subject was only reached rather late in Geneva negotiations and revealed considerable differences between governments (often as to what problems required attention, rather than how they should be resolved).[318]

The European Community Customs Code Committee resorts to the general definition of the term "royalties" in Article 12(2) of the OECD Model Double Taxation Convention on Income and Capital (1977). Such definition reads:

> payments of any kind received as a consideration for the use of, or the right to use, any copyright of literary, artistic or scientific work including cinematograph films, any patent, trademark, design or model, plan, secret formula or process, or of the use of, or the right to use, industrial, commercial or scientific equipment, or for information concerning industrial, commercial, or scientific experience.

It must be taken into account that, while the definition of the term "royalties" in the 1977 OECD MTC included payments "for the use of, or the right to use, industrial, commercial or scientific equipment," the reference to these payments was subsequently deleted from the definition. The Commentaries to Article 12(2) of the 1998 OECD MTC read:

---

between the two values. However, the adjustment is reduced to the extent the taxpayer establishes that the differences between the amount reported to the IRS and Customs are attributable to such items as freight, insurance, and American content which are not includible in dutiable value; and to differences in the valuation methods that can be objectively identified by the taxpayer. Also, the value taken into account for income tax purposes (that is compared to the value reported to Customs) must conform to the rules for determining cost basis or inventory cost under section 263A and section 1.471-11 of the Regulations. 2. If a taxpayer reports the exact same value to both Customs and the IRS, or a greater value to Customs than to the IRS, no adjustment may be made under section 1059A. However, if the IRS determines that the value reported to the IRS is not arm's length, an adjustment may be made under section 482." (US, Internal Revenue Service, *Private Ruling 9543048*, 1 August 1995).

318. *See* Sherman *supra* note 23, at 123.

> Given the nature of income from the leasing of industrial, commercial or scientific equipment, including the leasing of containers, the Committee on Fiscal Affairs decided to exclude income from such leasing from the definition of royalties and, consequently, to remove it from the application of Article 12 in order to make sure that it would fall under the rules for the taxation of business profits, as defined in Articles 5 and 7.

We are satisfied with the approach adopted by the European Community Customs Code Committee in defining the term "royalty" for customs valuation purposes. It shows a movement towards the integration of tax and customs concepts.

There are two conditions that must be met in order for a royalty or license fee to be added to Customs value:

1. the payment of the royalty or license fee must be related to the goods being valued;[319] and
2. such payment must constitute a condition of sale of the imported goods.[320]

There is a close economic relationship between these conditions.[321]

In Commentary 25.1, the TCCV explains that "...[t]he most common circumstances in which a royalty or licence fee may be considered to relate to the goods being valued is when the imported goods incorporate the intellectual property and/or are manufactured using the intellectual property covered by the licence. For example, if the imported goods incorporate the trademark for which the royalty or licence fee is paid, this would indicate that the fee relates to the imported goods."

Likewise, in the European Community, royalties and license fees are related to the imported goods where in particular, the rights transferred under the license or royalties agreement are embodied in the goods.[322]

The IRUCC provides that the method of calculation of the amount of the royalty or the license fee is not the decisive factor. However, where the method of calculation

319. In relation to this condition, the Technical Committee on Customs Valuation has provided guidance in Advisory Opinions 4.1, 4.4, 4.7, 4.8, 4.10, 4.11 and 4.12. *See* CVC *supra* note 38, at AO4.1/1-AO4.12/1. Commentary No. 3 of the European Community Customs Code Committee on the incidence of royalties and license fees in customs value states: "In determining whether a royalty relates to the goods to be valued, the key issue is not how the royalty is calculated but why it is paid, i.e., what in fact the licensee receives in return for the payment (in this connection *see* Article 161 of the Implementing provisions). Thus in the case of an imported component or ingredient of the licensed product, or in the case of imported production machinery or plant, a royalty payment based on the realisation on sale of the licensed product may relate wholly, partially or not at all to the imported goods."

320. In relation to this condition, the Technical Committee on Customs Valuation has provided guidance in Advisory Opinions 4.2, 4.3, 4.5, 4.6, 4.7, 4.9, 4.10, 4.11, 4.13 and 4.15. *See* CVC *supra* note 38, at AO4.2/1-AO4.15/1. Commentary No. 3 of the European Community Customs Code Committee on the incidence of royalties and license fees in customs value indicates: "The question to be answered in this context in whether the seller would be prepared to sell the goods without the payment of a royalty or license fee. The condition may be explicit or implicit. In the majority of cases it will be specified in the licence agreement whether the sale of the imported goods is conditional upon payment of a royalty or licence fee. It is not, however, essential that it should be so stipulated." [*see* CCVT *supra* note 105, at 15.]

321. *See* Sherman *supra* note 23, at 123.

322. *See* Article 136, paragraph 1, of the IRUCC.

of the amount of royalties or license fees derives from the price of the imported goods, it shall in the absence of evidence to the contrary be assumed that the payment of those royalties or license fees is related to the goods to be valued.[323] It should be noted that the addition to the customs value cannot be avoided merely by connecting the calculation of the royalty or the license fee to the later proceeds from the resale of the imported goods or of the goods produced from them or to any other basis.[324]

With respect to the "condition of sale" requirement, the TCCV indicates that a key consideration for determining whether the buyer must pay the royalty or the license fee as a condition of sale is whether the buyer is unable to purchase the imported goods without paying the royalty or the license fee. When the royalty or the license fee is paid to a third party related to the seller of the imported goods, it is more likely that the fee is paid as a condition of sale than when it is paid to a third party unrelated to the seller. However, in all the cases, each situation must be analyzed based on all the facts surrounding the sale and importation of the goods, including the contractual and legal obligations contained in relevant documents, such as the sales agreement and the royalty or the license agreement.

The European Commission adopted some of these concepts in paragraph 4 of Article 136 of the IRUCC, which provide:

> 4. Royalties and licence fees are considered to be paid as a condition of sale for the imported goods when any of the following conditions is met:
>
> (a) the seller or a person related to the seller requires the buyer to make this payment;
> (b) the payment by the buyer is made to satisfy an obligation of the seller, in accordance with contractual obligations;
> (c) the goods cannot be sold to, or purchased by, the buyer without payment of the royalties or license fees to a licensor.

The TCCV recognizes that, in general, the sales documentation does not include an explicit provision stating that the buyer cannot purchase the goods without paying the royalty. Therefore, in the view of the TCCV, other factors have to be considered in order to determine whether payment of the royalty is made as a condition of sale and, for such purposes, a review of all the facts surrounding the sale and importation of the goods is required. The TCCV mentions the following factors:

(a) There is a reference to the royalty or the license fee in the sales agreement or related documents;
(b) There is a reference to the sale of the goods in the royalty or the license agreement;
(c) According to the terms of the sales agreement or the royalty or the license agreement, the sales agreement can be terminated as a consequence of breaching the royalty or the license agreement because the buyer does not

323. IRUCC Article 136, paragraphs 1 and 2.
324. *See* Sherman *supra* note 23, at 126.

pay the royalty or the license fee to the licensor. This would indicate a linkage between the royalty or the license fee payment and the sale of the goods being valued;

(d) There is a term in the royalty or the license agreement that indicates if the royalties or license fees are not paid, the manufacturer is forbidden to manufacture and sell the goods incorporating the licensor's intellectual property to the importer;

(e) The royalty or the license agreement contains terms that permit the licensor to manage the production or sale between the manufacturer and the importer (sale for export to the country of importation) that go beyond quality control.

Charges for the "right to reproduce" the imported goods in the country of importation are not added to the customs value of the imported goods.[325] Commentary 19.1 of the Technical Committee on Customs Valuation[326] provides some guidance on the types of activities intended to be covered by the phrase "right to reproduce." The Technical Committee suggests that such phrase would seem to refer not only to the physical reproduction of the imported goods but also to the right to reproduce an invention, creation, thought or idea incorporated in the imported goods. In the opinion of the Technical Committee, it would also refer to originals and copies of scientific works, originals of literary works, models, prototypes and animal or plant species. The Technical Committee suggests an analysis of the following factors: (a) whether an idea or original work is incorporated in the imported goods; (b) whether the reproduction of the idea or work is the subject of a reserved right; (c) whether the right of reproduction has been assigned to the buyer in the contract of sale or through a separate agreement; (d) whether the holder of the reserved right has required a remuneration for the assignment of the right of reproduction.[327]

325. *See* Note to GVC Article 8.1(c).
326. *See* CVC *supra* note 38, at Com19.1/1.
327. We have observed that the Argentine Customs Service, in a number of duty re-determination procedures, made proportional adjustments to the price paid or payable for the imported goods without paying due attention to the relationship between the royalty or license fee and the goods. The position adopted by the Argentine Customs Service may produce erroneous results since it would give rise to adjustments to transaction value in every case in which an importer pays royalties or license fees to a foreign exporter, regardless of whether such royalties or license fees are related to the imported goods or, for instance, to a right to reproduce such goods. In one of such re-determination procedures, the Argentine Customs Service understood that a license fee paid in consideration for the right to breed certain parental seed and to produce commercial seed from such parental seed in Argentina had to be added to the price paid or payable for the imported parental seed. The license fee was calculated as a percentage on the sale of commercial seed produced from the multiplication (or reproduction) of the parental seed. The Argentine Customs Service understood that an appropriate apportionment was required since the license fee was related to the imported goods and to other ingredients that, together with the imported goods, were necessary to produce the commercial seed. In the Argentine Customs Service's view, the imported goods (parental seed) were an ingredient of goods "manufactured" in Argentina (the commercial seed), on the sale of which the royalty was calculated. We believe that this approach is incorrect and based on a wrongful interpretation of GVC Article 8.1(c) and its note. An apportionment of the license fee is required only if the license fee is related to the imported goods, but not where such license fee is related to a right to reproduce such goods in the country of importation. Being the license fees related to the

We have determined which royalties should be included in customs value. Now we will explore the most relevant issues arising from the existence of royalty payments when tax and customs values of imported goods are being compared.

A first issue to be considered when comparing tax and customs values of imported goods (or the rules for determining such values) relates to the definition of the term "royalty" under tax and customs laws. Even when "royalties" were added to or deducted from customs and tax values in the same manner, the customs value and the value of the imported goods for income tax purposes might not be equivalent if there were differences in the definition of the term "royalties" under tax and customs laws. Therefore, in order to compare tax and customs valuation results, the definitions of the term "royalties" – if any – under tax and customs laws should be examined. Differences between those definitions should be identified and accounted for through appropriate adjustments. In many cases, it may also be necessary to examine the definition of such term adopted under international tax treaties. For example, Article 12 of the MTC includes the following definition:

> 1. The term "royalties" as used in this Article means payments of any kind received as a consideration for the use of, or the right to use, any copyright of literary, artistic or scientific work including cinematograph films, any patent, trade mark, design or model, plan, secret formula or process, or for information concerning industrial, commercial or scientific experience.[328]

Since there is no definition of the term "royalties" under the GVC, the MTC and the OECD Guidelines may also provide guidance on the interpretation of such term under GVC Articles 1 and 8 (*see* above the position adopted by the EC Customs Code Committee). This may help avoid inconsistencies between the tax bases (or elements thereof) of customs duties and income taxes.

A second issue to be considered is whether the rules of valuation of goods laid down in the income tax statutes (e.g., for purposes of inventory cost of imported property) require such royalties (or some types of royalties) to be added to, or excluded from, the value of the goods. (Note that the rules of valuation of goods in some tax statutes may also provide for the exclusion of royalties that have already been included in the price paid or payable for the imported goods.). Identification of any difference between tax and customs rules is necessary to make appropriate adjustments to, and appropriate comparisons between, tax and customs values of imported goods.

A third issue, closely connected with the former, is whether the payment of such royalties is subject to income tax withholding under national tax statutes and/or treaty provisions. Payments made in consideration of the sale of goods for export to the country of importation are generally not subject to income tax withholding. Where such payments include charges for intellectual property, such part of the payment might be subject to income tax withholding. In this respect, the OECD Guidelines provide that:

---

right to breed the seed in Argentina (right that was protected by the law and exclusively owned by the developer/exporter of the seed), the Argentine Customs Service was not allowed to add such license fee to Customs Value.

328. MTC *supra* note 10, at 33.

> 6.98 In some situations intangibles or rights in intangibles may be transferred in combination with tangible business assets, or in combination with services. It is important in such a situation to determine whether intangibles have in fact been transferred in connection with the transaction. It is also important that all of the intangibles transferred in connection with a particular transaction be identified and taken into account in the transfer pricing analysis...
>
> 6.99 In some situations it may be both possible and appropriate to separate transactions in tangible goods or services from transfers of intangibles or rights in intangibles for purposes of conducting a transfer pricing analysis. In these situations, the price of a package contract should be disaggregated in order to confirm that each element of the transaction is consistent with the arm's length principle.[329]

One can identify, therefore, the following situations:

(1) Tax and customs valuation rules set out equivalent rules of determination of tax bases – or elements thereof – in particular, in relation to the treatment of royalty payments. In this case, no adjustment would usually be required for the purposes of comparison between customs and tax results.

(2) (a) Tax rules require deductions from transaction value (e.g., in respect of royalties which were already included in the price paid or payable) that are not allowed under customs rules.
   (b) Tax rules do not allow additions to transaction value (e.g., in respect of royalties related to the imported goods, that the buyer must pay to the seller as a condition of the sale of such goods) that are required under customs rules.
   (c) Tax rules allow additions to transaction value that are not required to be made under customs rules.
   (d) Tax rules do not allow deductions from transaction value that are allowed under customs rules.

In the situations mentioned in (2), a comparison between tax and customs values of the imported goods will usually require adjustments to account for the differences in the treatment of royalties under tax and customs rules. The situations described in (2) may appear combined, depending on the different income tax statutes. These could add complexity to any process of comparison.

16.2.5 Proceeds of Resale, Disposal or Use of the Imported Goods

GVC Article 8.1(d) provides for the addition to the customs value of the value of any part of the proceeds of any subsequent resale, disposal or use of the imported goods that accrues directly or indirectly to the seller.

329. *See supra* note 4 at 6.98 and 6.99.

Sherman explains that "more often than not, a royalty or licence fee is expressed as a percentage of resale price."[330] This author understands that "it would make no sense to go through the refined analysis called for by GVC Article 8.1(c) and conclude that the payment is not dutiable as a royalty only to find that the payment is dutiable under the companion provision of GVC Article 8.1(d) as proceeds of subsequent resale." He believes that the line of distinction which makes possible to reconcile GVC Articles 8.1(c) and (d) is that GVC Article 8.1(c) relates to payments for intangibles and GVC Article 8.1(d) relates to payments for the tangible imported goods. Therefore, he concludes that if a royalty for rights, information or services is not dutiable under GVC Article 8.1(c) it cannot be dutiable under GVC Article 8.1(d), even if it is measured or expressed as a portion of resale price.[331]

The European Community Customs Code Committee, in its "Commentary No. 3 on the Incidence of Royalties and Licence Fees in Customs Value," took a clear position in this respect:

> Non-applicability of Article 32(1)(d) of the Code
>
> 20. The provisions of Article 32(1)(a)–(e) of the Code, which concern additions to the price actually paid or payable for the imported goods, each have their own scope. Thus payments which fall within the definition of royalties and licence fees are to be examined solely in the light of Article 32(1)(c) of the Code. When the requirements of that provision are not met, such payments are not to be considered under Article 32(1)(d).

With the Hasbro Ruling,[332] the USCS – that had originally had the same understanding[333] – took the view that even if a royalty were not dutiable because it was not a condition of the import transaction, it nonetheless might be dutiable as proceeds of a subsequent resale if accruing to the benefit of the seller.[334]

Since the language of the GVC is ambiguous (especially if the Note to GVC Article 1 and GVC Articles 8.1(c) and (d) are read together) a clarification of this issue by the Technical Committee on Customs Valuation through an advisory opinion or commentary would be desirable not only for Customs administrations and practitioners, but also to promote uniform interpretation of the GVC.[335]

The analyses made in Section 16.2.4, in relation to adjustments and comparison between tax and customs values of imported goods, are also applicable for the

330. *See* Sherman *supra* note 23, at 144.
331. Sherman bases this understanding on a detailed analysis of the language of GVC Articles 8.1(c) and (d), the Brussels Definition of Value and the Notes to GVC Article 1. (*See* Sherman *supra* note 23, at 155).
332. USCS, Ruling 544436 (4 February 1991), Customs Bulletin Vol. 25, No. 18 (June 1991).
333. In Ruling 542900 (9 December 1982), the USCS had held that the existence of two separate categories, one specifically relating to royalty and license fees and the other to the proceeds of subsequent resale, use or disposal of the imported goods, clearly indicated that the two categories were not intended to cover the same set of circumstances. Thus, when the royalty or license fee was find not to be part of customs value as a royalty, no authority existed for including the fee in customs value as proceeds of subsequent resale (*see* CVE *supra* note 45 at chapter XXXVIII). *See also* Levey *supra* note 3, at 8.05[5][c][iv]. *See also* Neville *supra* note 326.
334. *See* Levey *supra* note 3, at 8.05[5][c][iv]. *See* Neville *supra* note 326.
335. *See* Article 18.2 and Annex IIA of the GVC.

purposes of this section. However, the customs treatment of certain royalties and license fees (e.g., those which are calculated as part of the proceeds of subsequent resale of the imported goods) depends on the interpretation by the Customs administrations and Courts of each country of GVC Article 8.1(d). Thus, whether or not certain adjustments in relation to such royalties are needed depends upon such interpretations.

16.2.6 Transportation and Related Charges

GVC Article 8 provides that "each Member shall provide for the inclusion in or exclusion from the customs value, in whole or in part, of the following: (a) the cost of transport of the imported goods to the port or place of importation; (b) loading, unloading and handling charges associated with the transport of the imported goods to the port or place of importation; and (c) the cost of insurance." Sherman explains that, the fact that most countries are on a CIF basis of customs valuation whereas the United States[336] and some others are on an FOB basis of customs valuation is reflected by this provision. The negotiators of the GVC decided not to undo this difference.[337]

Adjustments for the purposes of comparing tax and customs values under customs and income tax laws, would generally be necessary where a country has adopted an FOB basis of valuation for customs purposes, and the costs of transport and insurance are included in the value of the goods for income tax purposes (e.g., in the inventory cost of the imported goods). An example of this type of adjustment can be found in the regulations for Section 1059A. They provide that taxpayers, in determining the limitation on claimed basis or inventory cost of property, may increase the customs value of imported property by certain amounts. Freight charges and insurance are two of the four types of adjustments cited in the regulations.[338]

16.3 Deductions from Price Paid or Payable

The Note to GVC Article 1 provides for three deductions from customs value (C in our formula of customs value):

(a) charges for construction, erection, assembly, maintenance or technical assistance, undertaken after importation on imported goods such as industrial plan, machinery or equipment;

336. *See* 19 USC §1401a(b)(4)(A).
337. *See* Sherman *supra* note 23, at 159.
338. *See* Regulations for Section 1059A *supra* note 335. Such regulations read: "Adjustments to customs value. To the extent not otherwise included in customs value, a taxpayer, for purposes of determining the limitation on claimed basis or inventory cost of property under this section, may increase the customs value of imported property by the amounts incurred by it and properly included in inventory cost for – (i) Freight charges, (ii) Insurance charges ..." *See also* GAO *supra* note 251. Bear in mind that, pursuant to Section 1059A, the claimed basis or inventory cost for income tax purposes cannot exceed the customs value plus four classes of additions (adjustments).

(b) the cost of transport after importation; and
(c) duties and taxes of the country of importation.

However, in order for such elements to be deducted, they must be distinguished from the price actually paid or payable.[339]

All these elements represent costs and values added after the goods have been imported, reflecting the principle that customs value should not include values attaching after importation.[340]

When comparing tax and customs valuation results adjustment for these elements may be required. In effect, where national tax statutes include such elements in the cost of imported property (e.g., in its inventory cost or in its adjusted cost base), an adjustment to the tax or customs figures would be necessary to make such figures homogeneous, and to permit an appropriate comparison.

The Regulations for Section 1059A offer an example of these adjustments. In determining the limitation on claimed basis or inventory cost of property, charges for construction, erection, assembly, maintenance or technical assistance provided with respect to the property after its importation into the United States, constitute the third type of adjustment permitted under such regulations.[341]

16.4 Conclusions Regarding Customs Value

Throughout Sections 16–16.3, we have observed a number of interpretative problems derived from the concept of "customs value" and the adjustments thereto. We have also noted the relationship between this concept (as it affects the tax base of customs duties and other import taxes) and the value of imported goods for income tax purposes.

One can conclude that uniformity in applying the notion of customs value and its adjustments would be recommendable in order to undertake a process of harmonization between tax and customs valuation rules. As indicated above, the use of the OECD Guidelines in the context of GVC Article 1.2(a) aims at a uniform application of the GVC among the WTO members, as required by its Preamble. WTO members should undertake this process of harmonization paying special attention to the work of the Technical Committee on Customs Valuation of the World Customs Organization and to the way in which the different countries have been implementing the provisions of the GVC. We believe that the results of such process should be implemented by means of decisions of the Committee on Customs Valuation.

339. *See* Note to GVC Article 1.
340. *See* Sherman *supra* note 23, at 171.
341. *See* Regulations for Section 1059A *supra* note 335. Such regulations read: "Adjustments to customs value. To the extent not otherwise included in customs value, a taxpayer, for purposes of determining the limitation on claimed basis or inventory cost of property under this section, may increase the customs value of imported property by the amounts incurred by it and properly included in inventory cost for – [...] (iii) The construction, erection, assembly, or technical assistance provided with respect to, the property after its importation into the United States ..." *See also* GAO *supra* note 251.

CHAPTER 5

Price Review Clauses and Formula Pricing

17 INTRODUCTION

In Chapter 4 we explored the rules governing the tax base of customs duties, and examined the cases where a comparison between tax and customs values of imported property could not be made without appropriate adjustments to account for differences in the computation of such values.

In this chapter, we will examine some adjustments an importer may be required to make to the price originally declared to customs. This adjustments could be the consequence of a transfer pricing study for tax purposes. We will refer to this type of adjustments as "year-end adjustments."[342] From a customs standpoint, a year-end adjustment would involve a value declared to customs on a provisional basis - which is linked to variables which come into play some time after the goods have been imported - and a definitive value to be declared to customs subsequently, when such variables are finally known.

The year-end adjustment would be based on such variables. If the price is adjusted upwards, both the dutiable value and the amount of customs duties will be increased. If the price is adjusted downwards, the effect would be the opposite: both the dutiable value and the amount of customs duties will be decreased. In this latter situation, the importer may be entitled to a refund.[343]

Year-end adjustments may arise not only from adjustments made by the tax authorities under national tax regulations, but also when there is a cost-plus or resale-minus pricing and the customs entry is made when the costs and expenses have not been finalized.[344] In this regard, paragraph 2.71 of the OECD Guidelines reads:

342. *See* Levey *supra* note 3, at 8.05[10][f].
343. *Ibid.*
344. *Ibid.*

> Application of any arm's length method requires information on uncontrolled transactions that may not be available at the time of the controlled transactions [e.g., at the time of importation]. This may make it particularly difficult for taxpayers that attempt to apply the transactional net margin method at the time of the controlled transactions (although use of multiple-year data as discussed in paragraphs 3.75-3.79 may mitigate this concern). In addition, taxpayers may not have access to enough specific information on the profits attributable to comparable uncontrolled transactions to make a valid application of the method. It also may be difficult to ascertain revenue and operating expenses related to the controlled transactions to establish the net profit indicator used as the profit measure for the transactions...

In this chapter we will, therefore, analyze whether transaction values subject to year-end adjustments may be acceptable under GVC Article 1 and, if so, under which conditions such adjustments should be made.

This issue was first brought to the attention of the TCCV on a paper that we submitted at the TCCV's 20th Session.[345] In 2007, this issue was presented again, this time to the Focus Group on Customs Valuation and Transfer Pricing. This Focus Group included among its recommendations that a proposal be made to the TCCV at its next session that the following technical points be taken up for examination and consideration for further instruments: "... ii) Consideration of the customs valuation treatment of situations where a transfer pricing agreement indicates that the declared value be adjusted as necessary at a later date to achieve a pre-determined profit margin (known as price review clauses). This could be a development of earlier work of the TCCV on Price Review Clauses."

In working document VT0604E1a, the WCO Secretariat suggested that the TCCV needed to identify the objectives, the core issues, the ultimate goal and the way forward on the subject of customs valuation and transfer pricing. As a possible core issue, it suggested how to treat compensating or year-end adjustments of the tax authorities for adjusting the customs value by modifying the customs declarations at the point of importation, with reference to Commentary 4.1 dealing with price review clauses.

At the TCCV's 27th Session, we presented a draft case study which dealt, among other things, with year-end adjustments and price review clauses.[346]

In the Guide to Customs Valuation and Transfer Pricing, the WCO recognized the importance of this issue and that Commentary 4.1 could be a solution to such issue, as follows:

> It can be argued that given that the effect of a transfer pricing adjustment is to achieve an arm's length price, in some cases - depending on the type of transfer pricing adjustment– the adjusted price will be closer to the 'un-influenced' price actually paid or payable for Customs valuation purposes. In other cases, such as tax-only transfer pricing adjustments, it may demonstrate that the price was in fact influenced by the relationship. Put another way, Customs may not be able to make a final decision on the question of price influence until any adjustments have been

345. *See supra* note 55.
346. This draft case study was Case Study Nbr. 6 of the 11 draft case studies submitted to the Focus Group on Customs Valuation and Transfer Pricing.

> made (or quantified). It is therefore in Customs' interest to study the impact of transfer pricing adjustments on the Customs value.
>
> Customs' treatment of transfer pricing adjustments however is currently inconsistent around the world. Some Customs administrations consider both upwards and downwards price adjustments and make corresponding duty adjustments where appropriate, others do not, or only consider upwards adjustments (with additional duty payment) but do not consider downwards adjustments (duty refund). Some consider tax-only adjustments, whilst others only consider actual price adjustments. This inconsistency has been one of the main concerns expressed by the business community.
>
> It is desirable therefore that the Customs community strives to achieve a more consistent approach when considering the impact of transfer pricing adjustments on the Customs value.

An important principle is established in an instrument of the TCCV; Commentary 4.1 – Price review clauses (*see* Annex IV). This instrument considers the Customs value implications of goods contracts which include a "price review clause", whereby the price is only provisionally fixed at the time of importation; "the final determination of the price payable being subject to certain factors which are set forth in the provisions of the contract itself". It concludes that such clauses: "should not, of themselves, preclude valuation under Article 1 of the Agreement". This scenario can be compared to situations where the price declared to Customs at importation is based on a transfer price which may be subject to subsequent adjustment (for example to achieve a predetermined profit margin) and the possibility of a transfer pricing adjustment exists at the time of importation.[347]

18 PRICE REVIEW CLAUSES: FORMULA PRICING

Where a contract does not establish price review clauses or pricing formulae and the price is declared to customs at entry in a definitive manner, any subsequent modification to the price paid or payable would have the following customs consequences:

(a) where the modification of the price (e.g., a rebate not required under the contract) is made by the exporter, for whatever reason, but based on a new decision after the merchandise has been imported, the customs value would not be affected;[348] The US Customs Service has indicated that "retroactive price adjustments between related parties agreed to after importation of merchandise do not affect the transaction value of the goods, provided that it is determined that the parties' relationship does not influence the price."[349] (This condition would lead to the next customs consequence.).

(b) where the modification of the price is agreed to after importation due to *transfer pricing* (retroactive) adjustments, the originally declared transaction

347. *See supra* note 32 at 65.

348. *See* Sherman *supra* note 23, at 83. *See also* CVE *supra* note 45, at Chapter XXXIII, Rulings 542797 (19 May 1982), 543246 (30 April 1984), 543457 (9 April 1985) and 543537 (14 February 1986).

349. CVE *ibid.*, Ruling 542797 (19 May 1982).

> value could be regarded as being influenced by the relationship and, thus, rejected on the basis of appraisement under GVC Article 1. In effect, if the price has been definitively declared to customs based on a definitive price agreed upon by the related parties, any subsequent adjustment to comply with the arm's length standard would simply indicate that the originally declared price did not comply with such standard and, thus, that it has been influenced by the relationship.[350]

When this happens, the multinational enterprise finds itself at a crossroads. If at the time of importation the multinational enterprise declares that the relationship has not influenced the price paid or payable, but at the end of the tax year its transfer pricing studies call for a year-end adjustment to bring the price into compliance with the arm's length principle, the multinational will have made an incorrect declaration and will not only face a demand for unpaid import duties but may also be exposed to penalties for making an incorrect declaration under the national customs legislation. If, on the contrary, the multinational declares that the relationship has influenced the price, then the goods will have to be valued using the methods of Articles 2 to 7 of the GVC. Moreover, there may still be a risk of an incorrect declaration, but this time if no year-end adjustment is required at the end of the tax year, given that the transaction value originally declared would not have been influenced by the relationship.[351]

However, where the contract between the buyer and the seller establishes a pricing formula or price review clauses, the situation is radically different. Where there are pricing formulae, or price review clauses, *in effect at the time of importation* (although the actual price under the formula cannot be determined until later) the price actually payable for the imported goods can be established on the basis of the data specified in the contract. An example of this would be a cost-plus contract, if the cost figures are not yet available at the time of importation.[352] Therefore, in these cases, there is a transaction value and the pricing formula or the price review clause cannot be regarded as constituting a condition or consideration for which a value cannot be

350. We explained this problem at the 20th and 27th Sessions of the TCCV and at the First and Second WCO/OECD Joint Customs Valuation and Transfer Pricing Conferences. In the Guide to Customs Valuation and Transfer Pricing, the WCO indicates "...Regarding transfer pricing adjustments which affect only the tax liability (i.e., no actual change to the amount paid for the goods), Customs may consider whether this is an indication of price influence. In other words, there is an acknowledgement that the original price was not arm's length for transfer pricing purposes but the price actually paid has not been adjusted." (*Supra* note 32 at 66.)
351. *See supra* note 55.
352. Mayer and Outman indicate that the transfer pricing method of an APA "is, for all intents and purposes, a methodology in existence prior to the date of export which should form the basis upon which adjustments can be made, either up or down." These authors add that "Customs has, for example, ruled that where the price actually paid or payable is determined pursuant to a formula, a firm price need not be known or ascertainable at the time of exportation although is necessary for the formula to be fixed at that time so that a final sales price can later be determined." (*See supra* note 52 – HQ Ruling 542701 (4/28/82))

determined.[353] This statement finds support on an appropriate interpretation of Commentary 4.1 of the TCCV, based on the principles and objectives of the GVC.

The Technical Committee on Customs Valuation has said that, in contracts containing a price review clause, the transaction value of the imported goods must be based on the total final price paid or payable in accordance with the contractual stipulations. It concluded that "given that the Agreement recommends that, as far as possible, the transaction value of the goods being valued should serve as a basis for valuation, and given that Article 13 provides for the possibility of delaying the final determination of customs value, even though it is not always possible to determine the price payable at the time of importation, price review clauses should not of themselves, preclude valuation under Article 1 of the Agreement."[354] This last point is central in understanding the problems arising from year-end adjustments. Pricing formulae and price review clauses should be used to permit valuation under GVC Article 1, especially in case of related-party transactions. As noted by the Technical Committee, Articles 1 and 13 read together provide for the possibility of delaying the final determination of customs value. Transfer pricing year-end adjustments are often necessary to ensure the arm's length character of the transaction value agreed upon between related parties. The use of pricing formulae or price review clauses makes possible the introduction of such year-end adjustments to transaction value without affecting the acceptability of such value under GVC Article 1. This enables importers to declare appropriate arm's length prices and, consequently, to have their goods appraised under GVC Article 1. They also give the importer the opportunity to demonstrate that the relationship did not influence the price. In effect, where the transfer pricing method used by the taxpayer/ importer to determine its prices requires the use of data that is not available at the time of the import (e.g., cost-plus method), the importer will only be able to declare an arm's length price when such data becomes available. Obviously, it will not be able to demonstrate that the relationship did not influence the price if the Customs administration does not delay final determination of customs value until such data becomes available.[355]

At the time of importation (that is to say, during the tax period), the importer may do his best to estimate the most accurate price possible, but clearly cannot be required

353. *See* CVC *supra* note 38, at Com4.1/1 (Commentary 4.1 of the Technical Committee on Customs Valuation).
354. CVC *supra* note 38, at Com4.1/1.
355. Under the customs legislation of most countries (e.g. 19 U.S.C. §1592(d), Section 793 of the Argentine Customs Code), authority exists – subject to certain conditions – for Customs to seek restoration of duty payments where an underpayment has been made, notwithstanding that an entry has been liquidated and has become final. Where a transfer pricing upward adjustment affects the transaction value of an importation, Customs may be allowed to seek re-determination of the customs value on the basis of the price actually paid or payable after the upward adjustment. Preventing an importer from requesting such re-determination in the case of downward adjustments would appear not to be fair. In addition, an obligation on the tax administrations to consider the impact of downward adjustments on customs values for duty purposes (and, thus, to recognize any eventual refund of duties) would make tax administration's auditors be careful before undertaking a transfer pricing audit or a tax re-determination procedure, especially in those countries which keep high duty barriers or in those cases where valuation has not been used to obtain a tax advantage.

to predict all the data relating to the transfer pricing methodology (or formula). The logical consequence of this is that the importer will not be able to show that the price has not been influenced by the relationship if the Customs Service does not delay the final determination of the price until the data is available (i.e., until the end of the tax period).

It must be stressed the fact that the value of the goods for customs purposes should be based, to the greatest extent possible, on the transaction value of the goods being cleared.

In the 27th Session of the TCCV, the delegate of Argentina observed that Commentary 4.1 dealt with matters totally alien in nature to related-party transactions, and hence would not be relevant for the TCCV's purposes in dealing with transfer pricing situations.[356]

In our view, the legal support to sustain the acceptability of a price review clause which is based on the results of a transfer pricing methodology may be found in Article 13 of the GVC, in the General Introductory Commentary (which indicates that "the primary basis for customs value under this Agreement is 'transaction value' as defined in Article 1") and in the Preamble to the GVC (which indicates that "the basis for valuation of goods for customs purposes should, to the greatest extent possible, be the transaction value of the goods being valued"). Resorting to other instruments is actually not necessary if we follow the objectives of the GVC and, consequently, attempt to apply transaction value to the greatest extent possible. As indicated above, accepting a price review clause which is based on the results of an objective methodology of a transfer pricing study will permit the importer to have his goods valued under Article 1 of the GVC and, at the same time, to demonstrate that the relationship has not influenced the price.

It is clear that none of the examples of Commentary 4.1 refer to price review clauses which are dependent on the results of an OECD transfer pricing methodology and it is also clear that the members of the TCCV did not have in mind a price review clause of this type when they issued Commentary 4.1. But this does not mean that criteria underlying Commentary 4.1 are not valid and applicable in relation to this type of price review clause. The idea behind Commentary 4.1 is the possibility of delaying the final determination of customs value when it is not possible to determine the price payable at the time of importation, but when such price may be determined at a later point in time. Commentary 4.1 recognizes that: "... the Agreement recommends that, as far as possible, the transaction value of the goods being valued should serve as a basis for Customs valuation, and given that Article 13 provides for the possibility of delaying the final determination of Customs value ... price review clauses should not, of themselves, preclude valuation under Article 1 of the Agreement."

In addition, in the first example of Commentary 4.1, "... the final price will be determined on the basis of an agreed formula which recognizes increases or decreases of elements such as cost of labor, raw materials, overhead costs and other inputs incurred in the production of the goods."

356. WCO, Doc VT0663E1b.

These elements are as related to the goods being valued as those considered in the OECD transfer pricing methodologies. For example, the OECD cost-plus method is based on a formula which recognizes increases or decreases of cost of labor, raw materials, overhead costs and other inputs incurred in the production of the goods (i.e., the "cost" in the cost-plus formula). In fact, the year-end adjustments are generally necessary because the importer cannot predict the actual amounts for each of these elements prior to the end of the fiscal year. The "profit" element is as related to the production of the goods as the "cost" elements.

If the price review clause prescribes an objective mechanism to select the comparable companies and to make the appropriate economic adjustments to their financial information, then the formula is not within the control of the MNE. The whole process of fixing a transfer pricing policy is far from being under the control of the MNE. The most developed transfer pricing regulations are quite detailed on:

- how to make the comparability and functional analyses;
- how to select, accept and reject the comparables; and
- how to make economic adjustments to their financial information.

The MNE cannot just "choose" the comparables; it has to follow a screening process in public or private databases which is not at all discretionary. The MNE needs to follow strict rules in determining rejection or acceptance of the comparables, and the same is true for the economic adjustments to achieve adequate comparability. The adjusted financial information of these comparables will tell the MNE the profit margin which is required for the particular transaction to be at arm's length. The decreases or increases in the profit margins in a price review clause which is based on the results of an OECD transfer pricing methodology would not be within the control of the MNE.

Commentary 4.1 does not state that the elements listed in its examples are the only ones which may be considered in a price review clause. In our opinion, it is just the opposite. The wording used in the Commentary gives a clear idea that other elements may also exist.

What is important is that the price actually payable can be established on the basis of data or variables specified in the contract, and that those variables come into play some time after the goods have been imported. This is the case when the price review clause makes reference to a specific transfer pricing methodology based on the OECD Guidelines.[357]

One must bear in mind that the basis for valuation of goods for customs purposes should, to the greatest extent possible, be the transaction value of the goods being valued.[358] National legislation should provide for the possibility of declaring related-party transaction values, subject to eventual transfer pricing year-end adjustments to be introduced through pricing formulae or price review clauses.[359] Such pricing

357. *See supra* note 27.
358. *See* Preamble of the GVC.
359. In the Guide to Customs Valuation and Transfer Pricing, the WCO expressed the following views: "...Where the adjustment is initiated by the taxpayer and an adjustment is recorded in the accounts of the taxpayer and a debit or credit note issued, it could be, depending on the

formulae or price review clauses should be properly declared to customs at entry. This would logically imply the possibility of delaying the final determination of customs value. The purpose of this should always be to permit customs value to be determined under GVC Article 1 (i.e., to allow the importer to declare an appropriate arm's length price).[360]

With respect to the proceedings that have to be followed to introduce year-end adjustments, the WCO Guide to Customs Valuation and Transfer Pricing indicates that:

> ... Commentary 4.1 makes reference to Article 13 of the Agreement which provides for the possibility of delaying the final determination of Customs value. Article 13 requires Customs administrations to offer a facility to allow importers to clear their goods on provision of a security in cases where it becomes necessary to delay the final determination of the Customs value at the time of Customs clearance.
>
> The question arises whether it is necessary to require importers to lodge Customs declarations on the basis of a provisional declaration of value, covered by a security for the potential duty due. This creates a major resource implication for both business and Customs in terms of accounting and reconciliation procedures, particularly where a large number of Customs declarations are involved.
>
> This issue has been raised as a concern by business. As stated in the ICC's Policy Statement, Proposal 2:
>
> > "Companies should be permitted to perform customs value adjustments without being required to set up a provisional valuation procedure or being subject to penalties due to valuation adjustments."[361]
>
> Pending any international guidance on this point, it is for national Customs administrations to determine the Customs procedures required in these circumstances. As a basic requirement for Customs to consider an adjustment to the Customs value, it is clear that a transfer pricing policy should be in place prior to

---

nature of the adjustment, considered to have an impact on the price actually paid or payable for the imported goods, for Customs valuation purposes. In other cases, particularly where the adjustment has been initiated by the tax administration the impact may be only on the tax liability and not on the price actually paid or payable for the goods. Where such an adjustment takes place before the goods are imported then the price declared to Customs should take into account the adjustment. If, on the other hand, the adjustment takes place after importation of the goods, (i.e., it is recorded in the accounts of the taxpayer and the debit/credit note issued after Customs clearance of the goods), then Customs may consider that the Customs value is to be determined on the basis of the adjusted price, applying the principles established in Commentary 4.1..." (*See supra* note 32 at 66).

360. François Vincent suggested that "in the course of an APA, where the Canadian importer is using estimated purchase price during the year, for instance where a profitsplit method based on year-end results is the TPM [*transfer pricing method*], for customs purposes the price paid or payable should be that as finally determined and taking into consideration any compensating adjustment ... [W]hether in an APA context or otherwise, Canadian importers should be able to establish pricing mechanisms by which the final determination of the price paid or payable rests on some calculation to be done subsequently to the importation itself. This does not mean that this is a way by which rebates can indirectly be given effect for customs valuation purposes. However, it is definitively an avenue worth exploring for transfer pricing purposes and the legislation in play, the Customs Act and the ITA [Income Tax Act] may be reconcilable - contrary to past beliefs and positions." (Vincent, F., *Transfer Pricing in Canada*, notes furnished by Vincent to the author of the present work.)

361. The Guide indicates that the views and opinions expressed in the International Chamber of Commerce (ICC) Policy statement does not necessarily reflect those of the WCO or of the governments of its Members.

> the importation or clearance of the goods concerned, which indicates the criteria (or "formula") that will be applied to establish the final transfer price.
>
> Customs may require that the importer reports the existence of the transfer pricing policy in advance of importations. The policy may have been established in the context of an Advance Pricing Agreement. Customs would also typically require the business to report the final transfer price with details of the adjustment; this should be mandatory in the case of an upwards adjustment..."[362]

One timing issue that was raised during the First and Second Joint WCO/OECD Conferences on Transfer Pricing and Customs Valuation is that, when the TNMM is applied, typically the cost of goods sold ("COGS") is being tested and it is very unlikely that the COGS is the same as the purchases for the year. Thus, it was argued that the TNMM analysis for one given year could demonstrate that the COGS figure for such year was arm's length, but that this did not necessarily mean that the purchase prices of that year were also arm's length. In our view, this argument is not correct. The OECD Guidelines test prices, not COGS. The comparison of operating profit margins is an indirect way to test purchase prices. Even though it is true that there may be a mismatch between the COGS and the purchases of the year, this is part of the imperfect nature of this indirect mechanism for testing the arm's length character of a price, which affects tax and customs analyses in the same way. Either way, this imperfection of the method may be tackled, for customs purposes, by testing the prices of the transactions under examination using the transfer pricing study of the appropriate year which, eventually, could be the transfer pricing study of the year following the one in which the importation was actually made. For example, if the goods were imported in December of one year and sold during the next year, the customs administration could evaluate whether the relationship between buyer and seller influenced the price considering the transfer pricing analysis for the year in which the goods were sold. This would also be true in the case of price review clauses that are based on the results of transfer pricing studies. In the draft case study No. 6 (*see* above) presented to the Focus Group on Transfer Pricing and Customs Valuation on 26 October 2007 (which was also presented to the TCCV on 21 October 2008 during its 27th Session), we proposed a mechanism to allocate a year-end adjustment to the purchases of the year, considering the prices of goods included in the final inventory. However, in the author's view, this would add unnecessary complexity to the system and should only be used in those cases where the mismatch between the COGS and the purchases of the year is causing significantly unreliable results.[363]

19 CASE STUDIES

The following case studies were submitted by the author of this book to the Focus Group on Customs Valuation and Transfer Pricing, in the sidelines of the TCCV's 25th Session. They were intended to provide to the Focus Group and, later on, to the TCCV,

362. *See supra* note 32 at 68.
363. *See supra* note 27 (IBFD).

example on how to deal with transfer pricing year-end adjustments under Article 1 of the GVC applying the principles established in Commentary 4.1.

Case Study 6

APPLICATION OF ARTICLE 1.2

Facts of transaction

1. ICO, a distributor of country I, purchased and imported toasters from XCO, a related company of country X.

2. ICO did not purchase toasters or any other product from unrelated sellers. XCO did not sell toasters or goods of the same class or kind to unrelated buyers. There are no imports of identical or similar goods into Country I.

3. There is no available financial information about the sellers of goods of the same class or kind in country X.

4. There is available financial information about 2 distributors of blenders and rice cookers and 3 distributors of coffee makers and waffle makers in country I. The five distributors (the "Unrelated Distributors") purchased the goods from unrelated sellers of country X (the "Unrelated Sellers"). However, ICO indicated that accounting differences across ICO and the Unrelated Distributors in the treatment of costs affected the gross profit margin. ICO indicated that, in order to achieve consistent and reliable comparisons, it needed to adjust the gross profit margins arising from the transactions of the Unrelated Distributors. However, the information about the relevant costs was not readily available and, therefore, it was not possible to identify the particular costs for which an adjustment was required.

5. In particular, ICO, as well as the five Unrelated Distributors, offered a warranty with respect to all products so that the downstream price was uniform. The Unrelated Distributors, however, performed the warranty function but were, in fact, compensated by their Unrelated Sellers through a lower price. ICO did not perform the warranty function which was performed by XCO (products were sent back to the factory). However, XCO charged ICO a price that was higher than the price charged by the Unrelated Sellers to their Unrelated Distributors. The Unrelated Distributors accounted for the warranty expenses as operating expenses, and there was no detailed financial information, at an operating expense level, in order to identify and reclassify such warranty expenses.

6. ICO believed that there was a distortion in the gross profit margins, because the Unrelated Distributors accounted for the warranty expenses as operating expenses. If the Unrelated Sellers performed the warranty themselves, they would increase the transfer price, and therefore, the Unrelated Distributors' gross profit margins would be lower. Therefore, the margins of ICO and those of the Unrelated Distributors were not comparable until an adjustment was made to account for that difference. Since there was no detailed financial information, at an operating expense level, in order to identify and reclassify such warranty expenses, ICO believed that an adjustment could not be made.

7. ICO believed that it could, nevertheless, be possible to identify the net margin arising from the transactions and thereby ensure that a consistent measure is used. Consequently, ICO and XCO believed that the Transactional Net Margin Method, as described in Subchapter B of Part III of Chapter II of the OECD Guidelines was the most appropriate to examine the transaction value of the toasters.

8. ICO provided information showing that the net profit margins on the resale of toasters, blenders, rice cookers, coffee makers and waffle makers are generally the same in the small home appliances distribution industry.

9. The functional analysis showed that the number of functions performed by ICO, in connection with the toasters, was substantially similar to that of the five Unrelated Distributors. ICO and the five Unrelated Distributors distribute small home appliances. ICO and the five Unrelated Distributors have similar levels of inventories and fixed assets. The functional analysis showed that the risks assumed by ICO were substantially similar to those assumed by the five Unrelated Distributors.

10. In the prior fiscal year, the net profit margins of the five Unrelated Distributors when reselling their small home appliances were:

Unrelated Distributor 1	10 %
Unrelated Distributor 2	9 %
Unrelated Distributor 3	8 %
Unrelated Distributor 4	7 %
Unrelated Distributor 5	6 %

11. The median of the range was 8 %. The first and third quartiles were 7 % and 9 %, respectively.

12. ICO and XCO decided that the sales price would be a price that would allow ICO to make a net profit margin equal to the median of the range. However, they recognized that:

(i) The arm's length range of net profit margins of the Unrelated Distributors had to be determined on the basis of the Unrelated Distributors' financial information of the relevant fiscal year, and not of the prior fiscal year.
(ii) ICO's costs and expense figures would not be available at the time of importation but, rather, at the end of the fiscal year (once the cost of goods sold and the general sales and administrative expense figures are finished and reflected in the financial statements).

12. Therefore, they introduced in their Distribution Agreement a price review clause which provided that the price actually payable for the imported goods had to be established through a Transactional Net Margin Method (as described in the OECD Guidelines) on the basis of the information referred to in (i) and (ii) above. The Distribution Agreement provided that the parties would, at the beginning of the fiscal year, agree on a provisional transaction value (on the basis of the figures of the prior fiscal year and an estimation of the general sales and administrative expenses for the current fiscal year). However, the definitive transaction value – i.e., the price actually payable for the goods – was going to be determined within three months from the end of the fiscal year by applying the price review clause. The price review clause clearly prescribed an objective mechanism to select the comparable distributors and to make the appropriate economic adjustments to their financial information, and that it had to be applied in accordance with the transfer pricing regulations of country I. The Distribution Agreement also provided that the transaction value determined through the price review clause had to be the one used by ICO in determining its income tax liability in country I.

13. At the beginning of the fiscal year, ICO submitted the Distribution Agreement to Customs.

14. ICO sold the toasters to customers in Country I at 100 c.u. In order to fix the provisional transaction value, ICO and XCO agreed that ICO had to realize a net profit margin equal to the median of the prior fiscal year's arm's length range, i.e., 8%. ICO estimated that its general sales and administrative expenses (G&SA) per toaster for the current fiscal year would be approximately 20 c.u. Therefore, in order for ICO to realize a net margin of 8 %, XCO had to sell the toasters at a provisional transaction value of 72 c.u.

15. XCO sold the toasters to ICO during the fiscal year at the provisional transaction value of 72 c.u. and, at the end of the fiscal year, ICO had the following information in order to apply the price review clause:

Number of units sold to customers	1000
Price to customers	100 c.u.
Total sales	100.000 c.u.
Initial inventory	0 units
Purchases	1,000 units
Final inventory	0 units
Provisional transaction value (per unit)	72 c.u.
Cost of goods sold	**72,000 c.u.**
Gross margin	28,000 c.u.
Estimated GS&A per unit	20 c.u.
Actual GS&A (per unit)	15 c.u.
Total GS&A	**15,000 c.u.**
Net profits	13,000 c.u.
Net profit margin	13%

16. In the current fiscal year, the net profit margins of the five Unrelated Distributors when re-selling their small home appliances were:

Unrelated Distributor 1	9 %
Unrelated Distributor 2	8 %
Unrelated Distributor 3	7 %
Unrelated Distributor 4	6 %
Unrelated Distributor 5	5 %

17. The median of the range was 7 %. The first and third quartiles were 6 % and 8 %, respectively.

18. ICO and XCO applied the price review clause because ICO obtained a net profit margin which was above the median (and above the upper limit) of the current fiscal year's arm's length rate. The result of the adjustments was as follows:

Number of units sold to customers	1,000
Price	100 c.u.
Total sales	100,000 c.u.
Required net profit margin	7%
Required net profit	7,000 c.u.
Total GS&A	15,000 c.u.
Initial inventory	0 units
Purchases	1,000 units
Final inventory	0 units
Definitive cost of goods sold for required net profit	78,000 c.u.
PRICE PAID OR PAYABLE (PER UNIT) AFTER PRICE REVIEW CLAUSE	78 c.u.
Adjustment to provisional transaction value (per unit) to determine definitive transaction value	6 c.u.
Total adjustment to transaction values declared during the fiscal year	6,000 c.u.

16. Once the price was definitively settled, ICO submitted to Customs the transfer pricing documentation and the calculation of the definitive price payable to XCO. Since the definitive transaction value (78 c.u.) was above the provisional transaction value (72 c.u.) that was declared at the time of importation, ICO asked Customs to (i) accept the definitive transaction value as the basis for valuation of the goods imported during the fiscal year; (ii) receive the amended (reconciled) goods declarations for all the imports of the fiscal year; and (iii) liquidate Customs duties on the difference between the definitive transaction value and the provisional transaction value.

17. Commentary 4.1 indicates that the transaction value of imported goods, defined in Article 1 of the Agreement, is based on the price actually paid or payable for the goods. In the Interpretative Note to that Article, the price actually paid or payable is the total payment made or to be made by the buyer to the seller for the imported goods. Hence, in contracts containing a review clause, the transaction value of the imported goods must be based on the total final price paid or payable in accordance with the contractual stipulations. The Commentary provides, as an example, contracts which specify that the final price will be determined on the basis of an agreed formula which recognizes increases or decreases of elements such as cost of labor, raw materials, overhead costs and other inputs incurred in the production of goods. Since the price actually payable for the imported goods can be established on the basis of data specified in the contract, price review clauses of the type described in the Commentary should not be regarded as constituting a condition or consideration for which a value cannot be determined. Commentary 4.1 concludes that, given that the Agreement recommends that, as far as possible, the transaction value of the goods being valued should serve as a

basis for Customs valuation, and given that Article 13 provides for the possibility of delaying the final determination of Customs value, even though it is not always possible to determine the price payable at the time of importation, price review clauses should not, of themselves, preclude valuation under Article 1 of the Agreement.

18. However, Customs believed that the price review clause of the Distribution Agreement was not one of those described in Commentary 4.1, because the formula recognized increases or decreases of profit margins. Profit margins were not listed among the elements considered in Commentary 4.1 and, in addition, Customs believed that they were within the control of XCO and ICO.

In addition, Customs considered the fact that ICO had reasons to believe that an upward adjustment may be made to the price of the toasters as evidence that the relationship may have affected the price actually paid or payable. Consequently, transaction value was not considered to be the proper basis of appraisement.

Customs concluded, therefore, that recourse to an alternative method for determining Customs value of the toasters would be necessary.

Suggested determination of Customs value

19. The list of elements of Commentary 4.1 is illustrative and is not intended to comprise a complete list of the elements which may be included in an acceptable price review clause. In addition, if the increases or decreases of profit margins recognized in the price review clause agreed between ICO and XCO are based on objective market data, which may not be manipulated by the importer, then there is no reason to conclude that such a price review clause should preclude valuation under Article 1.

ADDITIONAL FACTS OF TRANSACTION FOR CASE STUDY 6

EFFECTS OF PRICE REVIEW CLAUSE ON FINAL INVENTORIES

Facts of transaction

1. Same as in CASE STUDY 6 except that, at the end of the fiscal year, ICO had the following information in order to apply the price review clause:

Number of units sold to customers	1,000
Price to customers	100 c.u.
Total sales	100,000 c.u.
Provisional transaction value (per unit)	72 c.u.
Initial inventory	0 units
Purchases	4,000 units (i.e. 288,000 c.u.)
Final inventory	3,000 units (i.e. 216,000 c.u.)
Cost of goods sold	72,000 c.u.
Gross margin	28,000 c.u.
Estimated GS&A per unit	20 c.u.
Actual GS&A (per unit)	15 c.u.

Total GS&A	15,000 c.u.
Net profits	13,000 c.u.
Net profit margin	13%

16. In the current fiscal year, the gross profit margins of the five unrelated distributors when reselling their small home appliances were:

Unrelated Distributor 1	9 %
Unrelated Distributor 2	8 %
Unrelated Distributor 3	7 %
Unrelated Distributor 4	6 %
Unrelated Distributor 5	5 %

17. The median of the range was 7 %. The first and third quartiles were 6 % and 8 %, respectively.

18. ICO and XCO applied the price review clause because ICO obtained a net profit margin which was above the median (and above the upper limit) of the current financial year's arm's length rate. The result of the adjustments was as follows:

Number of units sold to customers	1,000
Price	100 c.u.
Total sales	100,000 c.u.
Required net profit margin	7%
Required net profit	7,000 c.u.
Total GS&A	15,000 c.u.
Initial inventory	0 units
Purchases	4,000 units
Final inventory	3,000 units
Definitive cost of goods sold for required net profit	78,000 c.u.
Valuation of purchases	312,000 c.u.
Valuation of final inventory	234,000 c.u.
PRICE PAID OR PAYABLE (PER UNIT) AFTER PRICE REVIEW CLAUSE	78 c.u.
Adjustment to provisional transaction value (per unit) to determine definitive transaction value	6 c.u.
Total adjustment to transaction values declared during the fiscal year	24,000 c.u.

CASE STUDY 7

APPLICATION OF ARTICLE 1.2

Facts of transaction

1. Same facts as in CASE STUDY 6 but, in this case, ICO and XCO have not introduced a Price Review Clause in the Distribution Agreement. The price of 72 c.u. was fixed as a definitive price. No adjustment to the price paid or payable is made at the end of the fiscal year and, consequently, no additional invoice or debit or credit note is issued.

2. The transfer pricing documentation prepared by ICO at the end of the fiscal year is the same as in CASE STUDY 6. However, ICO does not make any adjustment to the cost of goods sold for income tax purposes because the tax legislation of country I does not allow transfer pricing adjustments reducing taxable income.

3. At the end of the fiscal year, ICO submitted to Customs the transfer pricing documentation and the calculation of the arm's length price. Since such arm's length price (78 c.u.) was above the price that was declared to Customs at the time of importation (72 c.u.), ICO asked Customs to (i) accept the arm's length price as the basis for valuation of the goods imported during the fiscal year; (ii) receive the amended (reconciled) goods declarations for all the imports of the fiscal year; and (iii) liquidate Customs duties on the difference between the arm's length price and the price declared to Customs at the time of importation.

Suggested determination of Customs value

4. Customs considered the conclusions of the transfer pricing documentation (and, in particular, the difference between the arm's length price and the price declared by ICO at the time of importation) as evidence that the relationship may have influenced the price actually paid or payable.

5. In the absence of a Price Review Clause, the price originally agreed by the buyer and the seller (which was declared to Customs at the time of importation) was definitive. Moreover, no additional amount was paid by ICO to XCO.

6. It was not possible to make a transfer pricing adjustment to the transaction value because such an addition to the price paid or payable in determining Customs value is forbidden under Article 8.4 of the Agreement.

7. Consequently, transaction value was not considered to be the proper basis of appraisement. Customs concluded, therefore, that recourse to an alternative method for determining Customs value of the toasters would be necessary.

20 YEAR-END ADJUSTMENTS IN THE UNITED STATES

The U. S. Customs Border Protection (CBP) had the opportunity to express its views on the issue of the year-end adjustments in several rulings.

In 1995, the U.S. Customs Service issued a "Notice to test the use of reconciliation for adjustments made to the price of imported merchandise by related-party companies under 26 U.S.C. 482."[364]

The Notice announced "a Customs plan to conduct a test for those related party importers which have reason to believe upward adjustments may be made to the price of imported merchandise for tax purposes pursuant to 26 U.S.C. 482."[365] The test was intended to facilitate the IRS/Customs decision as to whether reconciliation procedures provided a viable and appropriate circumstance for a taxpayer/importer to make a post entry upward adjustment to the price of imported merchandise.

The Notice explained that reconciliation would allow an importer to provide Customs with information not available at the time of entry summary filing and which is necessary to ascertain the final appraisement of imported merchandise. The reconciliation would have to be filed no later than 15 months from the date of the first entry summary filed under that reconciliation. A reconciliation would permit the liquidation of an entry despite the fact that undetermined information would be transmitted to Customs at a later time through reconciliation process.[366]

Interestingly, the Notice indicated that the valuation of the merchandise subject to reconciliation was not to be made under transaction value (i.e., GVC Article 1). The Notice established the following requisite:

> Each participant agrees that appraisement is under section 402(f) of the Tariff Act of 1930, as amended by the Trade Agreements Act of 1979 [*equivalent to the method laid down in GVC Article 7*], if, in fact, an upward section 482 adjustment is made for tax purposes.[367]

364. United States Customs Service, Department of Treasury, Vol. 60 Federal Register No. 128 (5 July 1995) 35105 [hereinafter "Notice"].
365. Suzanne Offerman indicates that this "Reconciliation Prototype was never implemented because there were no applicants." (Offerman Suzanne, "The Effect of Customs Reconciliation on Taxable Income" [1999] 25 Brooklyn J. Int'l L. 693). The "Announcement of National Customs Automation Program Test of Account-Based Declaration Prototype" (US Customs Service, Department of the Treasury, Vol. 62 Federal Register No. 59, 27 March 1997) indicated that "[i]n 1995 a notice was published in the Federal Register concerning a reconciliation prototype for related-party importers making upward adjustments to the price of imported merchandise, pursuant to 26 U.S.C. 482. This prototype did not become operational."
366. *See* Notice *supra* note 391.
367. This requisite was confirmed in "Notice to Test the Use of Reconciliation for Adjustments Made to the Price of Imported Merchandise by Related Party Companies under 26 U.S.C. 482" - Final Notice - (United States Customs Service, Department of the Treasury, Vol. 60, Federal Register No. 171, 5 September 1995). The US Customs Service expressed the following view: "Customs considers the fact that the related party importer has reason to believe that an upward adjustment may be made to the price of the imported merchandise as evidence that the relationship may have affected the price actually paid or payable for the merchandise. Therefore, transaction value will not be considered to be the proper basis of appraisement. The importer continues to have the right to have the hierarchy of appraisement applied to its transactions. However, if the importer claims another basis of appraisement, such as deductive value, then the importer will not be able to participate in the proposed test. This is due to the fact that the test is designed to determine how Customs can use the prices that the importer paid to the seller and the upward adjustments to those prices by using reconciliation. If a basis of appraisement is used that does not use these adjusted prices then the information is meaningless, for purposes of this test. Appraisement under section 402(f) of the Tariff Act of 1930, as amended by the Trade Agreements Act of 1979 allows Customs to utilize the importer's

One can clearly observe that the reconciliation test announced in the Notice was not one of the mechanisms that were suggested in this chapter for introducing year-end adjustments in transaction value. The purpose of pricing formulae and price review clauses - in addition to that of the mechanisms to delay final determination of the customs value under GVC Articles 1 and 13 - is to make possible a final appraisal of the imported goods under transaction value (as recommended in the Preamble of the GVC), and not to apply a new method of valuation under GVC Article 7.

The delay in the determination of the customs value should be directed towards the final declaration of an appropriate arm's length price under GVC Article 1.

Where adjustments to transaction value are made through pricing formulae or price review clauses, that have been properly declared at the time of the entry, there would be no reason to reject transaction value.

In effect, the price declared after the adjustment would be

(i) an arm's length transaction value;
(ii) the price actually paid or payable for the imported goods; and
(iii) the transaction value definitively declared to customs.[368]

---

information on the price it paid, and to reasonably appraise the merchandise using that information." However, Suzanne Offerman explains that "the legislative history of the Reconciliation program in the Mod Act indicates that reconciliation was a procedure implemented to help Customs and importers enter merchandise 'in a more business-like way, reducing paperwork and many of the administrative costs.' Nothing in its legislative history suggests that a reconciliation should change the manner in which transaction value is calculated. In fact, to the contrary, the legislative history of the Reconciliation program indicates that Congress wished to keep all Customs entry procedures the same, buy simply add the option to reconcile certain unknown value issues when they become available. Congress wrote 'a reconciliation will permit importers to submit information not available at the time of entry that is necessary ... to determine the correct amount of duty on a shipment' and yet, the method remains the same for: (i) determining transaction value for the underlying merchandise; (ii) liquidating merchandise at the time of the entry; and (iii) protesting Customs determinations. Given that valuation methods remain unchanged by the reconciliation program, entries flagged for reconciliation can be tested for an arm's length transaction price as any related party transaction is examined. A related party transaction is at arm's length when the price is uninfluenced by the relationship between the parties ... Moreover, an importer may file a reconciliation for entries imported from an unrelated party or a related party. The assumption that the relationship between the parties affected the price any time an importer flags for a reconciliation an entry imported from a related party prevents a related party from ever using reconciliation ... To discriminate against related parties is both unfair and unsupported in the legislative history of the Customs Valuation Statute and Reconciliation Program of the Mod Act, as a reconciliation is the sole manner by which an importer may liquidate entries and yet still hold open an unknown value. It follows that provided the circumstances of the sale show that the appraised value of the merchandise was not influenced by the relationship between the parties, there is no reason to treat entries that are flagged for reconciliation differently from an entry that is not." (Offerman *supra* note 392).

368. Meyer and Outman indicate that, in certain instances (e.g., where a taxpayer is audited for earlier years and a downward pricing adjustment is proposed), the ACS Reconciliation Prototype, implemented by the USCS (63 Fed. Reg. 6257) in the context of Section 637 of the North American Free Trade Agreement Implementation Act, may be used by a taxpayer/importer as a vehicle for maintaining customs flexibility until the transfer pricing issue has been solved (*See supra* note 52).

For this reason, we understand that the mechanisms to delay final determination of the customs value in cases of related-party transactions, should be based on the acceptance of transaction values subject to pricing formulae or price review clauses properly declared to customs at the time of the entry. In other words, where the importer believes that year-end adjustments may be made to the price of the imported goods, it must agree upon and declare the price subject to appropriate pricing formulae or price review clauses. Customs legislation should provide for appropriate procedures to enable importers to file provisional declarations of value and, subsequently - once year-end adjustments have been made pursuant to pricing formulae or price review clauses - to file definitive declarations of value on which final appraisal should be based.

In Ruling HQ W548314,[369] the CBP recognized that related-party transactions involve initial transfer prices that may be subject to adjustments after importation and that it is common for the transfer price to be determined in accordance with the company's transfer pricing policy/formula. CBP considered that the term "transfer pricing policy" referred to Advance Price Agreements, transfer pricing studies or legally binding inter-company agreements. It also recognized that, oftentimes, such policies provide the method for determining the transfer price, which could include the setting of an initial price and the making of various adjustments to the price after the importation based on specified criteria or year-end "compensating adjustments" to the transfer price to comply with the requirements of an APA entered into by the U.S. party and the IRS. CBP explained that, in previous rulings (HRL 544680) it had determined that if a transfer price was subject to post-importation adjustments and those adjustments were within the control of either the buyer or the seller, it would not be possible to consider that the price was determinable by an objective formula agreed upon prior to importation and, therefore, that transaction value was not applicable. In Ruling HQ W548314, CBP considered that, while the analysis of those previous rulings was consistent with CBP's interpretation at that time, it now concluded that notwithstanding that there may be some element of control, additional consideration had to be taken into account in evaluating whether an inter-company transfer pricing formula was an objective formula when it provides for post-importation adjustments to the price. CBP indicated that, when analyzing whether transaction value may be used between related parties, which could result in post-importation adjustments, the following factors should be examined to determine whether there is a fixed price, pursuant to a formula:

(1) a written "Intercompany Transfer Pricing Determination Policy" is in place prior to importation and the policy is prepared taking IRS code Section 482 into account;
(2) the U.S. taxpayer uses its transfer pricing policy in filing its income tax return, and any adjustments resulting from the transfer pricing policy are reported or used by the taxpayer in filing its income tax return;

369. CBP, 16 May 2012. Online: https://rulings.cbp.gov/index.asp?ru = w548314&qu = w548314& vw = detail.

(3) the company's transfer pricing policy specifies how the transfer price and any adjustments are determined with respect to all products covered by the transfer pricing policy for which the value is to be adjusted;
(4) the company maintains and provides accounting details from its books and/or financial statements to support the claimed adjustments in the United States; and,
(5) no other conditions exist that may affect the acceptance of the transfer price by CBP.

In the particular case, CBP found that since the Importer claimed adjustments for the fiscal years 2001 and 2002, and the written transfer pricing policy was executed by relevant parties on 11 February 2000, the agreement, and thus, the formula was in effect prior to the importations in question. CBP also noted that the formula had an impact on the reported Customs values and that the adjustments specifically resulted in lower declared values for the merchandise. Such transfer pricing adjustments indirectly related to the originally-reported price actually paid by the importer to the related seller and, based on the information provided by the importer, the related-party price (and the adjustments thereto) were determined pursuant to their transfer pricing policy. In addition, the importer had provided CBP with documentation that showed that adjustments were made on an entry-by-entry basis what demonstrated that adjustments were related to specific entries upon importation. Finally, the documents submitted by the importer showed how the adjustments were calculated and claimed.

CBP considered that, while some of the provisions of the transfer pricing policy could be considered to be within the "control" of the parties, the satisfaction of the factors mentioned above reduced the possibility of price manipulation and subjectivity in claiming post-importation adjustments. Therefore, CBP concluded that the importer's transfer pricing policy could be considered an objective formula in place prior to importation for purposes of determining the price for purposes of the transaction value method. In this sense, post-importation adjustments represented an element of the determination of the price actually paid or payable and simply reflected what should have been reported as the invoice price upon entry, had the exact price information of the imported merchandise been available at the time.

Interestingly, Ruling HQ W548314 indicates that the Importer used Reconciliation to report downward and upward post-importation adjustments to the value initially declared upon the importation of the goods. CBP explained that Reconciliation allows the importer, using reasonable care, to file entry summaries with CBP with the best available information, with the mutual understanding that certain elements, such as the declared value, remain outstanding. At a later date, when the specifics have been determined, the importer files a Reconciliation entry which provides the final and correct information. The Reconciliation entry is then liquidated, with a single bill or refund, as appropriate. The Reconciliation entry can be filed as late as 21 months from the date of the first entry summary filed under that Reconciliation with extensions of time as available to importers and considered that this flexibility makes Reconciliation an ideal vehicle to declare all upward or downward post-importation adjustments within the timeframe allowed by in the APA or a transfer pricing study or policy that directly (or indirectly) relate to the value of the merchandise.

In Ruling HQ H219515,[370] the issue under analysis was whether it was acceptable to take post-importation price adjustments (upward and downward) into account in determining transaction value. In that case, the importer had prepared its annual transfer pricing studies using the Comparable Profits Method (which is similar to the TNMM). As a consequence of utilizing the CPM approach, the importer believed that it could be required to make retroactive year-end (price) adjustments to meet its federal income tax obligations and to show that its prices are arm's length if the importer's profit margins fall outside the interquartile range specified in the transfer pricing study.

CBP found that the importer had a written transfer pricing study in place prior to importation and prepared in accordance with Section 482 of the IRS code, confirming the gross profits which were verified by other substantiating information. The importer also stated that it would use its transfer pricing study in filing its income tax return and report any adjustments to the IRS. The transfer pricing study covered all of the imported goods and specified the adjustments to be made. Under the CPM, adjustments would be made annually if needed to bring profits into the appropriate range, so that the final values of the imported goods declared to CBP would be at arm's length. Allocations of the adjustments would be proportionate for each product center so that each product center's gross margin conforms to the adjusted overall gross margin of the importer's U.S. distribution. The same methodology would be utilized to further allocate the gross margin of each product center to the gross margin of individual products. The company would book its adjustments as cost of goods sold affecting the value of the imported products.

CBP considered that, since these adjustments were adjustments to the profit and booked as cost of goods sold, the adjustments directly related to the value of the goods. Therefore, as long as the importer maintained and provided accounting details from its books and/or financial statements to support the post-importation adjustments upon making a claim, CBP found that the importer could claim downward and upward post-importation adjustments.

It is interesting to note that, even though CBP declined to rely solely on the importer's transfer pricing study in order to determine that the circumstances of the sale test was met, it concluded that this study further confirmed that the prices were already at arm's length since the importer's profit fell within the interquartile range, specified in the transfer pricing study. CBP concludes that "... were the importer to fall outside of the range of the acceptable gross profit margins (making the provisionally declared prices influenced by the relationship) and were the importer required to make adjustments to get within the range, transaction value would still be an appropriate method of appraisement because the importer already established that it meets the circumstances of the sale test based on the analysis in Section 2 above and which would be adjusted accordingly for the price to remain at arm's length for customs valuation purposes."

370. CBP, 11 October 2012. Online: https://rulings.cbp.gov/index.asp?ru = h037375&qu = H03737 5&vw = detail.

Conclusions

The existence of two different valuation regimes applied to the same transactions gave rise to the issue analyzed in the first chapter of this work: whether it is necessary and feasible to harmonize tax and customs transfer pricing regimes.

First, we decided which regimes were going to be analyzed, since in the tax field the existence of multiple pieces of tax legislation could make comparison extremely complex.

In the customs field, the GVC is the valuation system adopted by almost all the WTO members. Therefore, it seemed to be the appropriate example of customs valuation legislation. In the tax field, the MTC and the OECD Guidelines have been adopted (either partially or totally) by a great number of states (OECD members and non-OECD members). Although the OECD is not a legislative body that can dictate to its members, it enjoys a high level of prestige among its members, and most non-member states also hold it in high repute. Therefore, the MTC and the OECD Guidelines are an appropriate example of transfer pricing tax legislation. In addition, the OECD Guidelines are also a detailed set of rules that could be used to supplement the more general related-party provisions of the GVC.

Two arguments indicated that harmonization is, in fact, necessary or advisable. The first argument suggested that, where common principles and standards were adopted under both customs and transfer pricing regimes, the results obtained under such regimes should not be substantially different. The second argument, more practical in character, indicated that it did not appear to be reasonable (or at least, economically efficient) for an MNE to undertake two parallel valuation analyses for the same transaction.

In Section 3 we analyzed the question of whether harmonization was feasible. It was indicated that the GVC and the OECD Guidelines present many important differences which, in most cases, derive from the inhomogeneous nature of the instruments and taxes in question. However, it was also indicated that such differences were not so important where the interpreter focused on the related-party transactions of the GVC. We concluded that the fact that tax and customs rules shared common standards in relation to the treatment of related-party transaction, could make possible the process of harmonization.

In Chapter 2 we explored the standards for determining arm's length values and for examining whether the relationship influenced the transaction value. First, the definition of the arm's length principle was examined and it was concluded that such a principle is also reflected by GVC Article 1.2. We also observed that the example of Revenue Canada in its Memorandum D13-4-5 and that of the USCS in participating in the APA process, should be followed or even improved by the customs and tax administrations of those countries which have adopted the GVC and transfer pricing provisions based on the OECD Guidelines. We indicated that an advisory opinion or commentary from the Technical Committee on Customs Valuation of the World Customs Organization in line with this position would be recommendable and more than welcome by the trade community.

Second, we analyzed GVC Article 1.2(a), its Note and the other provisions of the GVC in order to determine whether the OECD Guidelines could be used to complement the related-party provisions of the GVC. We observed that importers and customs administrations could not be expected to solve complex transfer pricing problems solely on the basis of the general provisions of GVC Article 1.2 and its Note. This might produce inconsistent application of the related-party provisions of the GVC from one country to another, which is contrary to the principle of "uniformity and certainty" in the implementation of GATT Article VII. We concluded that the OECD Guidelines - being a detailed body of rules established for the purpose of applying the arm's length standard - could be applied broadly in the context of GVC Article 1.2. We also concluded that the use of the OECD Guidelines to supplement the provisions of Article 1.2 and its Note would help to harmonize not only tax and customs rules, but also implementation of the GVC's related-party provisions among the WTO Member countries.

Third, we explored the guidance provided by the OECD Guidelines concerning the application of the arm's length principle. We analyzed the application of the comparability analysis in the context of GVC Article 1.2, paying special attention to the provisions of the GVC relating to product comparability, to the functions performed by the parties to a transaction, and to the economic circumstances and business strategies of such parties. Finally, we evaluated the possibility of undertaking combined examination of separate transactions under the GVC, of the use of arm's length ranges and of the use of multiple-year data. In each case we determined that the OECD Guidelines are generally applicable, but that in certain circumstances (e.g., the combined examination of separate transactions), special care has to be taken since their application might not be consistent with GVC Article 1, or with the general objectives and principles of customs law. We also observed that these rules must only be applied for comparability purposes.

In Chapter 3 we examined the OECD arm's length methods in connection with GVC Article 1.2 and its Note. First, we distinguished such methods from those laid down in GVC Articles 2, 3, 5 and 6. However, we said that the principles underlying such articles could be useful to interpret the GVC's related-party provisions and that, therefore, they could provide guidance as to how the OECD arm's length methods should be applied in the context of Article 1.2.

Second, we explored the CUP method and the comparability criteria to be observed in applying such method. We indicated that the Guidelines follow criteria that are consistent with those underlying the GVC. In this context, we examined the solutions the OECD Guidelines provide for situations where there is a difference between the controlled and the uncontrolled price indicating that the conditions of the commercial and financial relations of the related parties are not arm's length. We observed that the solutions suggested by the Guidelines are not consistent with those of the GVC, since no substitute value could be determined under Article 1.2. It was concluded that this fact might produce inconsistencies between the results derived from the application of tax and customs rules. It was also concluded that the most consistent results could be achieved where the importer undertook a thorough transfer pricing analysis, prior to declaration of any transaction value to customs or tax authorities. In effect, the application of the OECD Guidelines is only possible where the importer can demonstrate that the relationship did not influence the price under Article 1.2(a). Where the importer is unable to demonstrate such circumstances, the transaction value is rejected and the methods of GVC Articles 2, 3, 5, 6 and 7 become applicable. The results obtained by the customs administrations under these methods might not be consistent with those arrived at by the tax administrations on the basis of the OECD Guidelines.

Third, we examined the resale price method in connection with GVC Article 1.2(a). We determined that this method is applicable under that article, and that, even though the GVC showed a preference for internal comparables over external comparables, the latter could also serve as a guide. Next, we analyzed the provisions regarding the application of the method. It was concluded that under the GVC, as well as under the OECD Guidelines, less product comparability might be required in using the resale price method. However, closer comparability of products would produce better results. It was also concluded that the resale price method depends on comparability of functions performed, since the amount of the resale price margin is often influenced by the level of activities performed by the re-seller. It was also determined that the provisions of the OECD Guidelines and of the GVC are consistent with regards both to the superdeductive method, and to the time elapsed between purchase and resale. Finally, we observed that, under the resale price method, customs administrations have to be prepared to examine the existence of transfers, licenses, ownership and/or development and maintenance of intangible property where profit margins have to be compared. This could constitute part of the circumstances surrounding the sale of tangible property.

Fourth, we analyzed the application of the cost-plus method in the context of GVC Article 1.2. We indicated that one of the examples of Article 1.2 could be regarded as derived from the application of such a method. It was concluded that the cost-plus method is applicable in the context of GVC Article 1.2, and observed that the OECD Guidelines, read together with the provisions of Article 6 and its Note, could provide useful guidance for applying such method in such context. Next, it was indicated that, even though the GVC shows a preference for internal comparables, external comparables could also serve as a guide in applying the cost-plus method. This statement was supported by, among others, the Note to GVC Article 6. We also analyzed the provisions of the GVC and OECD Guidelines regarding the effect of economic circumstances and relative efficiency of the enterprises being compared on cost-plus analyses. It was again found that such provisions are consistent. Finally, we determined that, in applying the cost-plus method under both the OECD Guidelines and the GVC, due account has to be taken of functions performed by the enterprises being compared, and of accounting consistency of the data used for the purposes of comparison.

Finally, we analyzed the transactional profit methods of the OECD Guidelines and their possible application in the context of GVC Article 1.2. We concluded that both the profit split method and the transactional net margin method, could only be used in determining whether the relationship influenced the price in cases where traditional transaction methods could not be reliably applied alone, or could not be applied at all. These would be considered methods of last resort. We observed that those methods have to be applied in a manner consistent with the general principles of the GVC.

The purposes of Chapter 4 were different from those of Chapters 1, 2 and 3. Under Chapter 4, we assumed that the OECD Guidelines were applicable in the context of GVC Article 1.2. Our point of departure was to distinguish transaction value from the tax base of customs duties, or from any of the different elements of the tax base of income taxes. Although the determination of an arm's length transaction value should be equivalent under tax and customs rules, the computation of the customs value and of the tax value of imported goods might be significantly different. Importers/taxpayers usually determine and declare tax bases. Likewise, tax and customs administrations have information about such tax bases and, consequently, base their examinations on such information. If, e.g., a customs administration determined that the customs values declared by the importer/taxpayer were acceptable under GVC Article 1.2(a), then this information could be useful for the tax administration to avoid double scrutiny of the same transactions. However, the tax administration could not use the information collected by the customs administration (usually, information about the tax base of customs duties) if the differences in computation of tax and customs values are not duly identified and accounted for. If the taxpayer has declared arm's length transaction values for tax and customs purposes, the customs value and the tax value (e.g. adjusted cost base, inventory cost or COGS) should be equivalent, once the differences between such values have been identified, and appropriate adjustments to account for such differences have been made. A taxpayer could present this argument to prevent customs and tax administrations from taking inconsistent positions in determining the appropriate arm's length transaction value. The purposes of Chapter 4 were (i) to analyze the tax base of customs duties (as defined by the GVC), (ii) to identify additions to or deductions from such a tax base that are required or allowed under the GVC, and that are not usually required or allowed under income tax statutes, and (iii) to indicate in which situations adjustments have to be made to account for differences in tax bases of customs duties and income taxes.

We analyzed, among other things, the provisions of the GVC, advisory opinions and decisions concerning discounts and interest charges. We identified the cases in which discounts do not affect transaction value for purposes of GVC Article 1, and indicated that, where such discounts affect the value of the imported goods for income tax purposes, an appropriate adjustment is required in order to compare tax and customs values. We also identified the cases in which interest charges are to be included in transaction value for the purposes of GVC Article 1, and the possible adjustments that could be required – in comparing tax and customs results – to account for such inclusion.

Subsequently, we examined the additions to customs value required under GVC Article 8. We observed that certain elements, such as buying commissions and certain types of assists and royalties which are not required to be added to customs value under Article 8, might be required to be added to the tax value of imported goods under some income tax statutes. In these cases, an adjustment to account for these elements might be necessary in comparing tax and customs values. It was also observed that adjustments to account for the exclusion of transport and insurance costs from customs value, are often necessary in cases of countries that adopted an FOB basis of valuation for customs purposes pursuant to GVC Article 8.

Then, we examined the deductions from transaction value allowed under the Note to GVC Article 1. It was indicated that, when comparing tax and customs values, an adjustment for such elements may also be required to make customs and tax figures homogeneous.

Finally, we concluded that uniformity in applying the notion of customs value and its adjustments would be recommendable in order to undertake a process of harmonization between tax and customs valuation rules. WTO members should undertake this process of harmonization paying special attention to the work of the Technical Committee on Customs Valuation of the World Customs Organization and to the way in which the different countries have been implementing the provisions of the GVC.

Under Chapter 5, we examined some adjustments an importer might be required to make to the price that is originally declared to customs, as a consequence of transfer pricing studies or determinations (usually for tax purposes). Year-end adjustments may be necessary when there is a cost-plus pricing and the customs entry is made when the costs have not been finalized. The importer would not be able to declare an arm's length price unless customs administrations permit him to introduce year-end adjustments to transaction value.

It was concluded that the use of pricing formulae or price review clauses is an appropriate way to introduce year-end adjustments to transaction value. Such pricing formulae or price review clauses have to be agreed upon prior to the entry of the goods through customs, and properly declared to customs at the time of such entry. Where adjustments to the transaction value are made under such conditions, the adjusted transaction value should be accepted as basis of appraisal under GVC Article 1, since such transaction value would be: (i) an arm's length value; (ii) the price actually paid or payable for the imported goods; and (iii) the transaction value definitively declared to customs. It was also concluded that customs legislation should provide for appropriate procedures to enable importers to submit provisional declarations of value, and subsequently to submit definitive declarations of adjusted values on which final appraisal should be based. In other words, customs administrations should delay the final determination of transaction value, in order to appraise the imported goods on the basis of the total final price paid or payable in accordance with the contractual stipulations.

Appendix: Additional Case Studies

CASE STUDY 8

Facts of transaction

1. ICO, a distributor of country I, purchased and imported concentrate (A) from XCO, a related company of country X.
2. Concentrate (A) is simply diluted with ordinary water and consumer packed before sale.
3. Concentrate (A) is sold only to ICO in country I and there are no importations of identical or similar goods into country I.
4. ICO purchased and imported Concentrate (B) from an unrelated seller in country X. Concentrate (B) is also simply diluted with ordinary water and consumer packed before sale.
5. Concentrates (A) and (B) may be considered as goods of the same class or kind.
6. ICO provided Customs with a transfer pricing study which was prepared on the basis of a resale price method, as described in Subchapter C(ii) of Chapter II of the OECD Guidelines.[1]
7. Since ICO does not buy Concentrate (A) from unrelated sellers, then the gross profit margin was established by reference to the gross profit margin that was earned in comparable transactions of Concentrate (B).
8. The functional analysis showed that the number of functions performed by ICO, in connection with Concentrate (A), was substantially similar to that performed in connection with Concentrate (B). ICO had similar levels of inventories of Concentrates (A) and (B) and used the same fixed assets.
9. In the relevant fiscal year, the gross profit margin of ICO when reselling Concentrate (A) was 30.5 %. In the same fiscal year, the gross profit margin when reselling Concentrate (B) was also 30.5%

1. OECD Transfer Pricing Guidelines 1998.

10. In order to calculate the gross profit margin realized by ICO in the particular sales under examination, ICO had to use its financial statements for the relevant fiscal year because it did not prepare financial statements for sub-periods within a fiscal year (e.g. quarterly financial statements). Likewise, the calculation of cost of goods sold was made on an annual basis, taking into account initial inventories, purchases during the year and final inventories. Consequently, the calculation of the gross profit margin in each particular transaction had to be made with reference to the gross profit margin calculated for the complete fiscal year.
11. In addition, ICO provided information to Customs showing that the purchase prices of Concentrates (A) and (B) have not changed during the relevant fiscal year.
12. XCO owns a trademark which may or may not be applied to Concentrate (A) when it is sold after dilution depending on the terms of a particular sale for importation. The fee for use of the trademark is paid on a per unit basis.
13. ICO resold Concentrate (A) with trademark. As a condition of the sale for import there was a requirement for payment of the fee. During the relevant fiscal year, ICO paid a fee of 30 c.u. per unit.
14. XCO licensed the trademark to three unrelated licensees in countries J, K and L. ICO's transfer pricing documentation shows that the transactions with the three unrelated licensees are in most aspects comparable to the transaction with ICO. Firstly, ICO and the unrelated licensees could expect similar benefits from the intangible property. Secondly, there were no substantial differences in the geographic markets of the transactions and the rights were not licensed on an exclusive basis. Thirdly, ICO and the licensees had similar distribution networks.
15. With respect to the trademark fee, ICO's transfer pricing documentation tested the arm's length character of that fee on the basis of a Comparable Uncontrolled Price Method, as described in Chapter II.C(i) and paragraph 6.23 of Chapter VI.C(iii) of the OECD Guidelines.[2]
16. During the relevant fiscal year, the three unrelated licensees also paid a fee of 30 c.u. per unit. Therefore, the transfer pricing study concluded that the license fee charged by XCO to ICO was at arm's length.

Suggested determination of Customs value

17. The methods of the OECD Guidelines should be accepted in the context of Article 1.2, as long as they are useful and reliable in determining whether the relationship influenced the price. On these grounds, importers and Customs administrations would be authorized - where appropriate - to use the resale price method in examining the circumstances surrounding the sale.

2. *Ibid.*

18. An adequate level of product comparability – as required under the resale price method – is observed among the transactions of Concentrates (A) and (B).
19. Customs established that the prices charged to ICO for Concentrate (A) were adequate to recover all ICO's costs. It also established that ICO's gross profit margin in sales of Concentrate (A) was equal to the gross profit margin realized in sales of Concentrate (B). This shows that ICO's gross profit margin in sales of Concentrate (A) is adequate to recover a profit that is representative of the profit realized in sales of goods of the same class or kind. This also shows that the price charged by XCO to ICO in sales of Concentrate (A) is at arm's length. In accordance with paragraph 3 of the Interpretative Note to Article 1.2, transaction values in respect of Concentrate (A) may be acceptable for Customs purposes.
20. Since the license fee is required by XCO as a condition of the sale for import of Concentrate (A), then such license fee must be added to the price actually paid or payable for Concentrate (A). (See Advisory Opinion 4.6)
21. This addition to the price paid or payable does not affect the examination of the circumstances of sale under Article 1.2 or the use of the transfer pricing documentation in that context. In order to determine whether the relationship influenced the price, a comparison between the prices or profit margins of the controlled and uncontrolled transactions can be made before the license fee is added to the price paid or payable.

CASE STUDY 9

Facts of transaction

1. Same facts as in CASE STUDY 8, except that:
   (i) During the relevant fiscal year, the three unrelated licensees paid a fee of 40 c.u. per unit. Therefore, the transfer pricing study concluded that the license fee charged by XCO to ICO was not at arm's length.
   (ii) The Tax Administration of country X required XCO to make a transfer pricing adjustment increasing the license fee charged to ICO during the relevant fiscal year to 40 c.u.
   (iii) XCO made the transfer pricing adjustment and required ICO to make the corresponding adjustment. The Tax Administration of country I accepted the corresponding adjustment under Article 9.2 of the Convention to Avoid Double Taxation between countries X and I.
   (iv) The adjustments, however, were technical in character. XCO did not charge to ICO the extra 10 c.u. per imported unit and, consequently, ICO did not pay any additional amount to XCO.

Suggested determination of Customs value

2. The transfer pricing adjustment does not affect the examination of the circumstances of sale under Article 1.2 or the use of the transfer pricing documentation in that context. As in CASE STUDY 8, in order to determine whether the relationship influenced the price, a comparison between the prices or profit margins in the controlled and uncontrolled transactions can be made independently from the examination of the arm's length character of the license fee.
3. Since ICO did not pay the extra 10 c.u. per imported unit to XCO, then the technical transfer pricing adjustment to the license fee must not be added to the price actually paid or payable.

CASE STUDY 10

Facts of transaction

1. Same facts as in CASE STUDY 9 but, in this case, the transfer pricing adjustment was not technical. XCO charged to ICO the extra 10 c.u. per imported unit and, consequently, ICO did pay the additional 10 c.u. per imported unit to XCO.

Suggested determination of Customs value

2. As in CASE STUDY 9, the transfer pricing adjustment does not affect the examination of the circumstances of sale under Article 1.2 or the use of the transfer pricing documentation in that context. In order to determine whether the relationship influenced the price, a comparison between the prices or profit margins in the controlled and uncontrolled transactions can be made independently from the examination of the arm's length character of the license fee.
3. Since ICO did pay the extra 10 c.u. per imported unit to XCO, then the transfer pricing adjustment to the license fee must be added to the price actually paid or payable.

CASE STUDY 11

Facts of transaction

1. ICO, a distributor of country I, purchased and imported concentrate (A) from XCO, a related company of country X.
2. Concentrate (A) is simply diluted with ordinary water and consumer packed before sale.
3. Concentrate (A) is sold only to ICO in country I and there are no importations of identical or similar goods into country I.

4. UCO, another distributor of country I, purchased and imported Concentrate (B) from an unrelated seller in country X. Concentrate (B) is also simply diluted with ordinary water and consumer packed before sale. Concentrate (B) was sold under a trademark, which was owned by the unrelated seller.
5. Concentrates (A) and (B) may be considered as goods of the same class or kind.
6. ICO provided Customs with a transfer pricing study which was prepared on the basis of a resale price method, as described in Subchapter C(ii) of Chapter II of the OECD Guidelines.[3]
7. Since ICO does not buy Concentrate (A) from unrelated sellers, then the gross profit margin was established by reference to the gross profit margin that was earned by UCO in comparable transactions of Concentrate (B).
8. The functional analysis showed that the number of functions performed by ICO, in connection with Concentrate (A), was substantially similar to that performed by UCO in connection with Concentrate (B). ICO and UCO had similar levels of inventories of Concentrates (A) and (B), respectively, and used the same fixed assets.
9. In the relevant fiscal year, the gross profit margin of ICO when reselling Concentrate (A) was 35 %.
10. In the same fiscal year, the gross profit margin of UCO when reselling Concentrate (B) was 30 %.
11. XCO owns a trademark which may or may not be applied to Concentrate (A) when it is sold after dilution depending on the terms of a particular sale for importation. The fee for use of the trademark is paid on a per unit basis.
12. ICO resold Concentrate (A) with trademark. As a condition of the sale for import there was a requirement for payment of the fee. During the relevant fiscal year, ICO paid a fee of 30 c.u. per unit.
13. XCO did not license the trademark to unrelated licensees.
14. The trademarks owned by XCO (in respect of Concentrate A) and by the unrelated seller (in respect of Concentrate B) were comparable in most aspects, including the value added by the trademark to the product, taking into account consumer acceptability, geographical significance, market share and sales volume.
15. Therefore, in order to achieve comparability between the gross profit margins in transactions of Concentrates (A) and (B), ICO adjusted its gross profit margin by adding the license fee paid to XCO to the purchase price of Concentrate (A).
16. After the adjustment, ICO's gross profit margin was equal to UCO's gross profit margin (i.e. 30 %).

3. *Ibid.*

Suggested determination of Customs value

17. The methods of the OECD Guidelines should be accepted in the context of Article 1.2, as long as they are useful and reliable in determining whether the relationship influenced the price. On these grounds, importers and Customs administrations would be authorized - where appropriate - to use the resale price method in examining the circumstances surrounding the sale.
18. An adequate level of product comparability – as required under the resale price method – is observed among the transactions of Concentrates (A) and (B) (except for the incidence of a trademark in the purchase price of Concentrate (B) for which an adjustment was made).
19. The OECD Guidelines indicate that "in the sale of goods incorporating intangible property, it may also be possible to use the CUP or resale price method following the principles in Chapter 2. When marketing intangibles (e.g. a trademark) are involved, the analysis of comparability should consider the value added by the trademark, taking into account consumer acceptability, geographical significance, market shares, sales volume, and other relevant factors."
20. On the basis of the transfer pricing documentation, Customs established that the prices charged to ICO for Concentrate (A) were adequate for ICO to recover all its costs. It also established that ICO's adjusted gross profit margin in sales of Concentrate (A) was equal to the gross profit margin realized by a comparable unrelated distributor in sales of Concentrate (B). This shows that ICO's adjusted gross profit margin in sales of Concentrate (A) is adequate to recover a profit that is representative of the profit realized by unrelated distributors in sales of goods of the same class or kind. This also shows that the price charged by XCO to ICO in sales of Concentrate (A) is at arm's length. In accordance with paragraph 3 of the Interpretative Note to Article 1.2, transaction values in respect of Concentrate (A) may be acceptable for Customs purposes.
21. Since the license fee is required by XCO as a condition of the sale for import of Concentrate (A), then such license fee must be added to the price actually paid or payable for Concentrate (A). (See Advisory Opinion 4.6)
22. This addition to the price paid or payable does not affect the examination of the circumstances of sale under Article 1.2 or the use of the transfer pricing documentation in that context. In order to determine whether the relationship influenced the price, it was necessary to add the license fee to the price paid or payable to achieve an adequate level of comparability between the profit margins of the controlled and uncontrolled transactions.

Bibliography

International Material

World Trade Organization

International Agreements

Agreement on Implementation of Article VII of the General Agreement on Tariffs and Trade 1994 included in *The Final Act Embodying the Results of the Uruguay Round of Multilateral Trade Negotiations*", 15 April 1994, at 171, online: <http:// www.wto.org:80/wto/english/ docs_e/legal_e/final_e.htm> (date accessed: 3 August 2000).

Decisions

WTO, Committee on Customs Valuation, Decision 3.1, *Treatment of Interest Charges in the Customs Value of Imported Goods*, WTO Doc. Val/6/Rev.1.

WTO, Committee on Customs Valuation, *Decision regarding cases where customs administrations have reasons to doubt the truth or accuracy of the declared value WTO*, Doc. G/Val/1 (27 April 1995).

Reports

WTO, Council for Trade in Goods, *WTO Trade Facilitation Symposium (9/10 March 1998), Report by the Secretariat, Panel 2 – Import and export procedures and requirements, including customs and border crossing problems – D – Compendium of all presentations – "Practical Problems for traders in the area of customs valuation"*, WTO Doc. G/C/W/115 (19 May 1998), online: <http:// www.wto.org/wto/ddf/ep/public.html> (date accessed: 3 August 2000).

European Community

Conventions

EC, *Convention 90/463/EEC of 23 July 1990*, [1990] O.J. L. 225, 20.8.1990.

Regulations

EU, *Regulation No 952/2013 of the European Parliament and of the Council of 9 October 2013 laying down the Union Customs Code*, O.J.L 269/1 10 October 2013 *EU, Commision Implementing Regulation 2015/2447 of 24 November 2015 laying down detailed rules implementing certain provisions of Regulation (EU) No 952/2013 of the European Parliament and the Council laying down the UCC*, O.J.EUL 343/558 29 December 2015

Legislation

Argentina

Constitución de la Nación Argentina, as amended in 1994.

Ley de Impuesto a las Ganancias, t.o. 1997 y sus modificaciones (Argentina), Article 15, as amended by *Ley 25.239* (B.O. 31 December 1999).

Ley de Impuesto a las Ganancias, t.o. 1997 y sus modificaciones (Argentina), Article 93, as amended by *Ley 25.239* (B.O. 31 December 1999).

United States

19 U.S.C. §1401, 1997 edition.

Internal Revenue Code, 26 U.S.C. §482 (1.5.99).

Internal Revenue Code, 26 U.S.C. §1059A (1.5.99).

26 CFR §1.1059A-1 (revised as of 1 April 2000).

US, United States Customs Service, Department of the Treasury, *Announcement of National Customs Automation Program Test of Account-based Declaration Prototype*, Vol. 62 Federal Register No. 59, 27 March 1997.

US, United States Customs Service, Department of Treasury, *Notice to Test the Use of Reconciliation for Adjustments made to the Price of Imported Merchandise by Related Party Companies under* 26 U.S.C. 482, Vol. 60 Federal Register No. 128 (5 July 1995) 35105.

US, United States Customs Service, Department of the Treasury, *Notice to Test the Use of Reconciliation for Adjustments Made to the Price of Imported Merchandise by Related Party Companies under* 26 U.S.C. 482 – *Final Notice*, Vol. 60, Federal Register No. 171, 5 September 1995).

Canada

Customs Act [1986, c.1 assented to 13 February 1986].

Jurisprudence

Brittingham v. *Commissioner*, 66 TC 373 (1976), aff'd [1979], 598 F2d 1375 (5th Cir. 1979). (United States).

ESSO S.A.P.A. v. *A.N.A. s/ recurso de apelación* (7 October 1993) Tribunal Fiscal de la Nación, Sala G, File No. 6872-A (Argentina).

Shell Canada Ltd. v. *Canada* [1999] 3 S.C.R. 622 (Canada).

Hauptzollamt Karlsruhe v. *Gebrüder Hepp GmbH & Co. KG* (25 July 1991), European Court reports 1991 page I-04301 (European Community).

Nissho Iwai American Corporation v. *United States*, 98 F.2d 505 (1992) (United States).

Rosenthal-Netter, Inc. v. *United States*, 12 CIT 77, 679 F.Supp. 21 (1988) aff'd 861 F.2d 261 (1988) (United States).

Jay-Arr Slimwear, Inc. v. *United States*, 12 CIT 133, 681 F.Supp. 875 (1988) (United States).

Moss Manufacturing Co. Inc. v. *United States*, 13 CIT 420, 714 F.Supp. 1223 (1989) (United States).

Advisory Opinions, Commentaries, Rulings and Memoranda

Canada Border Services Agency, Memorandum D13-4-5 "Transaction value method for related persons" (17 September 2015) [hereinafter "Memorandum"] online: <http://www.cbsa-asfc.gc.ca/publications/dm-md/d13/d13-4-5-eng.html> (date accessed: 8 July 2017).

US, Internal Revenue Service, Private Ruling No. 9543048 (1 August 1995).

US, United States Customs Service, Ruling No. 546211 (10 June 1996), online: <http://www.customs.ustreas.gov/impoexpo/impoexpo.htm> (date accessed: 3 August 2000).

US, United States Customs Service, Ruling No. 544436 (4 February 1991), Customs Bulletin Vol. 25, No. 18 (June 1991).

US, United States Customs Service, Rulings: 542122 (4 September 1980), 542141 (4 February 1981), 542261 (11 March 1981), 542302 (27 February 81), 542412 (27 March 1981), 542696 (22 February 1982), 542797 (19 May 1982), 542900 (9 December 1982), 543070 (18 July 1995), 543246 (30 April 1984), 543324 (8 August 1984), 543457 (9 April 1985), 543537 (14 February 1986), 543568 (30 May 1986), 543820 (12 December 1986), 543951 (23 September 1987), 543984 (22 February 1988), 544686 (31 August 1994), 544781 (4 March 1994), 544809 (1 June 1994), 545361 (20 July 1995), 545638 (13 February 1995), 545800 (28 June 1996), 545813 (11 September 1996), 546037 (31 January 1996), 546285 (7 June 1996), 546449 (6 January 1998) (*Customs Valuation Encyclopedia*, USCS, 1998).

WCO, Technical Committee on Customs Valuation, Advisory Opinions No. 1.1, 4.1 to 4.13, 5.1, 5.3, 7.1, 12.1, and 16.1 (*Customs Valuation Compendium*, Brussels, WCO, 1997).

WCO, Technical Committee on Customs Valuation, Commentaries No. 1.1, 4.1, 8.1, 9.1, 14.1, 15.1, 17.1, 19.1, 23.1 and 25.1 (*Customs Valuation Compendium*, Brussels, WCO, 1997).

WCO, Technical Committee on Customs Valuation, Case Studies No. 1.1, 2.1, 2.2, 10.1 and 14.1 (*Customs Valuation Compendium*, Brussels, WCO, 1997).

EC, European Commission, Directorate General XXI - Customs and Indirect Taxation, Customs Code Committe, Commentaries No. 3, 5, and 7 (*Compendium of Customs Valuation Texts*, Brussels, EC Customs Code Committee, 1997).

Secondary Material: Books

Alsina *et al.*, *Codigo Aduanero. Comentarios – Antecedentes – Concordancias*, Vol. 4 (Buenos Aires, Abeledo Perrot).

Bakker, A and Obuoforibo, B. (editors), *Transfer Pricing and Customs Valuation. Two worlds to tax as one.* (IBFD, 2009).

Hammer *et al.*, *International Transfer Pricing – OECD Guidelines* (WL, 2000), online: WL (Hammer, Lowell, Burge & Levey, Transfer Pricing Treatises).

Inama, S. and Vermulst, E., *Customs and Trade Laws of the European Community* (London, Kluwer Law International, 1999).

Jarach, D., *El Hecho Imponible*, 3rd ed. (Buenos Aires, Abeledo-Perrot, 1982).

Jarach, D., *Finanzas Publicas y Derecho Tributario* (Buenos Aires, Ed. Cangallo, 1985).

Krishna, V., *Fundamentals of Canadian Income Tax* (Toronto, Carswell, 1993).

Lasok, D., *The Trade and Customs Law of the European Union*, 3rd ed. (London, Kluwer Law International, 1998).

Levey, M., *Taxation of Foreign Controlled Business* (WL, 2000), online: WL (Levey, Taxation of Foreign Controlled Business, Tax Treatises).

Lowell, Burge & Brieger, *US International Transfer Pricing* (WL, 2000), on line: WL (Lowell, Burge & Brieger, US International Transfer Pricing) (date accessed: 28 May 2000).

Sherman, S. and Glanshoff, H., *Customs Valuation. Commentary on the GATT Customs Valuation Code* (New York, Kluwer Law and Taxation Publishers, 1988).

Terra, B. and Wattel, P., *European Tax Law*, 2nd ed. (London, Kluwer Law International, 1997).

Secondary Material: Articles

Ellis, J., "Aggregation of Income and Losses from Various Sources" in *Canadian Taxation* (Toronto; Richard de Boo, 1981) at 446.

Jovanovich, J. M. "Transfer Pricing for Customs and Tax Purposes" (Periódico Económico Tributario - No. 333, 334, 335 y 336) - La Ley, Buenos Aires, 2005). Paper submitted to the TCCV at its 20th Session.

Musso de Zunino, C., *Valoración aduanera en las importaciones. Problemas que se suscitan en relación a la aplicación del actual régimen de valor* (Derecho Tributario, 9, 227).

Neville, M., "Customs planning may avoid conflict with IRS transfer pricing rules" (1993) 4 J. Int'l Tax'n 70, online: LEXIS (date accessed: 5 July 2000).

Offerman Suzanne, "The Effect of Customs Reconciliation on Taxable Income" [1999] 25 Brooklyn J. Int'l L. 693.

Dennis I. Meyer and William D. Outman, "U.S. Tax and Customs Consequences of Dealing with a Related Foreign Supplier" (November 2001) 12 J. Int'l Tax'n 30, online: <http://www.bakernet.com> (date accessed: 25 April 2002).

Wrappe, Pike and Chung, "Joint APA Effort Signals New Level of IRS–Customs Coordination" (29 November 2000) 9 Transfer Pricing 551.

Government Documents

Canada, *Report of the Royal Commission on Taxation* (Carter Report), Vol. 4 (Ottawa: Queen's Printer, 1966) at 252–255.

US, General Accounting Office, *International Taxation: IRS' Administration of Tax – Customs Valuation Rules in Tax Code Section 1059A*.(4 February 1994). GAO/GGD-94-61, online: <http://www.unclefed.com/GAOReports/gao94-61.html> (date accessed: 15 July 2000).

US, Staff of Joint Comm. on Taxation, General Explanation of the Tax Reform Act of 1986, 100th Cong., 1st Sess. 1062 (1987).

OECD Publications

Organization for Economic Cooperation and Development, *Transfer Pricing Guidelines for Multinational Enterprises and Tax Administrations* (Paris: OECD, 2017).

OECD, Committee on Fiscal Affairs, *Model Tax Convention on Income and on Capital*, June 1998 condensed version (Paris: OECD, 1998).

OECD, Committee on Fiscal Affairs, *Transfer Pricing and Multinational Enterprises* (Paris: OECD, 1979).

WCO Publications

World Customs Organization (WCO), Technical Committee on Customs Valuation, *Customs Valuation Compendium* (Brussels, WCO, 1997).

World Customs Organization (WCO), *Guide to Customs Valuation and Transfer Pricing* (2015 - WCO). Available at: http://www.wcoomd.org/en/topics/key-issues/revenue-package/~/media/36DE1A4DC54B47109514FFCD0AAE6B0A.ashx

USCS Publications

United States Customs Service, *Customs Valuation Encyclopedia* (USCS, 1998).

United States Customs Service, *Customs Valuation Rulings under the Trade Agreement Act of 1979* (December 1984), Trade Agreement Act Decision 17.

U.S. CBP Publications

United States Customs Border Protection, *Determining the acceptability of transaction value for related party transactions* (April 2007).

Unpublished Material

Jovanovich, J.M., 11 Case Studies on Customs Valuation and Transfer Pricing submitted to the Focus Group on Customs Valuation and Transfer Pricing (2007).

Kaplan, J., "Transfer Pricing in Customs Valuation", paper delivered at the Transfer Pricing Seminar organized by Insight Information Co. (26–27 April 1999).

Levey, M., "Transfer Pricing", paper delivered at the Transfer Pricing Course organized by Baker & McKenzie (28–29 April 1999).

Vincent, F., "Transfer Pricing in Canada", paper furnished by Vincent to the author of the present work (April 2000).

Index

SERIES ON INTERNATIONAL TAXATION

1. Alberto Xavier, *The Taxation of Foreign Investment in Brazil,* 1980 (ISBN 90-200-0582-0).
2. Hugh J. Ault & Albert J. Rädler, *The German Corporation Tax Law with 1980 Amendments,* 1981 (ISBN 90-200-0642-8).
3. Paul R. McDaniel & Hugh J. Ault, *Introduction to United States International Taxation,* 1981 (ISBN 90-6544-004-6).
4. Albert J. Rädler, *German Transfer Pricing/Prix de Transfer en Allemagne,* 1984 (ISBN 90-6544-143-3).
5. Paul R. McDaniel & Stanley S. Surrey, *International Aspects of Tax Expenditures: A Comparative Study,* 1985 (ISBN 90-654-4163-8).
6. Kees van Raad, *Nondiscrimination in International Tax Law,* 1986 (ISBN 90-6544-266-9).
7. Sijbren Cnossen (ed.), *Tax Coordination in the European Community,* 1987 (ISBN 90-6544-272-3).
8. Ben Terra, *Sales Taxation. The Case of Value Added Tax in the European Community,* 1989 (ISBN 90-6544-381-9).
9. Rutsel S.J. Martha, *The Jurisdiction to Tax in International Law: Theory and Practice of Legislative Fiscal Jurisdiction,* 1989 (ISBN 90-654-4416-5).
10. Paul R. McDaniel & Hugh J. Ault, *Introduction to United States International Taxation* (3rd revised edition), 1989 (ISBN 90-6544-423-8).
11. Manuel Pires, *International Juridicial Double Taxation of Income,* 1989 (ISBN 90-6544-426-2).
12. A.H.M. Daniels, *Issues in International Partnership Taxation,* 1991 (ISBN 90-654-4577-3).
13. Arvid A. Skaar, *Permanent Establishment: Erosion of a Tax Treaty Principle,* 1992 (ISBN 90-6544-594-3).
14. Cyrille David & Geerten M.M. Michielse (eds), *Tax Treatment of Financial Instruments,* 1996 (ISBN 90-654-4666-4).
15. Herbert H. Alpert & Kees van Raad (eds), *Essays on International Taxation,* 1993 (ISBN 90-654-4781-4).
16. Wolfgang Gassner, Michael Lang & Eduard Lechner (eds), *Tax Treaties and EC Law,* 1997 (ISBN 90-411-0680-4).
17. Glória Teixeira, *Taxing Corporate Profits in the EU,* 1997 (ISBN 90-411-0703-7).
18. Michael Lang et al. (eds), *Multilateral Tax Treaties,* 1998 (ISBN 90-411-0704-5).
19. Stef van Weeghel, *The Improper Use of Tax Treaties,* 1998 (ISBN 90-411-0737-1).
20. Klaus Vogel (ed.), *Interpretation of Tax Law and Treaties and Transfer Pricing in Japan and Germany,* 1998 (ISBN 90-411-9655-2).
21. Bertil Wiman (ed.), *International Studies in Taxation: Law and Economics; Liber Amicorum Leif Mutén,* 1999 (ISBN 90-411-9692-7).
22. Alfonso J. Martín Jiménez, *Towards Corporate Tax Harmonization in the European Community,* 1999 (ISBN 90-411-9690-0).

23. Ramon J. Jeffery, *The Impact of State Sovereignty on Global Trade and International Taxation*, 1999 (ISBN 90-411-9703-6).
24. A.J. Easson, *Taxation of Foreign Direct Investment*, 1999 (ISBN 90-411-9741-9).
25. Marjaana Helminen, *The Dividend Concept in International Tax Law: Dividend Payments Between Corporate Entities*, 1999 (ISBN 90-411-9765-6).
26. Paul Kirchhof, Moris Lehner, Kees van Raad, Arndt Raupach & Michael-Rodi (eds), *International and Comparative Taxation: Essays in Honour of Klaus Vogel*, 2002 (ISBN 90-411-9841-5).
27. Krister Andersson, Peter Melz & Christer Silfverberg (eds), *Liber Amicorum Sven-Olof Lodin*, 2001 (ISBN 90-411-9850-4).
28. Juan Martin Jovanovich, *Customs Valuation and Transfer Pricing: Is It Possible to Harmonize Customs and Tax Rules?*, Second Edition, 2018 (ISBN 978-90-411-6134-5).
29. Stefano Simontacchi, *Taxation of Capital Gains under the OECD Model Convention: With Special Regard to Immovable Property*, 2007 (ISBN 978-90-411-2549-1).
30. Michael Lang, Josef Schuch, & Claus Staringer (eds), *Tax Treaty Law and EC Law*, 2007 (ISBN 978-90-411-2629-0).
31. Duncan Bentley, *Taxpayers' Rights: Theory Origin and Implementation*, 2007 (ISBN 978-90-411-2650-4).
32. Sergio André Rocha, *Interpretation of Double Taxation Conventions: General Theory and Brazilian Perspective*, 2008 (ISBN 978-90-411-2822-5).
33. Robert F. van Brederode, *Systems of General Sales Taxation: Theory, Policy and Practice*, 2009 (ISBN 978-90-411-2832-4).
34. John G. Head & Richard Krever (eds), *Tax Reform in the 21st Century: A Volume in Memory of Richard Musgrave*, 2009 (ISBN 978-90-411-2829-4).
35. Jens Wittendorff, *Transfer Pricing and the Arm's Length Principle in International Tax Law*, 2010 (ISBN 978-90-411-3270-3).
36. Marjaana Helminen, *The International Tax Law Concept of Dividend*, Second Edition, 2017 (ISBN 978-90-411-8394-1).
37. Robert F. van Brederode (ed.), *Immovable Property under VAT: A Comparative Global Analysis*, 2011 (ISBN 978-90-411-3126-3).
38. Dennis Weber & Stef van Weeghel, *The 2010 OECD Updates: Model Tax Convention & Transfer Pricing Guidelines - A Critical Review*, 2011 (ISBN 978-90-411-3812-5).
39. Yariv Brauner & Martin James McMahon, Jr. (eds), *The Proper Tax Base: Structural Fairness from an International and Comparative Perspective—Essays in Honour of Paul McDaniel*, 2012 (ISBN 978-90-411-3286-4).
40. Robert F. van Brederode (ed.), *Science, Technology and Taxation*, 2012 (ISBN 978-90-411-3125-6).
41. Oskar Henkow, *The VAT/GST Treatment of Public Bodies*, 2013 (ISBN 978-90-411-4663-2).
42. Jean Schaffner, *How Fixed Is a Permanent Establishment?*, 2013 (ISBN 978-90-411-4662-5).

43. Miguel Correia, *Taxation of Corporate Groups*, 2013 (ISBN 978-90-411-4841-4).
44. Veronika Daurer, *Tax Treaties and Developing Countries*, 2014 (ISBN 978-90-411-4982-4).
45. Claire Micheau, *State Aid, Subsidy and Tax Incentives under EU and WTO Law*, 2014 (ISBN 978-90-411-4555-0).
46. Robert F. van Brederode & Richard Krever (eds), *Legal Interpretation of Tax Law*, Second Edition, 2017 (ISBN 978-90-411-8473-3).
47. Radhakishan Rawal, *Taxation of Cross-border Services*, 2014 (ISBN 978-90-411-4947-3).
48. João Dácio Rolim, *Proportionality and Fair Taxation*, 2014 (ISBN 978-90-411-5838-3).
49. Paulo Rosenblatt, *General Anti-avoidance Rules for Major Developing Countries*, 2015 (ISBN 978-90-411-5839-0).
50. Gaspar Lopes Dias V.S., *Tax Arbitrage through Cross-Border Financial Engineering*, 2015 (ISBN 978-90-411-5875-8).
51. Geerten M.M. Michielse & Victor Thuronyi (eds), *Tax Design Issues Worldwide*, 2015 (ISBN 978-90-411-5610-5).
52. Oktavia Weidmann, *Taxation of Derivatives*, 2015 (ISBN 978-90-411-5977-9).
53. Chris Evans, Richard Krever & Peter Mellor (eds), *Tax Simplification*, 2015 (ISBN 978-90-411-5976-2).
54. Reuven Avi-Yonah & Joel Slemrod (eds), *Taxation and Migration*, 2015 (ISBN 978-90-411-6136-9).
55. Alexander Bosman, *Other Income under Tax Treaties: An Analysis of Article 21 of the OECD Model Convention*, 2015 (ISBN 978-90-411-6610-4).
56. John Abrahamson, *International Taxation of Manufacturing and Distribution*, 2016 (ISBN 978-90-411-6664-7).
57. Frederik Boulogne, *Shortcomings in the EU Merger Directive*, 2016 (ISBN 978-90-411-6713-2).
58. Angelika Meindl-Ringler, *Beneficial Ownership in International Tax Law*, 2016 (ISBN 978-90-411-6833-7).
59. Andreas Waltrich, *Cross-Border Taxation of Permanent Establishments: An International Comparison*, 2016 (ISBN 978-90-411-6832-0).
60. Sergio André Rocha & Allison Christians (eds), *Tax Sovereignty in the BEPS Era*, 2017 (ISBN 978-90-411-6707-1).